The HERITAGE *of the* MIDDLE WEST

The HERITAGE
of the MIDDLE WEST

EDITED BY JOHN J. MURRAY

NORMAN : UNIVERSITY OF OKLAHOMA PRESS

LIBRARY OF CONGRESS CATALOG CARD NUMBER: 58-11607

Copyright 1958 by the University of Oklahoma Press, Publishing Division of the University. Composed and printed at Norman, Oklahoma, U.S.A., by the University of Oklahoma Press. First edition.

To
the men and women of Coe College
who contributed to
The Heritage of the Middle West

INTRODUCTION

WHAT IS the Middle West? A leading dictionary defines it as "that part of the United States occupying the northern half of the Mississippi River basin." This definition may well serve the cartographer, but it is highly inadequate for the historian, the economist, the educator, the politician, or any of the millions of people who live there. Ask ten middle westerners to define the area in which they live, and you will get ten different answers. A rancher in the fringes of the Dakota badlands will not think of the Middle West in the same terms as a dairy farmer in Wisconsin, yet both are middle westerners. Nor will a Chicagoan and a resident of Summersville, Missouri, agree in their opinions of middle western life. The politician will view the Middle West as a block of votes, and the economist will see it as a solid cornerstone in the economic structure of the nation. To each of these people, the Middle West is something entirely different, and to define it properly would be to list all of the things which make it what it is to them, for these are the things which differentiate it from every other part of the United States.

The purpose of this book is not to catalogue all of the distinguishing characteristics of the Middle West, but to examine some of the factors which have produced them. As one middle western scholar has recently pointed out, the forces which influenced the growth and development of the Middle West are not unique—they are the same forces which shaped the course of civilization in other parts of the United States and the world —but the effects of their combination at the right time and in the right place *are* unique; otherwise there would be no Middle West. The truth of this statement is perhaps best illustrated in terms of heritage, that vital agent which mixed the necessary social, political, economic, religious, and cultural ingredients together in the mold from which the Middle West was cast.

Each of the twelve contributors to this volume presents a different view of the Middle West in terms of its heritage. Those selected were chosen not only for their competence in their respective fields, but also for their ability to discuss specific aspects of middle western growth and development. Conferences were held at various historical association meetings so that each author had a clear indication of what the others were doing. The result of their efforts is a series of detailed observations of the Middle West from twelve distinctive points of view—education, politics, immigration, the humanities, and community living, to name a few. From these there emerges a new and different picture of the Middle West which, because of its depth and latitude, cannot be found in the better-known histories.

Needless to say, such a project as this tends to be somewhat uneven and, in some cases, even contradictory. Some phases of middle western development, as in science and technology, should perhaps have had sections devoted to them, and it is quite understandable that some readers would prefer to see certain sections omitted and others added. So be it. Perhaps they are right. Nevertheless, the authors, the editor, and the publisher hope that this book will be useful to the professional and amateur historian alike, and that it will help to shed some light upon the heritage of the Middle West for readers who live both in and out of the area.

On behalf of the authors, I should like very much to thank the many people who contributed time, advice, and energy to this project. Paul Glad and Richard Pinney gave considerable assistance, as did Howell H. Brooks, president of Coe College, and Harry M. Gage. Thanks are also due Owen Elliott chairman of the board of trustees of Coe College and the members of the board. Special thanks go to the Coe College Conference on the Heritage of the Middle West and the Margaret Pilcher Fund, whose generous assistance made this book possible. Eugene Kingman, director of the Joselyn Art Museum, and Professor Marvin Cone of the Coe College art department have helped with the selection of the illustrations. To all, we are deeply grateful. They are not only heirs of the heritage of the Middle West, but contributors to it.

JOHN J. MURRAY

Cedar Rapids, Iowa
June 17, 1958

CONTENTS

ILLUSTRATIONS

The HERITAGE *of the* MIDDLE WEST

I

INHERITANCE
FROM THE OLD WORLD
John J. Murray

AN OLD Chinese proverb says "When you plant for a year, plant grain. When you plant for ten years, plant trees. And when you plant for a hundred years, plant men." No saying dealing with the European heritage of the Middle West could be more appropriate. Europe indeed gave of herself when she gave of her people to fill the valleys of the Ohio, the Mississippi, the Missouri, and a host of lesser rivers. They came across the woodlands of the Old Northwest and into the plains beyond the Great River; into the lush, rolling farmlands of Iowa; into the badlands of the Dakotas; into the cattle lands of Arkansas, Kansas, and Nebraska; into the verdant forest lands of Wisconsin; into lands teeming with riches and wealth.

How do you evaluate the thirty-five million Europeans who have come to the United States since 1820, when the states of the Middle West were in the making? Four and one-half million Irishmen; four million Englishmen; six million Teutons from the area which later was to become the German Empire; two million Scandinavians; eight million Poles, Jews, Hungarians, Bohemians, Slovaks, Ukrainians, and Ruthenians; five million Italians; and three million Greeks, Macedonians, Croats,

3

Albanians, Syrians, and Armenians.[1] These were the people "who built America";[2] these were a new type of pioneer who came to the New World when the land lay open to the West.

Into the great central heart of the nation they came in large numbers—some the corps of the "ragged regiments of Europe," others tired, huddled masses yearning to breathe freedom's air—refuse of Europe's teeming shore, homeless and tempest tossed. There were many great men among them who sought individualism and who needed only a free climate in which to express themselves. Providing a yeast for the peasant dough were scientists, doctors, and men of letters and the arts, all of whose efforts aided the rapid rise of the Middle West. They took much from the land of their adoption, but they returned a great deal more. Affected by the frontier, they in turn affected the growing heartland of the United States. As Oscar Handlin discovered, "to describe the course and effects of immigration involved no less a task than to set down the whole history of the United States."[3]

Most of the immigrants were peasants who came to the New World to seek freedom to buy or to sell, to work or to loaf, to become rich or to remain poor. Their chief aim was economic emancipation from the restrictions upon individual economic enterprise which they had endured in their own countries, rather than freedom of speech or press. Many wanted to evade military service, and others wanted to live under republican institutions. Often accused by American nativists of being radicals, the immigrants, for the most part, were just the

[1] Oscar Handlin, *The Uprooted: The Epic Story of the Great Migrations that Made the American People* (Boston, 1951), 35.

[2] For an elaboration of this theme, see Carl Wittke, *We Who Built America: The Saga of the Immigrant* (New York, 1945).

[3] Handlin, *The Uprooted*, 3.

4

opposite. Placing great emphasis upon success, "they did not want to level down the gradations of society; they had no idea of dividing up wealth; they were not socialists nor communists."[4] They were believers in the democracy of the republic, with the brand of government that facilitated the acquisition of property and position and which protected that property and position once they had been acquired.

The immigrant's economic motivation for coming to the United States was a contributory factor to the traditional conservatism of the Middle West. Even though the naturalized voter might be without economic security or property, even though he lived in the squalor of the sordid and filthy tenements of the East Side and South Side, no matter how wretched his condition, he was a capitalist at heart. "Like a sea that tempers the heat and cold of the surrounding land, the ocean of immigrants moderated the cold of political reaction and the heat of democratic reform."[5] A few revolutionaries exiled from Europe gave the immigrant a bad name, but it is well to remember that after the bombing during the Haymarket riots, mass meetings of Swedish and German groups condemned the terrorists and reiterated firm and fervid devotion to American ideals. More immigrants were lost to socialism after their arrival in this country than were ever won from the rank and file of labor by the newcomers. The cessation of mass immigration, instead of fostering conservatism, actually promoted radicalism. American workers then became more like those of Europe and used political power to obtain economic and social objectives.[6]

Few students of United States history will take issue today

[4] Marcus Lee Hansen, *The Immigrant in American History* (Cambridge, 1940), 80–82.
[5] *Ibid.*, 95–96.
[6] *Ibid.*, 85–95.

with the boast of Adam Dam, a Danish immigrant poet who proclaimed:

> *We came not empty-handed here*
> *But brought a rich inheritance.*

Actually, the people who filled the Middle West carried with them as a legacy the cultural heritage of western Europe. To be sure, we have taken that legacy, twisted it, changed it, and sometimes warped it, but fundamentally, American culture is a modification of European culture, especially that which we refer to in survey history courses as Western civilization. We still draw cultural and spiritual nourishment from abroad. Recently having come of age, we are assisting in the task of preventing the mortgaging off of the old homestead. Much sweat and brawn were expended in making the immigrant dream of economic and political freedom a reality. In the striving, old cultures changed direction. Some were altered or fused with new and often quite different ones, and the resulting product is the United States of today.

One thing that all immigrants brought with them, no matter what their station in life, was their language. The first English settlers along the Atlantic Seaboard had spoken, for the most part, "the tongue that Shakespeare spake," and had held the faith and morals which Milton held. English, with noticeable variations, was to become the language of the new republic. As the nation flexed its muscles and waxed larger, the spread of the language advanced proportionately. It became the chief medium through which the culture of western Europe was handed down to young America. The writings of Chaucer, Shakespeare, Donne, Addison, Milton, Locke, Bacon, More, and a host of other British authors and translators became the intellectual food of the United States. Americans responded first by imitation, then by variation, and finally by initiation. The impact of the King James Version of the Bible upon the politicians and orators of the United States is worthy of further study by intellectual historians: "With malice toward none, with charity for all." "You shall not crucify mankind upon a cross of gold." "We stand at Armageddon and we battle for the Lord." Senator John J. Ingalls of Kansas evidently was in error when he proclaimed: "The Decalogue and the Golden Rule have no place in a political campaign."[7] Word associations, ideas, references, the magnificent cadences of many of our political speakers, prophetic righteousness, and a sense of destiny link American politics and political oratory closely to the Bible. These relationships have strongly colored American political ideals in the past and will continue to do so in the future. This single book is indeed a goodly heritage whose importance is not always recognized or appreciated by the majority of Americans.

To exploit more fully the great intellectual gift we inherited from Europe, young middle westerners were exposed to the classics. Latin and Greek opened new treasures to the bright young men who in the red-brick colleges of the Middle West were striving "to be up and doing, with a heart for any fate." The Babel of Tongues found in crowded city and isolated village added to the cultural enrichment of the land. Not only was the literature of all Europe introduced into this country, but the immigrant also produced literature, in his native tongue, to be re-exported to the homeland. Of this group, Ole Rölvaag is the prime example.

[7] Henry L. Stoddard, *As I Knew Them* (New York and London, 1927).

7

Alien in speech, the immigrant set up his own foreign-language newspaper. The library of the University of Illinois contains copies of American newspapers printed in 33 different languages. At one time Milwaukee published six daily papers in German, which in linguistic importance ranked second to English. The Norwegians, who were by no means the largest racial group in this country, established in the land of their adoption more than 400 Norwegian journals. This diffusion of knowledge through the various tongues added a spiciness and a richness to mid-America.[8]

By the turn of the century, nativism, intermarriage, and the desire to conform brought about a decline in the use of languages other than English. By the middle of the century, the decline was reflected not only in the people, but also in the educational system, which more and more saw the teaching of foreign languages being restricted. Americans had lost by default the great cultural advantage of language diversity which had been theirs. At a time when internationalism might represent the sole hope for the world's survival, professional pedagogues were pushing out through the curriculum door the very keys to international understanding. So deficient had the Americans become in their ability to handle foreign languages that during World War II, special schools had to be set up to teach German-Americans German, Italian-Americans Italian, etc.

The problems coincident with the immigrant's attempts to adjust to unfamiliar surroundings gave to American letters a new theme, which was to be exploited by Willa Cather, Ham-

[8] The statistics dealing with the foreign-language press were derived from Wittke, *We Who Built America*, 229, and Hansen, *The Immigrant in American History*, 28.

lin Garland, Ruth Suckow, Ellen Glasgow, and others. The newcomers provided variety, color, and dash to American speech as well as to American literature. Foreign place names, foreign dishes, foreign articles of clothing, and foreign tools became incorporated into the American language. What was once an alien word became a part of the American dialect as the various racial groups became interwoven with the expanding pattern of middle western life. What would our humor and tall tales have been without Pat and Mike, Reginald Snodgrass, Jock McTavish, Abe Cohen and Sammy Goldberg, those dumb Swedes, Ole Olson and "Yonnie Yohnson," or that volatile "Eytalian," Luigi?

A recent Dutch observer of the American scene while a visiting professor at a middle western university was shattered in the convictions that he had previously held regarding American materialism. After extensive travel and research, he arrived at the opinion that the United States was perhaps one of the more religious countries of the world. Instead of being crass pursuers of the almighty dollar, Americans were held by the sociologist from the Netherlands to be a people of message and mission, a people with a great sense of destiny.[9] Such attributes are also a part of our European heritage.

The Danish Nobel Prize–winning novelist, Johannes V. Jensen, in *The Long Voyage*, traced the coming of the first Europeans to the New World as a continuation of European folk migrations dating back to prehistoric times. Without a doubt one can draw parallels between Jensen's Gest and Ole Rölvaag's Per Hansa. Spiritually, however, a better progression is from More's *Utopia* to the unknown poet in Virginia who could write during the starving time: "We hope to plant a

[9] P. J. Bouman, *Volk in Bewegung* (Assen, 1951), 107–111.

9

nation where none had stood before." Thence we could come down to the "O Pioneers" of Walt Whitman's poetry and Willa Cather's novels. Hundreds of associations come to mind. Drake sailing out of Plymouth Harbor and a handful of Pilgrims on a bleak New England shore—Plymouth, England; Plymouth, Massachusetts; Plymouth, Ohio; Plymouth, Indiana; Plymouth, Illinois; Plymouth, Iowa. German inspirationalism —in Hesse, in Upper New York, in Amana, Iowa.

As the American saga unfolds, it reveals the names of hundreds of men filled with dreams, daring schemes, and great visions. Inspired by religious fervor, they sought to build utopias wherein their own concepts of God and politics would be predominant. They echoed in their hearts, if not with their tongues, the thought of Brigham Young: "This is the place." Prophets could and did move into the political arena: a gangling storekeeper from Illinois who hated racial injustice and who later signed the Thirteenth Amendment; an immigrant governor from the same state who refused to allow his sense of right to be stampeded in the Haymarket riots and who, with all due respect to the poet Vachel Lindsay, became an eagle who was not forgotten; a farm boy from West Branch, Iowa, who risked a large personal fortune in order that the starving people of Belgium might be fed; a shirt salesman from Independence, Missouri, who pushed the economic recovery of Europe and the ideals of international co-operation; a military man, born of a pacifist mother from Abilene, Kansas, who directed a bloody crusade that liberated half of Europe and who is now leading peaceful efforts to free the other half. To disassociate these men from their God is to misunderstand them completely.

The religions of America, for the most part, have their roots in Europe. In many ways, the transplanted churches of these religions were very much like their European counter-parts. But there were differences, too. As Marcus Lee Hansen has pointed out, the "ministers and synods of immigrant churches have always been less liberal in theology and ecclesi-astical practice than the brethren they left behind; and laymen who before emigration had only a casual connection with the church entered with enthusiasm into the problems of congre-gational finance and orthodoxy."[10] Yet the economic experi-ments fostered by certain religious societies were American, and the agriculturists who took part in them entered upon an entirely new way of living.[11] The church, however, remained as a strong tie between the new American citizen and his for-mer homeland.

Puritan ethics influenced both American religion and American life. They spread from the Northeast to the Middle West, capturing some of the pulpits of the older denominations and forcing many of the immigrant churches to conform to Puritan ideas and standards of conduct. Immigrant ministers, in their desire to have their churches considered respectable, forbade their parishioners to do certain things or engage in certain activities which had been considered socially acceptable in the old country. Immigrant denominations soon found that ministers trained in Europe, and thus not apt to be so imbued with Puritanism, were strangers to their New World flocks, both in theology and in ecclesiastical practice. A new minister soon found that it was better to preach "Boston morals" than to discuss theology.[12]

Religion and Puritan ethics have both been influential in

[10] Hansen, *The Immigrant in American History*, 97–126.
[11] Handlin, *The Uprooted*, 83.
[12] Hansen, *The Immigrant in American History*, 97–126.

the development of education in the Middle West. Hundreds of colleges sprang up throughout the area as various religions, often following national lines, attempted to preserve their spiritual and cultural identities. These denominational schools drew much of their inspiration from Europe but were modified to meet the needs and conditions of life in the United States. Norwegian colleges, such as Luther in Iowa, St. Olaf and Concordia in Minnesota, and Augustana in South Dakota; Swedish colleges, such as Bethany in Kansas, Augustana in Illinois, Luther in Nebraska, and Gustavus Adolphus in Minnesota; and Dutch colleges, such as Hope and John Calvin in Michigan and Central in Iowa have given a unique cultural stamp to higher education in the United States. The same can be said for the denominational institutions, which, in their beginnings, drew their religious inspiration from creeds in Great Britain. Representative colleges are Kenyon in Ohio (Anglican), Coe in Iowa (Presbyterian), Beloit in Wisconsin (Congregational), Northwestern in Illinois (Methodist), the University of Chicago (Baptist), Notre Dame in Indiana (Catholic), and Friends in Kansas (Quaker). Northwestern and the University of Chicago are examples of colleges that have evolved into great secular universities. Notre Dame has also become a great university, but it has maintained its religious connection. As for the smaller denominational colleges, the tendency generally has been toward secularization.

The very concepts of colleges and universities go back into the Middle Ages, when traditional learning burst forth from the cathedral schools and brought the institution of higher education into being. Academic gowns, the idea of a curriculum wherein a certain amount of material is covered in a specific amount of time, the idea of the residential college, the organization of universities according to faculties, the granting of degrees, the degrees themselves (with the exception of some of today's fancy ones), administrative titles (such as dean, chancellor, and rector), and other facets of academic life have come down to us from medieval times. Although we have made many adjustments and changes since the twelfth century, none of our attempts at modernity have found a suitable substitute for colleges and universities as communities of professors and students dedicated to the twin tasks of teaching and learning.

Many middle western colleges are, through Harvard and William and Mary, direct descendants of Cambridge and Oxford, while the original charters of the universities of Indiana and Michigan drew heavily from the French ideas on education devised by the government of Napoleon and expressed in the University of France. The seminar method for the instruction of graduate students, and in some cases juniors and seniors, was adopted by the majority of middle western universities and a considerable number of colleges. A constant stream of American students yearly went abroad to study, and thus a cross-fertilization between Old World and New World was achieved. The greatest gifts, however, that Europe gave to American institutions were the cultural achievements in the arts and the humanities, the discoveries in the sciences, and the theories of the social sciences which became so basic to higher education.

European influences can also be discerned in the elementary and secondary levels of education. These are often difficult to trace because at times, ideas from Europe hastened native developments already under way rather than initiated new ones. Still, there are instances where the European influence was direct, or at least it supplied the jargon which clarified—or in some instances confused—American thinking on educational matters. In the United States during the 1860's, there was tremendous enthusiasm over the ideas of Johann Pestalozzi, especially as they had been practiced by his followers in Prussia. The great Swiss educator gave a direct stimulus to lines in education already laid down in this country.

Perhaps of more importance were the teachings of Johann Herbart, who held that the chief purpose of education was to develop personal character and to prepare one for social usefulness. Herbart's ideas, which "took like wildfire," gave more import to content than did those of Pestalozzi, and they won a great many converts in the normal schools located in the Upper Mississippi Valley. To the Herbartians, we are indebted for the important concept of teaching history by showing its relationship to literature and geography. Herbart's followers advocated that history be taught in all elementary grades and that a moral aim be supplied to learning in addition to the mere acquisition of facts. Yet they did not ignore facts which they recognized to be not only useful, but also necessary. They never intended that content be taken out of education.

Another European, Emanuel von Fellenberg, believed that manual labor should be combined with schooling, and his adherents can still be found today. The adoption of this philosophy led to the establishment of many institutes on the secondary level, some of which became colleges. Western Reserve, Oberlin, Franklin, Wabash, and Knox colleges fall into this category. The ideas of von Fellenberg appeared later in modified form as middle westerners demanded that the mechanic arts and agriculture be taught on both the secondary and university levels.

Manual training received its first general introduction into the United States at the Centennial Exposition of 1876, where students of the Imperial Technical School at Moscow displayed their handicraft in wood and iron. Eventually, we adopted the Russian idea and extended it downward from the high-school and university levels to the junior high school. Our teaching of drawing and design in the high school resulted from another exposition, one held in 1851 at the Crystal Palace in England. Also from England came the idea of the Sunday school and the Lancasterian system of instruction.

Kindergartens in the United States—in fact the very name —can be traced to German educator Friedrich Froebel and to the German immigrants who transplanted his educational ideas in the New World. Froebel, who introduced advanced concepts of play and handiwork activities, believed that motor activity and learning by doing were of utmost importance in child development. One of his pupils, Mrs. Carl Schurz, established the first American kindergarten, which was located at Watertown, Wisconsin, and in which German was the language of instruction. When Mrs. Schurz and her husband moved to Missouri, she took her enthusiasm for the education of preschool-age children with her, and St. Louis shortly became the center from which was diffused the idea of public support for kindergartens.

France did the pioneering work in educating the deaf and perfected the use of sign language. Denmark did the same thing for the rehabilitation of cripples. Germany performed yeoman spadework in the treatment and education of the feeble-minded, although Edward Sequin, the French "Apostle of the Idiot," made more significant contributions in this field. From France also came the idea that the blind could be educated and thus trained to perform useful lives, and the adaptation of the American Braille system of reading has done a great deal to bring cultural light into the lives of those doomed to a life of darkness. In all fields of specialized and general education, we borrowed much from Europe, adapted it to our own needs and usage, and in many cases made significant contributions of our own. The necessity of assimilating the immigrant, then, was not the least of the specific problems which led to the formation of American educational philosophy.[13]

Our debt to Europe in the fine arts, especially music, cannot be calculated. The immigrant made a strong impact on native culture in the field of music, and foreign-born music teachers soon became familiar figures in American towns, especially in the Middle West. Perhaps of even greater significance were the Europeans who made sojourns here. Outstanding European musicians and conductors who have graced our concert stages and the European composers whose works have become a part of our musical tradition have much enriched American life. So did the nameless immigrant artists who, between the duties of shop and farm, had time for music. In *My Ántonia*, Willa Cather introduces us to Mr. Vanni, who played the harp at the dance hall, and Mr. Shimerda, who died of homesickness when the music went out of his soul. In *O Pioneers!*, Nels Jensen played on his *dragharmonika*, and Raoul Marcel sang Gounod's *Ave Maria*.

What a riot of song in our musical heritage from Europe! Beethoven in Symphony Hall in Chicago. Dvořák and Smetana at the "Bohemie Hall" in Cedar Rapids. German drinking songs at the Volkfeste in St. Louis. Elizabethan ballads sung by hillbillies high in the Ozarks and "river rats" going down the Ohio

---

[13] Most of the material dealing with education was taken from Ellwood P. Cubberley, *Public Education in the United States* (Boston, 1934).

and Mississippi. Welsh lullabies hummed to fretful children as
the covered wagon moved west. The nostalgic melodies of
immigrant Scandinavian and Slav that told of home to weary
workers on the farms or in the crowded cities. A German
Christmas carol, an Irish jig, a Hungarian dance. Plaintive advice—"O come back to Erin" or "You take the high road and
I'll take the low road." Service clubs singing "America" to the
tune of "God Save the King." Music, music, music! Sung by
immigrant choral groups and impromptu orchestras made up
of the Shimerdas, Marcels, and Vannis who helped make these
United States a more delightful place in which to live.

Europe permeates life in these United States: a Georgian
home on an Ohio street or a Georgian hall on a Wisconsin
campus. Gothic arches and gargoyles in the libraries of the University of Chicago and Northwestern University. Tall Gothic
spires on Catholic cathedrals in the large cities and delicate
steeples on Congregational churches in the small towns. Log
cabins whose design was imported from Sweden—they became
the symbol of life in the Old Northwest. Classical columns on
buildings which center the courthouse squares. Germantown
in Missouri, Holland in Michigan. In the Middle West, almost
every type of European art and architecture is reflected. Our
own artists and architects have given this inheritance a decided
American twist.

Because our cultural borrowings are legion, the best that
a survey of this sort can do is to bring to mind certain representative items in order that we may realize more fully the
scope of the cultural transference. Let us take the common
function of eating as our example. Nowhere but in the United
States do the cookbooks list such a variety of dishes. Nowhere
else are there so many restaurants that cater to such a multitude

of tastes. The dishes at our command would fill a dictionary devoted to international gastronomical adventures. An elaborate, but possible, formal dinner party might have the following menu: First, a Martini cocktail made with London dry gin and French vermouth, with an olive from Portugal. Guests who find a Martini too strong might be given sherry. What about hors d'oeuvres? Thin crackers covered with English Cheddar cheese or perhaps Edam or Gouda. Vienna sausages or perhaps spreads of *pâté de foie gras* or caviar. Others might prefer marinated herring from Norway. Enough of the preliminaries. Let us leave the living room and go into the dining room for the meal itself.

The table is covered with an Irish-linen tablecloth, the furniture shows European influences in its design, and the dishes were made at Josiah Wedgwood's factory in England. The first course consists of French onion soup, although it could just as well be bouillon, Vichyssoise, consommé, or borsch. Then roast beef, Yorkshire pudding, and vegetables. Unless the vegetables are corn, squash, or potatoes, the chances are that they were transplanted from Europe. Our salad can be plain lettuce with French, Russian, or Roquefort dressing. Wine with the meal? Burgundy, Bordeaux, or claret are some of the red wines from which we might choose. Being somewhat less formal, we might offer beer. Munich, Pilsener, or lager could be offered, according to the tastes of our guests. For dessert we could offer Danish pastry or perhaps crepes suzette. Some of the guests might prefer crackers and cheese—Swiss Gruyère, Danish blue, or perhaps Camembert.

After dinner a liqueur might be offered with the coffee—a liqueur which was probably made according to formulae worked out by the Bols or De Kuyper companies in the Neth-

THE BEGINNINGS: Belleview, or Mr. Dougherty's Agency
on the Missouri, as seen by Carl Bodmer.

THE FIRST TRAIN: Arrival at Cedar Rapids, 1857. From
the painting by Edward Bruns.

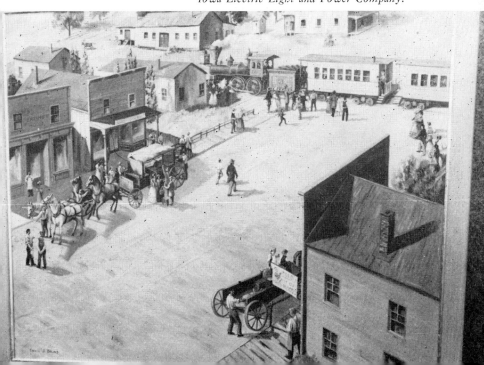

O PIONEERS: Nebraska Family and Sod House a Century Ago.

BEFORE THE TRACTOR: Oxen as high as a man's head at Amana Colony.

erlands. Someone may ask for French brandy, while another may like his brandy mixed with Benedictine, a cordial made by a monastic order dating from the sixth century. Others may want a highball and may specify a preference for Scotch or Irish whisky.

And so it goes with our eating habits. Swedish smörgåsbords, Italian spaghetti with Chianti and garlic Vienna bread, *Wiener Schnitzel*. It all depends upon where one goes to eat. One can have Czech kolaches with his coffee at breakfast, a frankfurter or hamburger for lunch (varied perhaps with a braunschweiger or liverwurst sandwich), and end his day with a dinner such as has been outlined above.

European authors, lecturers, and artists on the local stage or in the Chautauqua tent helped to share habits and tastes in the Middle West during its formative period. French fashions were copied by middle western women, while their spouses aped the latest styles from London. Our European heritage trickles down to the minutiae of life: from a Sheffield knife in the kitchen to a blanket in the bedroom—shades of Sir Thomas Blanket, medieval cloth manufacturer.

Early manufacturers in the Middle West drew heavily upon English experience. The same can be said for our financial system, although much of the economic practice that we received from England had earlier been exported to London from the Netherlands. Many of our ideas on stocks, bonds, insurance, and banking had their roots in Europe, especially in Italy, the Low Countries, and Great Britain. The three balls which today signify a pawnbroker's shop were also the sign of the banking house of the Medicis, who flourished in Florence in the fourteenth, fifteenth, and sixteenth centuries. From Holland came some of our earliest actuarial tables and theories of life and marine insurance. As far as stocks and bonds are concerned, there is a direct historical progression from the Amsterdam Bourse to Exchange Alley, to Wall Street, and to the Chicago Stock Exchange.

Europe's role in the economic development of the Middle West was not confined solely to the export of theories relating to finance. The assistance was often more tangible and measurable. The Louisiana Purchase was made possible by a loan floated in Holland.[14] After the War of 1812, British capital began to pour into the United States in increasingly large amounts. This fact is well illustrated by Leland H. Jenks's statement that "before 1836 over ninety million dollars had been invested in canals and railroads of which more than half was a charge upon the public credit."[15] Most of this money came from Britain, and a goodly portion of it went into the comprehensive state canal systems of the Old Northwest. Much of the opposition to the Bank of the United States arose from the fact that foreigners held eighteen thousand of its twenty-five thousand shares.[16] Between 1841 and 1842, Michigan, Indiana, Illinois, and Arkansas were among the states repudiating debts to English investors under a "gloss of patriotic sanctity."[17]

From 1869 on, Britain was not only a lender to American railroads, but also a supplier of metal and equipment.[18] British capitalists were slow to invest in industrial developments because American middle western factories competed with the

[14] Leland Hamilton Jenks, *The Migration of British Capital to 1875* (New York, 1927), 65.

[15] *Ibid.*, 75.

[16] Davis Rich Dewey, *Financial History of the United States* (11th ed., New York, 1931), 127.

[17] Jenks, *The Migration of British Capital to 1875*, 103.

[18] Sir John Clapham, *The Bank of England* (Cambridge, 1945), II, 291.

English merchant-prince investors who owned the factories in Britain. Still, the capital which promoted transportation and westward expansion indirectly financed industry. In addition, American merchants could draw upon British capital for unspecified ventures, and many such loans were put into industrial development. In this relation, it was possible for the New York *Express* to say that "millions of foreign capital are invested in manufactures in this country."[19] Between 1871 and 1873—years of great importance in the industrial development of the Middle West—the export of British capital and capital goods to the United States reached its maximum.[20]

"Department store" banking in the United States found its precursor in France's *crédit mobilier,* a finance company which promised the investors profits both from promotion and underwriting. There also arose business concerns whose owners were themselves impersonal entities owned by other limited-liability companies in infinite series. This system reached Britain for the first time in 1863, when the International Financial Society, Ltd., was founded. There occurred in list of directors the name Morgan, a name destined to play a significant role in American financial history.[21] The subsequent role of *crédit mobilier* in American political and financial history was noteworthy, and it forms an excellent illustration of the correlation of European finance with the political and industrial development of the United States in general and of the Middle West in particular.

The export of European capital to the United States conformed closely to fluctuations in the movement of immigration.

---

[19] Quoted in Jenks, *The Migration of British Capital to 1875,* 77.
[20] Clapham, *The Bank of England,* II, 271.
[21] Jenks, *The Migration of British Capital to 1875,* 240–48.

The immigrant influenced the national economy by supplying a labor force that allowed industry to expand without pauperizing its native American workers. It was possible for the cost of production to decrease at the same time the capacity to consume rose. A fluid social system resulted which allowed each new group to thrust its way upward to the level of its predecessor.[22] European capital, equipment, and labor laid the foundation for the tremendous industrial and financial structure of the United States which today periodically provides a prop to the world's economy.

As important as economic aid and theory was the political heritage that the Middle West received from Europe. It would indeed be imprudent for a European historian to disagree with Professor Turner's thesis that frontier individualism promoted democracy from the very beginning, but on the other hand, I must again emphasize that the foundation upon which constitutional government was built was laid in Europe, especially England. Our very concepts of parliamentary government have a long history which includes the dooms of the Anglo-Saxon kings, the charter of Henry I and the Magna Charta of John, the Parliaments of Henry III, the Model Parliament of Edward I, the first meeting of the Virginia burgesses, the Petition of Right signed by Charles I and the Bill of Rights agreed to by William III, the constitution of Massachusetts drawn up in 1780, and the constitutions of the middle western states as they are in 1956. Those cherished limitations on government found in our national constitution and in the state constitutions of the Middle West can be attributed to frontier democracy in only one respect: European political philosophies found fertile climates of opinion on the middle western frontier. I would

[22] Handlin, *The Uprooted*, 5, 72.

almost wager that the frontier states, in their political ado-
lescence, did not produce a single political concept that was
not previously kicked around by the pamphleteers and the
"Godly preaching ministry" who flourished in seventeenth-
century England. Undoubtedly, nineteenth-century mid-
America reached some of these political conclusions indepen-
dently, and I might have added "without benefit of clergy"
were I not fairly sure that the role of the minister in molding
political opinion on the frontier could perhaps stand the same
sort of historical scrutiny to which the divines of seventeenth-
and eighteenth-century England have been exposed.

The legal procedures and theories of the Middle West
are based upon the common law of England, with Glanville,
Bracton, Littleton, Coke, and Blackstone all influencing our
legal development. Still, as Roscoe Pound has pointed out, the
common law was in force only so far as it was applicable to
our conditions and institutions.[23] The same statement, however
—with some modifications could be applied to the legal system
of modern Britain as compared with law as it existed there prior
to the American Revolution. The same relationship can be
applied to natural law, which shines forth in all its splendor
in the Declaration of Independence. America accepted natural
law with a variant. In Europe, natural law dealt with the nature
of man. In this country it dealt with the nature of government,[24] but we must not forget that John Locke, the political
theorist perhaps most influential in molding American political
thought, was also concerned with natural law and its relationship to government.

[23] Roscoe Pound, *An Introduction to the Philosophy of Law* (New
Haven, 1924), 50.
[24] *Ibid.*

Political influences from Europe have not always been good. The insidious collectivist doctrines, which have been rejected by the American people and which have so sorely plagued the world, still remain with us, tempting the wild-eyed professional liberal and the reactionary conservative. In the main, however, the Republic has said, "A plague on both your houses," and has continued to support those concepts of individual liberty under law that we have primarily derived from Great Britain.

There are also other weaknesses in our political structure. The tendency of our politicians to appeal to the nationalism of various hyphenated groups in America constitutes a running sore on the body politic and at times poses a danger to the Republic itself. Professor Marcus Hansen once referred to a well-known public official in Chicago who had some twenty speeches, each of which dealt "with the contribution of a particular nationality to American civilization."[25] Many of our groups have organized themselves into associations and organizations whose main efforts are spent in exaggerating the cultural contributions of their own particular nationalities to a point which is far out of proportion to the facts. I hope that my last statement will not be construed to mean that I am against all American-European societies. On the contrary, I think that, in themselves, they are contributions to the American heritage. Yet at times these groups have formed political blocks which, by overly patriotic devotion to the land of their fathers, have unwittingly hurt the land of their children and their children's children.

Professor Thomas Bailey, in his works on American diplomacy, has called attention to this tendency in our foreign

[25] Hansen, *The Immigrant in American History*, 27.

policy.[26] There were times in the nineteenth century when the anti-English activities of nationalistic groups might have embroiled us in a costly war with Britain, but, fortunately, in each emergency wise counsel prevailed on both sides of the Atlantic and prevented overt acts of war from causing a major conflict. In explosive situations, however, politicians played upon the emotional sensibilities of certain nationalities in order to gain votes. Again, politicians, often lacking political integrity, have catered to outspoken radical elements in the United States and have, by their actions, endangered the safety of the Republic.

Fortunately, good has outweighed bad as far as our cultural heritage from Europe is concerned. There is no correlation between the contribution of a group and the loudness of its shouting and the enthusiasm of its breast-beating. For example, the English element in the United States has no society to perpetuate and elaborate the American debt to Britain, but British contributions are greater than those from any other racial or national group.

When large-scale immigration stopped, most groups rapidly assimilated. The constant movement of the American population was a factor in the breaking down of the tendency of specific groups to congregate in specific areas. The non-British groups, for instance, modified the ideals we took from England. As Professor Hicks has pointed out, the older institutions were never quite the same after the non-British people began to come to this country in large numbers.[27] It was fortunate that we had a political framework in the Constitution and a political philosophy in the Declaration of Independence into which the

[26] See especially Thomas A. Bailey, *The Man in the Street: The Impact of American Public Opinion on Foreign Policy* (New York, 1948).
[27] John D. Hicks, *The American Tradition* (Boston, 1955), 9.

various groups could be fitted.[28] This changing of the American scene by newcomers in their search for liberty and their pursuit of happiness was a part of the Middle West's coming of age. Goldberg, Livingston, Schmidt, Nye, Schaffer, O'Shaughnessey, Petersen, Bjelland, Bjornson, Westergaard, Hoekstra, Shimerda, Beneš, Brooks, Billington—middle westerners. Citizens in every walk of life. Builders of a diversified society who have resolved to make the United States a better place because of their being a part of it. Recipients of a goodly heritage and builders of another, these middle westerners are determined that the inheritance they have received from Europe and from the economic and political environment of the frontier shall flow endlessly onward like the mighty and powerful waters that divide the area.

[28] Bouman, *Volk in Bewegung,* 12.

II

THE GARDEN OF THE WORLD: FACT AND FICTION

Ray Allen Billington

THOSE WHO SEEK to appraise the influence of the Middle West's frontier heritage must recognize that throughout America's pioneer era not one, but two frontiers existed. One was a frontier of fact, where sweating dirt farmers toiled endlessly to triumph over nature's obstacles and the greed of their fellow-men. The other was a frontier of myth, existing only in the minds of eastern humanitarians, western promoters, and romanticists everywhere, but no less influential both at that time and since. Each of these frontiers has affected life and thought in the United States from the eighteenth century to the present; their heritage can be understood only by recognizing that the frontier which men *thought* to exist bore little resemblance to the frontier that actually *did* exist, yet was just as real in the minds of men.

John B. Newhall, a middle western booster of the 1840's, reflected generations of mythmakers when he surveyed Iowa's rich lands and exclaimed: "It is not the Garden of America, but of the World!"[1] The sentiments that he voiced were as

---

[1] John B. Newhall, *A Glimpse of Iowa in 1846; or, the Emigrant's Guide* (St. Louis, 1846), 2.

27

old as Benjamin Franklin, Thomas Jefferson, and other eight-eenth-century agrarians, all of whom fervently believed that the westward thrust of population in America would create a social order based on simplicity, virtue, and contentment. There, in the broad West, man would slough away the jeal-ousies and meanness bred of competition in lands unblessed by nature's plenty, finding contentment and brotherhood as his natural lot. Wrote Joel Barlow in *The Vision of Columbus:*

> *Each rustic here, that turns the furrow'd soil,*
> *The maid, the youth, that ply mechanic toil,*
> *In freedom nurst, in useful arts inured,*
> *Know their just claims, and see their rights secured.*[2]

And St. John de Crèvecour added happily: "We have no princes, for whom we toil, starve, and bleed: we are the most perfect society now existing in the world."[3]

During the early nineteenth century this concept of the West as a land of plenty and equality was sharpened as a rising spirit of nationalism, romanticism, and humanitarianism awak-ened Americans to the role of the frontier in their destiny. Nationalists, swept along by the heady concept of manifest destiny, pictured their land and its institutions as God perfected and calmly prophesied the day when the whole continent, and even the world, would share in its glories. Romanticists such as James Fenimore Cooper peopled the frontier with noble savages and virtuous husbandmen, all touched with the wand of perfectionism by mere contact with the forest, thus helping

[2] Joel Barlow, *The Vision of Columbus, A Poem in Nine Books* (Hart-ford, 1787), 204.
[3] St. John de Crèvecoeur, *Letters from an American Farmer* (London, 1782), 46–48.

plant in the popular mind the belief that nobility of character somehow permeated all who crossed the Appalachians. Humanitarians with little knowledge of either human nature or lands beyond the settlements similarly viewed the West as a haven from the East's economic storms where all could achieve prosperity and equality. Horace Greeley only caught the spirit of his day when he urged those dispossessed by the Panic of 1837: "Go West, young man, go forth into the country." Thus there emerged in the American consciousness a belief that the West was not only the hope and salvation of the needy, but was truly the Garden of the World.[4]

At the same time, and especially after the 1830's, the Garden was defined and delimited by eastern humanitarians and nationalists. With the rise of antislavery sentiment, advocates of the myth could hardly picture their Eden populated by fellow humans held in bondage. Hence they divorced the lands of the Southwest from their Garden, which they confined now to the Upper Mississippi Valley. There alone, they cried, could the world's oppressed find a haven from the rigors of factory life and the evils of slavery. There alone, in the words of a contemporary poet, could men come

> *To seek a competence, or find a grave,*
> *Rather than live a hireling or a slave.*[5]

In the newer states of the Old Northwest—Illinois, Michigan, and Wisconsin—and in the new territories beyond the Mississippi—Minnesota and Iowa—lay the Garden of the World.

[4] This concept is admirably developed in Henry Nash Smith, *Virgin Land: The American West as Symbol and Myth* (Cambridge, 1950), 123–64.
[5] James K. Paulding, *The Backwoodsman, A Poem* (Philadelphia, 1818), 11. Quoted in *ibid.*, 136.

This concept was immeasurably strengthened by the first pioneers to invade these lands. From the day of their arrival, an articulate minority among the frontiersmen directed a torrent of words toward the East, all painting the West in such inviting terms that none (it was hoped) could resist its lure. Motivating some of this propaganda was a genuine belief in the new-found land, but more veiled were the personal ambitions of its authors. Whether newspaper editors seeking more subscribers, merchants wanting customers for their gimcracks, speculators after buyers for their holdings, or merely ordinary farmers anxious to unload that unneeded quarter-section on a newcomer, all stood to gain through immigration. Hence their message—in the form of letters to friends, guidebooks, advice to immigrants, and newspaper accounts—was one of unadulterated praise for the Garden of the World, where kind fate had thrust them. As this permeated the East, the concept of the West as a modern (and somewhat improved) Eden was fastened more firmly in the popular mind.

More than this, however, the flood of propaganda directed eastward from the Upper Mississippi Valley emphasized three special appeals of the West, all of them inherent in the myth of the Garden but never before so exactly delineated. In America's vast heartland, easterners were told, they would find a land so rich and so beautiful that Paradise paled by comparison, an atmosphere so wholesome that every man's character was transformed for the better, and economic opportunities so abundant that the lowest wage slave could achieve affluence by scarcely turning a hand. The literature of pioneer Iowa abounded with instances in which these three themes were emphasized until they merged into the concept of the Garden of the World.

Certainly no land in all creation could rival Iowa in beauty —if its pioneer propagandists may be believed. Situated between two of the nation's mightiest rivers, both navigable for miles beyond its borders, and connected with the East by every possible means of transportation, Iowa was indeed a settlers' heaven. Its "beautiful rolling prairies" waited the plow, "like a rich old meadow, cleared of every roughness and obstruction, inviting the Eastern farmer to a good home, well-stored granaries, and a life of comparative freedom from the many disappointments and health-destroying labors connected with the cultivation of the weak and uncertain soils of the crowded Eastern states."[6] A letter-writer reminded his friends in the East: "It is said that the Sioux and Fox Indians, on beholding the exceeding beauties of this region, held up their hands, and exclaimed in an ecstasy of delight and amazement, 'I-O-W-A' —which in the Fox language means, 'this is the land!' "[7] Another, despairing of evaluating the riches of a land so good, concluded his paeons of praise with: "Her resources are inexhaustible, her advantages are beyond the scope of calculation."[8]

As though beauty were not enough, a benevolent nature had bestowed on Iowa a balmy climate that assured both comfort and health to all its inhabitants. "Our spring," wrote one enthusiast, "usually commences in March, and by the middle of May the prairies are green, with mild beautiful weather. In May, all the face of nature is covered with flowers and the foliage of the prairie bends before the breeze like the waves of an enchanted lake, whilst the whole atmosphere is scented

[6] John G. Wells, *Pocket Hand-Book of Iowa* (New York, 1857), 27–28; Albert M. Lea, *The Book That Gave Iowa Its Name* (Iowa City, 1935), 11.
[7] Buffalo *Journal*, quoted in *Niles' Register*, Vol. LVI (March 16, 1839), 48.
[8] Wells, *Pocket Hand-Book of Iowa*, 25–26.

with the breath of flowers."[9] During the summer, the heat that seared less favored climes was dispersed by cool breezes, "sweeping over the prairies, bearing health and rich perfume from the green verdure and brilliant flowers that clothe the earth like a fair vesture."[10] Disease, of course, was unknown in such a land the "miasmic" gases released from the decaying vegetation of forested areas to spread malaria and pulmonary diseases were dissipated on Iowa's zephyr-swept prairies.[11]

Not only would immigrants to this blessed land enjoy comfort and health, but they would also undergo a basic transformation—if the prophets of the Garden-of-the-World myth could be believed. Living in a land where nature's abundance stifled the competitive instinct and where a benevolent government bestowed on all who sought them farms at the pittance of $1.25 per acre, men accustomed to constant battle for their daily bread were transmuted into a wondrous new breed—the yeomen farmers of America. There was little evil or meanness in these idealized figures. Robust and strong, with skin deeply tanned and muscles rippling beneath clean blue shirts, they worked with a song on their lips as they raked sweet-scented hay or milked sleek, contented cows that placidly chewed their cuds. With care and want unknown, they drifted down the gentle stream of life, at peace with all the world and living virtuous lives that contrasted strongly with those of their less fortunate fellows in the East's crowded cities. "I have," wrote Stephen A. Douglas on one occasion, "found my mind liberalized and my opinions enlarged when I get out on

9 Nathan H. Parker, *The Iowa Handbook for 1857* (Boston, 1857), 9.
10 Nathan H. Parker, *The Iowa Handbook for 1856* (Boston, 1856), 11.
11 Newhall, *A Glimpse of Iowa in 1846*, 19–20; John B. Newhall, *Sketches of Iowa; or, the Emigrant's Guide* (New York, 1841), 25–26; Parker, *The Iowa Handbook for 1856*, 13–14.

those broad prairies, with only the heavens to bound my vision, instead of having them circumscribed by the narrow ridges that surround the valley where I was born."[12] To which Timothy Flint added in 1827: "Compare the cheeks of the milk maids with the . . . pale faces in the great manufactures. Farmers and their children are strong, innocent and moral almost of necessity."[13]

On Iowa's broad prairies this transformation was especially rapid; one had only to "compare the easy, social, unassuming deportment of the western pioneer, with the stiff, reserved, haughty and domineering manners of a southern black leg, or a northern coxcomb" to realize the change that had taken place.[14] A few communities there had, it was reported, erected jails out of a sense of duty, but they languished without occupants in that land where morality reigned supreme.[15] One Keokuk editor recorded his pleasure at watching the changes wrought as the pioneer shook off the traits that he had brought from the "old-fogy settlements" of the East—"to see his mind expand, his eye light up with the fire of a new energy, and his whole nature grow to the liberal standards of Nature's doings in the West."[16]

Part of this transmutation asserts that which the Garden myth ascribed to the perfect equality that all men enjoyed in the boundless West. This was achieved, not by degrading the elite, but by elevating the masses. Sharing equally in nature's vast riches, all ascended the social ladder so rapidly that class

[12] Quoted in William J. Peterson, *The Story of Iowa* (New York, 1952), I, 355–56.
[13] *Western Monthly Review*, Vol. I (July, 1827), 169–70.
[14] Isaac Galland, *Iowa Emigrant* (Iowa City, 1950), xi.
[15] Wells, *Pocket Hand-Book of Iowa*, 133–34.
[16] Keokuk *Whig*, quoted in Nathan H. Parker, *Iowa As It Is In 1857* (Chicago, 1857), 31.

differences disappeared overnight. Iowa, one writer insisted in the early 1850's, had already "placed the early adventurer on the throne of fortune,"[17] and others were certain to follow as the tapping of the region's riches went on, "bearing her sons and daughters to loftier, and still loftier, peaks, and revealing to their gaze still wider and richer vistas."[18] Nor would this process ever cease, for "as the multitudinous throngs hasten toward these goals of promise—as they crowd with eager steps, and work with untiring hands—they find that far from being drained, her resources deepen and increase in proportion as they take from them—not merely keeping pace with their accumulating wants, but ever exceeding them."[19]

This was inevitable in a land so singularly blessed by nature. Iowa's soils were so rich, propagandists maintained, that no other part of America, or of the world, yielded such bountiful crops with so little effort. One reported a field of corn that had produced 168 bushels to the acre, potatoes 16 inches in circumference, beets 27 inches long, apples weighing 1 ½ pounds each, and squash harvested at 100 pounds.[20] A visitor from Ohio, standing awe struck as he gazed on a field of wheat a mile in extent, with luxuriant stalks and heads heavy with kernels, wrote feelingly: "We would go for a day's ride to see such a field of wheat as that."[21]

Best of all, these blessings were within the reach of all, for basic to the myth of the Garden was the concept of the frontier as a safety valve. Westerners and easterners alike had, since the days of Thomas Jefferson, firmly believed that in

---

[17] Parker, *The Iowa Handbook for 1856,* 137.
[18] Nathan H. Parker, *Iowa As It Is In 1856* (Chicago, 1856), xv.
[19] *Ibid.,* xiv.
[20] Parker, *The Iowa Handbook for 1856,* 17–18.
[21] *Niles' Register,* Vol. LVI (June 29, 1839), 277.

SOD BUSTING: Single-bottom, Horse-drawn Walking Plow
about 1900.

TRAINING GROUND FOR STATESMEN: Early School House in Nebraska, about 1875 (District 12).

SCHOOL, NEW MODEL: Thomas Jefferson Senior High School, Cedar Rapids.

times of economic stress, dispossessed factory workers had only to move westward, buy the government's cheap land, and begin life anew in the Mississippi Valley. "Whenever," Jefferson had written, "it shall be attempted by the other classes to reduce them to the minimum of subsistence, they will quit their trades and go to labouring the earth."[22] With the passing years, this belief had become an integral part of America's folk belief. Horace Greeley only spoke for his generation when he wrote: "When employment fails or wages are inadequate, they may pack up and strike westward to enter upon the possession and culture of their own lands on the banks of the Wisconsin, the Des Moines, or the Platte, which have been patiently awaiting their advent since creation."[23] There they would not only find a haven from the crowded East's economic storms, but would also undergo the transformation into contented yeoman farmers, the lot of all who were fortunate enough to settle in that happy land.

This was the West pictured by eastern agrarians and western boosters who subscribed to the myth of the Garden of the World: a West of breath-taking beauty and gentle climate, where boundless opportunity elevated the transplanted factory worker into a prospering farmer and endowed him with virtues and morality unknown to the rest of mankind. How closely did this stereotype conform to the realities of frontier life? Iowa's pioneer years provide a striking example of the wide gulf between fancy and reality.

When its occupation began in the early 1830's, some 500,000 persons had already settled in the adjacent states of

[22] Quoted in Smith, *Virgin Land,* 204–205.
[23] New York *Herald Tribune,* February 18, 1854, quoted in Carter Goodrich and Sol Davison, "The Wage Earner in the Westward Movement," *Political Science Quarterly*, Vol. L (June, 1935), 179–80.

Illinois and Indiana. As this westward-moving tide lapped against the region's rolling prairies, federal officials realized that it could not long be restrained. Hence they seized on the opportunity provided by the brief and tragic rebellion known as the Black Hawk War to force from the Sac and Fox Indians the fifty-mile-wide strip along the Mississippi known as the Black Hawk Purchase. On June 1, 1833, this was officially opened to settlement, although long before that date overeager homeseekers had illegally crossed the river to appropriate choice town sites at Keokuk, Burlington, Sandusky, and Fort Madison or to occupy prized wooded lands adjacent to open prairies. All that summer, as one pioneer wrote, "the roads were literally jammed with the long blue wagons of the emigrants wending their way over the broad prairies . . . often ten, twenty and thirty wagons in company."[24] By autumn some 2,000 persons lived in Iowa, while the tide continued to flow so steadily that the population numbered 10,564 in 1836, when the first census was taken, and 23,242 two years later.[25] By that time pioneers' cabins were springing up on the banks of the Iowa River. So great was their pressure that the government, in 1837, bought an additional 1,250,000 acres from the Sac and Fox Indians just west of the Black Hawk Purchase.

Few among these newcomers found the Paradise that the propagandists of the Garden myth had led them to expect. The countryside was to their liking in that pleasant land of prairies and timber patches, but the promised "gentle zephyrs" failed to cool the summer's heat or stop the ravages of ague and the itch; life expectancy there was hardly more than forty years.[26] Nor was human nature magically glorified, as honest

[24] Quoted in LeRoy R. Hafen and Carl C. Rister, *Western America* (New York, 1941), 383.
[25] Marie Haefner, "The Census of 1838," *The Palimpsest*, Vol. XIX (April, 1938), 187.

immigrants found to their sorrow when gangs of cutthroat horse thieves and counterfeiters used their river-town nests for raids on the countryside.[27] These discomforts might have been endured, for the frontiersman accepted illness and disorder as his lot, but the government's failure to provide him with land was more serious. Not until 1836, when more than ten thousand persons lived in Iowa, did surveys begin; not until 1838, when the population was more than twenty-three thousand, was the first acre offered for sale. If the pioneer was to have a home, he must "squat" on the land, despite a law of 1807 (specifically applied to Iowa in 1833) forbidding anyone to settle on the public domain until surveys were completed.

Illegal or not, squatting was universally practiced in Iowa's early days. Travelers everywhere reported eager-eyed pioneers, equipped with a few tools and a week's provisions, wandering over the countryside, seeking a choice spot that could be transformed into a farm and home. Once this was located —usually in timbered areas, for despite the propagandists, frontiersmen distrusted the wind-swept prairies, with their lack of fuel and building materials[28]—the squatter marked out his farm and hastily threw up a temporary log cabin. Then his family moved in, the land was slowly cleared, a permanent cabin erected, and rail fences laboriously fashioned to mark off boundaries. All of these improvements were made without any title to the land, but with the hope that eventually its purchase would be possible.[29]

[26] Peterson, *The Story of Iowa*, I, 355–56.
[27] Benjamin F. Gue, *History of Iowa from the Earliest Times to the Beginning of the Twentieth Century* (New York, 1903), I, 331–35.
[28] Earle D. Ross, *Iowa Agriculture: An Historical Survey* (Iowa City, 1951), 13–14.
[29] The process is described in the *Iowa News*, May 26, 1838, quoted in Roscoe L. Lokken, *Iowa Public Land Disposal* (Iowa City, 1942), 68–69.

As this continued throughout eastern Iowa, troubles began to multiply for the squatters. In instance after instance bullies tried to drive settlers from choice farms, or government surveyors informed them that lands on which they had labored had been set aside for schools and must be surrendered. Frequently, too, rival claimants fought bitterly over a piece of property, burning cabins, destroying fences, and not infrequently killing each other. In 1836, two groups of men, all armed to the teeth, met to decide the ownership of a farm near Toolesboro; bloodshed was averted only when an old settler managed to patch up a truce. Such incidents, however, convinced the sober elements in the population that something must be done.[30]

Following the usual pattern of frontiersmen who found themselves beyond the pale of the law, they began meeting to form claim clubs or claim associations. Each of these adopted a written constitution which provided for such elected officers as a "recorder of claims" and a "bidder," and each laid down strict regulations concerning the marking and holding of claims. Most ruled that a squatter could hold his land for six months by breaking five acres to the plow and for another six months by building a cabin "eight logs high with a roof."[31] When each member had registered his claim with the recorder, he was protected against "claim jumpers" by the entire strength of the community. In one instance in the Iowa River Valley, a jumper who refused to leave had his cabin pulled down about his ears by the entire membership of a claim club;[32] in another

---

[30] Cyrenus Cole, *A History of the People of Iowa* (Cedar Rapids, 1921), 151.

[31] Newhall, *Sketches of Iowa,* 54; Benjamin F. Shambaugh, "Frontier Land Clubs or Claim Associations," in American Historical Association *Annual Report for 1909* (Washington, 1901), I, 67–85.

in Scott County, an intruder who announced that he would shoot it out with the association changed his mind when a yoke of oxen was hitched to the corner of his home and started pulling.[33] There can be no question that the clubs protected their members' claims, despite their complete illegality. "Although 'claim-law' is no law derived from the United States, or from the statute book of the territory," wrote an observer, "yet it nevertheless *is* the law, made by and derived from the sovereigns themselves, and its mandates are imperative."[34]

With the first land sales in 1838, the claim clubs assumed an equally important new duty. Long before the announced dates—November 5 at Dubuque and November 19 at Burlington—dozens of speculators had roamed the countryside, selecting choice spots for purchase and preparing to bid for them at the auctions.[35] That these plots were already occupied by squatters made no difference to the speculators; indeed, such sites were especially desirable, since the improvements made upon them had increased their value. Somehow the settlers had to raise the $1.25 per acre needed to pay the government its minimum prices for their farms and at the same time prevent speculators from bidding the price above this sum. If they could not, they would lose the homes on which they had toiled for three or four years.

Simply raising the money was difficult enough, for the government would accept only "land-office money" at the auctions: specie or notes on a few sound banks in denomina-

[32] Benjamin F. Shambaugh, *Constitution and Records of the Claim Association of Johnson County, Iowa* (Iowa City, 1894), xiv–vi.
[33] Willard Barrows, "History of Scott County, Iowa," *Annals of Iowa,* First Series, Vol. I (April, 1863), 61.
[34] Newhall, *Sketches of Iowa,* 56.
[35] *Wisconsin Democrat,* December 22, 1836, quoted in Benjamin H. Hibbard, *History of Public Land Policies* (New York, 1934), 217.

tions of $20 or more. For months before the fatal day, every penny was carefully hoarded. "The precious 'mint drops,'" a settler wrote, "take to themselves wings, and fly away from the merchant's till to the farmer's cupboard. Times are dull in the towns; for the settler's home is dearer and *sweeter* than the merchant's sugar and coffee."[36] When hoarding failed, as it often did, the squatters had no choice but to borrow from the loan sharks who descended upon Iowa for the occasion. Although usury laws forbade interest of more than 7 per cent, these worthies openly asked—and received from 35 to 50 per cent a year, at the same time protecting themselves by taking full title to the property until the loan, with interest, had been repaid in full.[37] Yet so desperate were the squatters' needs that even with these terms an Illinois loan shark boasted of loaning $100,000 at the Burlington sale alone, while other smaller lenders were equally active.[38] "During that land sale, indeed," recorded an eastern visitor, "I beheld so much of the selfishness, the petty meanness, the detestable heartlessness, of man's nature, that I turned away disgusted, sick at heart for the race of which I was a member."[39]

No one could protect the pioneers from loan sharks, but the claim clubs did rescue them from the clutches of speculators. At both Dubuque and Burlington, the members of each association attended the sales in a body, sometimes armed with clubs or guns and all grimly determined to prevent land jobbers from securing lands wanted by themselves. On an occasional

[36] Newhall, *Sketches of Iowa*, 57–58.
[37] *Iowa Territorial Gazette*, November 3, 1838, quoted in J. A. Swisher, "The First Land Sales," *The Pamlipsest*, Vol. XIX (November, 1938), 475.
[38] *Ibid.*, 475–76; Hawkins Taylor, "Squatters and Speculators at the First Land Sales," *Annals of Iowa*, First Series, Vol. VIII (July, 1871), 273–74.
[39] Edmund Flagg, *The Far West* (New York, 1838), I, 176.

piece of property not occupied by a squatter, bidding sometimes forced the price above the $1.25 minimum, but woe unto
any "overbidder" who boosted the price of occupied land.
Few tried; instead, the official "bidder" chosen by each club
stood with record book in hand, droning out his monotonous
"one twenty-five" as each parcel was placed on sale, without an
opposition bid being heard.[40] The rare speculator who defied
the associations was summarily dealt with. In extreme cases
he might be severely beaten or driven from town; more commonly he was outlawed by the community, with every citizen
pledged "not to borrow of him, nor lend to him, nor sell to
him, nor to associate with him in any manner whatsoever."[41]
One observer wrote: "So general has this usage become, and
so united are the interests of the settlers, that it would be
deemed extremely hazardous, as well as highly dishonorable,
for a speculator or stranger to bid upon their 'claims.' "[42]
The claim clubs did protect their members, but there was little
in their extralegal practices that conformed to the stereotype
of the Garden of the World, where a generous government
bestowed cheap lands impartially on all who needed them.

Conditions in Iowa, however, were no worse than elsewhere in the Middle West, and so migration there continued
and multiplied. By 1840, its population numbered 43,112, almost doubling in two years.[43] So great was the pressure for
lands that on May 1, 1843, the federal government opened a
new Indian purchase embracing most of the central portion of

[40] Newhall, *Sketches of Iowa*, 54–58; Swisher, "The First Land Sales,"
The Palimpsest, Vol. XIX (November, 1938), 477.

[41] Shambaugh, "Frontier Land Clubs or Claim Associations," in American Historical Association *Annual Report for* 1900, I, 78.

[42] Newhall, *Sketches of Iowa*, 54.

[43] *Census of Iowa for 1880* (Des Moines, 1883), 200–201, 210–15.

the territory. For months before that date, as one observer noted, "every main road leading to the new purchase was . . . almost literally lined with men, women, and children, with their flocks and herds, eager to be among the first to take possession,"[44] while within the territory, troops patrolled in a vain effort to keep back the premature squatters. On the night of April 30, the eastern border of the purchase was crowded for miles with homeseekers, held back by soldiers until midnight, when guns were fired to signal the official opening. The rush that followed was remarkably similar to that of the Boomers into Oklahoma District fifty years later; by sundown on the first of May, 1,000 pioneers had staked out their farms in one county alone, while such towns as Addyville, Ottumwa, and Agency City were complete with streets, lots, and the tents of their new occupants.[45] Seven years later, the Census of 1850 showed that nearly 150,000 persons had moved to Iowa during the decade.

Yet more were to come, for the state's boom decade was that of the 1850's. As "Iowa Fever" raged through Ohio, Indiana, and Illinois or as the tensions bred of eastern industrialization and a drought in the Ohio Valley uprooted the dissatisfied, increasing thousands turned their steps toward this promised land. Editor after editor reported that every train bound for the West was jam packed with Iowa immigrants,[46] that the roads were crowded with their wagons, and that at the river ferries, homeseekers camped for weeks to wait their turn on

---

[44] *The Home Missionary*, Vol. XVI (June, 1843), 39; Newhall, *Sketches of Iowa*, 45.

[45] Cardinal Goodwin, *The Trans-Mississippi West* (New York, 1922), 253–54.

[46] Parker, *The Iowa Handbook for 1856*, 151; Dan E. Clark, "The Westward Movement in the Upper Mississippi Valley During the Fifties," *Mississippi Valley Historical Association Proceedings*, Vol. VII (1913–1914), 216.

boats that operated day and night but still could not keep pace with the demand.[47] So many crowded through the streets of Davenport on their way to the western part of the state that the local editor was reminded of "an invading army . . . armed with implements for a pitched battle with the soil of Iowa."[48] The peak of the migration occurred between 1854 and 1856, when 190,000 persons were added to the population. "By the side of this exodus," wrote a Keokuk resident, "that of the Israelites becomes an insignificant item, and the greater migrations of later times are scarcely to be mentioned."[49] When it was over, the state's population had grown by 482,699, or 251 per cent, during the decade, while that of the Upper Mississippi Valley as a whole had increased by 167 per cent.[50]

To contemporaries, this migration to the Garden of the World clearly demonstrated the role of the West as a safety valve; dispossessed workers from the smoking factories of Europe and the Atlantic Seaboard, they believed, were moving en masse to the agrarian Paradise that was Iowa. Nothing could be further from the truth. Until 1850, more immigrants arrived from the Southern States than from the Northeast; only 5,535 of those living in the territory that year had been born in industrial New England, while 24,506 were from the Middle States and 30,954 from the plantation South. More significant was the fact that 59,098 persons had migrated from the agricultural Old Northwest, with Ohio contributing 30,713, Indiana 19,925, and Illinois 7,274. Nor do these figures reveal

[47] *Ibid.*, 214–19.
[48] Parker, *The Iowa Handbook for 1856*, 150.
[49] Quoted in Goodwin, *The Trans-Mississippi West*, 263.
[50] Clark, "The Westward Movement in the Upper Mississippi Valley," Mississippi Valley Historical Association *Proceedings*, Vol. VII (1913–1914), 212–14.

their true meaning until it is known that 17,165 of the 30,954 southerners in Iowa came from Tennessee, Kentucky, and Missouri.[51] Thus by 1850, the state had attracted 76,263 persons from near-by agricultural states and only 43,840 from New England, the Middle States, and the Southeast. Of these, probably two-thirds were from farming areas hard hit by competition with western farms. Neither Iowa nor the rest of the Upper Mississippi Valley was a safety valve for dispossessed factory workers during those years.

Nor did the decade of the 1850's substantially alter this picture. By 1860, Iowa's population included 377,684 persons born elsewhere in the United States. Of these, only 54,006 came from the South, with Kentucky, Tennessee, and Missouri again contributing the largest number, while 193,005 had migrated from the other states of the Upper Mississippi Valley, 103,173 from the Middle States, and 25,040 from New England. Ohio contributed more than any other state, with 60,000 pioneers, followed by Indiana, New York, Pennsylvania, and Illinois.[52] Then, as in the earlier period, the golden opportunities of Iowa proved more attractive to adjacent farmers than to distant city dwellers.

That this was the case is not surprising. Unemployed factory workers had neither the inclination nor the skills needed to forsake one form of life for another; successful farming required technical knowledge that could be gained only by a long apprenticeship. Moreover, establishing a farm required cash outlays far beyond the reach of the average worker. A

[51] F. I. Herriott, "Whence Came the Pioneers of Iowa," *Annals of Iowa,* Third Series, Vol. VII (July, 1906), 463–64.

[52] William J. Peterson, "Population Advance to the Upper Mississippi Valley, 1830–1860," *Iowa Journal of History and Politics,* Vol. XXXII (October, 1934), 334–36.

contemporary in the 1850's estimated that a new arrival in Iowa would need $200 for a quarter-section of land, $350 for the simplest cabin, $100 for sheds, a like sum for a yoke of oxen, $175 for a reaping machine, $200 for a thresher, $320 for fencing, $480 to hire the special plow needed to break the prairie sod, and smaller sums for livestock, a well, hand implements, and a variety of other needs. These were astronomical figures for factory workers, whose average wage was only a little more than $1 per day.[53] Actually, the West was never, during the national period, a safety valve in the sense that Horace Greeley believed it to be, although the constant shift of population from older states to the newer ones did leave gaps that could be filled by the more aggressive of the East's discontented.

Nor did those who migrated to Iowa in the 1840's and 1850's find waiting there the cheap lands promised them by propagandists of the myth of the Garden, for as in all periods of heavy migration, land speculators were there before them— and in such numbers that the individual purchaser had little chance to obtain choice sites. Wrote an Iowan in 1857: "Comparatively few of the immigrants to Iowa locate upon lands obtained directly from the government. During the last year, speculators have visited us and entered their thousands and hundreds of thousands of acres of public lands. These they have sold to . . . the actual settlers, who are emigrating in large numbers to take possession of them."[54] Indeed, so feverish was the speculative mania during the 1850's that some favored closing the land offices for the years needed to sell off the jobber-held land,[55] while others expressed alarm lest all other activities

[53] Parker, *The Iowa Handbook for 1856,* 159–61.
[54] Davenport *Gazette,* quoted in *ibid.,* 149.
[55] *Ibid.,* 150.

cease. "Farms were neglected," wrote one editor, "debts were left to run on unasked about, goods and groceries were bought on credit, lands alone selling for ready money at exorbitant prices. In short, every one was a professional speculator, and the good results which always flow from a proper division of labor, skill and capital were entirely dried up."[56]

This was due in part to the ease with which land jobbers could secure the best sites before the actual settlers. Some took advantage of a clause in the Pre-emption Act of 1841 which allowed a claimant to hold a quarter-section of land for a year simply by declaring his intention to settle upon it. Often these "claim-makers," as they were called, operated in pairs, with each transferring his holding to the other at the end of twelve months, thus holding the land for two years while its price increased.[57] Claim-making, a universal evil on the Iowa frontier, resulted in the withdrawal of thousands of acres from occupancy. Additional thousands were withheld from use by farmers who purchased more than they needed against the day when their excess holdings could be sold off at a profit. "One man," wrote a Charles City editor as he watched this process, "buys land at $1.25 an acre, sells it at $2.50 or $3.00, and invests again 'further west.' The second purchaser makes some improvements upon the lands and sells for $5.00 an acre. In the meantime some other 'speculator' has built a mill nearby and lays out a village, and the third purchaser sells the tract of which we have been speaking at $15 or $20 per acre."[58] Although the small operators guilty of these practices were

[56] Charles City *Intelligencer,* September 1, 1859, quoted in Hibbard, *History of Public Land Policies,* 216.
[57] Lokken, *Iowa Public Land Disposal,* 136–41.
[58] Charles City *Intelligencer,* August 20, 1857, quoted in Hibbard, *History of Public Land Policies,* 222.

universally resented, the principal wrath of the settlers was reserved for the wealthy speculators who engrossed vast estates in their quest for profits.

The most common device employed by these large jobbers was to obtain land with military bounty warrants. Beginning in 1847, the federal government issued to all Mexican War veterans script entitling the holder to 160 acres of government land; a short time later, bounties were authorized for veterans of the Indian wars, and, at the same time, the warrants were made transferable. Because relatively few who received them wanted to settle in the West, the warrants rapidly declined in value until by the end of 1848, one worth $200 at face value could be purchased for $125. In this form they were eagerly bought up by speculators, who used them to obtain rich acres at less than the minimum price of $1.25 an acre. One million acres of Iowa land were sold for warrants in 1849 and 2,000,000 acres in 1850; each year thereafter the amount increased until a total of 14,000,000 acres of the Iowa public domain had been alienated in this way.[59] That virtually all warrants were used by speculators was shown by the size of the estates they purchased. One such estate embraced 250,000 acres, another 200,000, while the average for the 140 largest purchases during the 1850's was 9,860 acres.[60]

Jobbers also were able to buy great tracts of the public domain that had been turned over to the state by the federal government. In all, Washington officials gave Iowa 2,000,000 acres of land to be used for the support of education, more than 1,000,000 acres to finance improvements designed to make the Des Moines River navigable, 1,600,000 acres of so-called

[59] Lokken, *Iowa Public Land Disposal*, 136–41.
[60] Hibbard, *History of Public Land Policies*, 224–25.

"swamp lands" to aid local road-building, and more than 4,000,000 acres as land grants to encourage railroad-building. Most important among these gifts were the railroad grants; these were allotted the state in 1856 and two years later were parceled out among four roads in the form of alternate sections on either side of the right of way.[61] In each instance the grants were either held by the railroad against a price increase or sold in large parcels to other speculators who similarly withheld them from the market. The inevitable result was revealed when an Iowan wrote that every inch of land within four miles of the projected Mississippi and Missouri Railroad was in speculators' hands and was being offered at from five to ten dollars an acre.[62]

Amidst this scramble the individual farmer had little chance to buy cheap government land in the Garden of the World. In all, the United States disposed of 36,000,000 acres of Iowa land. Of this amount, fewer than 12,000,000 acres were sold for cash, while 1,000,000 acres in the state's northwestern corner were given away under the Homestead Act of 1862. Of these 13,000,000 acres, perhaps one-third was engrossed by speculators or was held by speculative farmers against a price increase. Of the remainder, 14,000,000 acres were distributed through military-bounty warrants, 2,000,000 acres through educational allotments, and 7,000,000 acres as gifts to aid internal improvements.[63] Virtually all of this found its way into speculative channels. Thus of the state's 36,000,000 acres, roughly 27,000,000 reached actual users through land jobbers; for every farmer who bought directly from the gov-

[61] Lokken, *Iowa Public Land Disposal*, 126.
[62] Parker, *Iowa As It Is In 1856*, 69.
[63] Lokken, *Iowa Public Land Disposal*, 154, 267–69.

ernment at $1.25 an acre, four were forced to pay excessive premiums to speculators.

The effect of this carnival of greed on the Middle West's heritage was both immediate and enduring. The immediate result was the retardation of the physical—and hence the cultural—development of the region through the withdrawal of land from cultivation. In 1850, of the land that had been sold or granted in Iowa, only 30.1 per cent was improved; by 1856 the amount had shrunk to 23.9 per cent, and in 1860 it had risen to 38.8 per cent.[64] Some of these unimproved lands simply waited the pioneer's plow, but more were being held for an expected price rise. This was shown by the decline in the percentage of improved lands in 1856, when the speculative boom was at a height, and the increase in 1860, when the speculative bubble had been pricked by the Panic of 1857, which forced jobbers to sell off their holdings. For years, however, some of the state's best land had been withheld from production, dooming its farmers to excessive taxes and so separating them from each other that cultural progress was handicapped.

More serious was the long-term result. By charging high prices for the best lands and those nearest transportation outlets, speculators forced many immigrants into two professions hardly to be expected in the Garden of the World: farm laborers and farm tenants. Thus Iowa in 1860, although barely fourteen years a state and with two-thirds of its prairies still unbroken, had 40,827 farm laborers—about 6 per cent of its population. More to the point: of every 100 persons then engaged in agriculture, 23 were farm laborers, and by 1870, the number had increased to 37.[65] And this at a time when such

[64] *Census of Iowa for 1880,* 179.
[65] Paul W. Gates, "Frontier Estate Builders and Farm Laborers," in Walker D. Wyman, ed., *The Frontier in Perspective* (Madison, 1956).

a laborer had a lower social status than a European peasant and when land ownership was considered the birthright of every individual, no matter his origin.

Farm tenancy was another unfortunate outgrowth of speculative activity. An analysis of two central Iowa counties in 1870 reveals that almost one-half the farmers were tilling lands they did not own. If the farm laborers are added to these tenants, the startling fact emerges that more than 80 per cent of those engaged in agriculture were either tenants or laborers. By 1880, 23 per cent of all Iowa farms were tenant operated, and 43 per cent of those earning their living on farms were non-owners.[66] Statistical evidence indicates that the principal basis for Iowa tenancy was high land prices, for the percentage of tenants tended to decline as population thickened or towns multiplied and to increase in direct proportion to the increased price of land.[67] Nor was Iowa the exception, for in 1880, only 2,964,306 of the 7,670,443 persons engaged in farming throughout the United States owned the land they tilled—about 40 per cent.[68]

Speculators were primarily, although not solely, responsible for this situation. Thousands of immigrants, lured to the Mississippi Valley by the Garden myth, found on arrival that they did not have the money needed to pay a jobber five or ten dollars an acre for a farm, let alone the additional sums needed for housing, tools, and livestock. Many of these people became laborers, hoping in this way to save the amount needed to become independent. Others found that speculators, beset as they

[66] *Ibid.*

[67] Edwin Thomas, "An Analysis of the Importance of Selected Factors in Tenancy, Southeast Iowa, 1890" (Unpublished term paper, Northwestern University, 1956).

[68] Thomas P. Gill, "Landlordism in America," *North American Review*, Vol. CXLII (January, 1886), 56.

were by mounting taxes, were willing to rent out land in forty- or eighty-acre plots, usually with the tenant paying the owner one-half or one-third of the crop yearly. Like the laborers, the renters hoped to save enough to buy the farms they operated, but since land prices tended to increase more rapidly than savings, few were able to make this transition. Those who could not either stayed on as tenants or moved westward to buy cheaper lands. This migration from Illinois and Iowa during the 1870's and 1880's helps to account for the growing conservatism of the Upper Mississippi Valley as the center of farm unrest shifted westward between the era of the Grange and the era of Populism.[69]

Thus the Middle West that emerged from its pioneer period bore little resemblance to the Garden of the World pictured by propagandists a generation before. With its unrivaled riches still only partially tapped, with almost half its population unable to buy excessively priced lands and reduced to the menial status of tenants or farmers, and with the more energetic renters fleeing still farther westward in hope of finding a purchasable farm, the region was saddled with a heritage of debt and dissatisfaction rather than one of prosperity and hope. Little wonder that its settlers, viewing this vast gulf between dream and reality, have felt justified in demanding a larger share of the national income through political action, from the days of the Grange and Populism to those of farm parity and soil banks.

Yet the Middle West's heritage stems not only from the frontier of fact, but from the frontier of myth as well; American thought has always been influenced by what the people

[69] Gates, "Capitalist Estate Builders," in Walker D. Wyman, ed., *The Frontier in Perspective.*

51

believed the frontier to be as much as by what the frontier actually was. To those bred in the belief that the West was the Garden of the World, where the dispossessed could tap nature's bounties as they underwent a transformation into the sturdy yeomen who formed the backbone of the nation, the passing of the frontier at the close of the nineteenth century meant a psychological readjustment that is still going on. Certainly the problems posed by the passing of the era of cheap land seemed terrifying real when, in 1890, the director of the census announced that an unbroken line between the settlements and the wilderness no longer existed. How could a nation accustomed to continual expansion adjust to life within fixed borders? How could farmers, long geared to an economy of exploitation, assume European habits of conservation? How could workers who (it was believed) had always escaped economic storms by fleeing westward cope with periods of depression now? And, most important of all, how could security and prosperity be provided for a people who had always secured these ends by exploiting the abundant resources of new frontiers?

During the era of farm prosperity which ushered in the twentieth century and which reached its peak in World War I, these problems could be ignored, but with the pricking of the inflationary bubble in 1920, they became uncomfortably real. Farm income, which had soared to $17,500,000,000 in 1919, slumped to $10,000,000,000 in 1920 and to less than $7,000,000,000 a decade later; by this time the industrial depression that began in 1929 was posing the additional problem of millions of unemployed factory workers who could no longer escape through a frontier safety valve. Belatedly, the nation awakened to the fact that it could not relax while cheap lands solved its problems; positive action by the government was required to provide citizens with the security and prosperity formerly found in the Garden of the World. This was the realization that underlay the conservation policies and "trust busting" of Theodore Roosevelt, the "New Freedom" of Woodrow Wilson, the "New Deal" of Franklin D. Roosevelt, the "Square Deal" of Harry S. Truman, and much of the domestic program of Dwight D. Eisenhower. Franklin Roosevelt only summed up the nation's reaction to the explosion of the Garden myth when he declared in 1935: "Today we can no longer escape into virgin territory; we must master our environment."

III

~~~~~~

FROM POVERTY TO PROSPERITY
Paul Sharp

ALEXIS DE TOCQUEVILLE, one of the most perceptive European visitors to the Middle West, judged the valley of the Mississippi to be the "most magnificent dwelling place prepared by God for man's abode." His observation was also a prophecy, for the region of which he wrote possessed both the land and the resources out of which men have created an economy of abundance. In doing so, the Middle West has fulfilled Franklin D. Roosevelt's prophecy that "we must master our environment."

It is not regional chauvinism to point out that the Middle West[1] is one of the most important and clear-cut case studies in economic growth in modern history. Within a century American enterprise transformed a mid-continental region from a wilderness sustaining fewer than 100,000 aborigines to a complex, dynamic economy supporting 37,000,000 people and producing industrial and agricultural surpluses that seek national and international markets. And during the same years, Chicago grew from a town of less than 30,000 to the region's

---

[1] I am using a rather restricted definition of the region accepted by Odum and Moore (*American Regionalism: A Cultural-Historical Approach to National Integration* [New York, 1938]) to include only the states of Ohio, Michigan, Indiana, Illinois, Wisconsin, Minnesota, Iowa, and Missouri. Obviously, portions of neighboring states possess sufficient similarity to be included in the larger Middle West.

metropolis of nearly 4,000,000—"proud to be Hog Butcher, Tool Maker, Stacker of Wheat, Player with Railroads and Freight Handler to the Nation."

What forces impelled this amazing growth in little more than a century? What factors explain our high standard of living, so widely distributed, our high level of productivity, and our economic strength? The answer lies in our economic heritage.

Heritage is a word foreign to the vocabulary of the economic historian, one not easily used. Its poetic quality, its imprecision, and, perhaps even more, its public-relations connotations frighten the serious student of the past, leaving him wary of what is to follow. Perhaps if we think of it as our inheritance, that complex mass of economic habits, attitudes, and forces shaping our behavior from day to day, we come close to defining our task. Along with systems of production, consumption, and exchange, the values by which men live determine their economic performance. In the Middle West, the curious amalgam of Puritanism and Poor Richard, the dedication to the desirability and possibility of material improvement, and the dominance of the spirit of progress are as important as per capita statistics and technologies in the fulfillment of the goals they visualize. Our economic heritage, to put it simply, is the precipitate of history, the residue that helps us to share our present and predict our future.

An easy answer to our questions, although no truer for its simplicity, is that middle westerners have inherited their wealth from a bountiful nature. European critics of our economic institutions have made rather too much of this point, arguing that we stumbled into riches and have enjoyed them, whatever the level of our performance. Many of us who have sought to explain the nature of our economy to students in foreign universities have found this a stereotyped explanation of America's productivity. Our only claim to achievement is our good fortune in possessing a continent rich in fertile soils, great mineral and power resources, extensive river and lake systems, and a favorable climate.

There is now no question of the importance of resources in economic growth, but as every schoolboy knows, American Indians starved and froze, surrounded by the same natural resources that feed our industries. And the region's first settlers subsisted on a standard not much higher than that of the Indians they displaced. Human ingenuity, technological skills, and driving incentives developed through the years to utilize the wealth that primitive people had neither the means nor the desire to use.

Abundant resources of a wide range of economic use, however, are the base on which middle western development rests. Perhaps the most graphic method of demonstrating this fact is to look at those nations, young like our own, lacking similar natural wealth. Australian pioneers, once across the Blue Mountains, found a bleak continent of sand and rock; no fertile Middle West awaited their enterprise. Population and industry were pinned to the seacoast, thus restraining economic development in a country whose land mass is somewhat larger than our own.

Similarly, Canadian farmers pushed inland to reach an equally barren Pre-Cambrian shield, a land of rock and scrub. For Canada there could be no Middle West either, and population and capital accumulation lagged far behind her neighbor to the south as rich farms and burgeoning industries appeared in the Old Northwest.

During the initial years of settlement, the cultivation of millions of acres of virgin lands comprised the great addition to national wealth and regional development. Frederick Jackson Turner rested much of his case for the pervasive influence of the frontier upon forces released by the rapid expansion of agriculture in his native region. "The western wilds, from the Alleghenies to the Pacific, constituted the richest free gift that was ever spread out before civilized man," he wrote in one of his most famous essays.[2]

Land, however, was only one of many resources whose abundance in the Middle West contributed to economic growth. Although it was the first to be placed into production, other resources were equally important, and their exploitation stimulated further expansion of the middle western economy long after frontier farmers had plowed and fenced the last free land. As David M. Potter has recently pointed out, the abundance of frontier resources, not just the presence of unused land, comprised the basic influence upon our economy during the formative years of settlement.[3] Timber, copper, lead, iron, water power—these and many other gifts of nature were appropriated as advancing technology, improved communications, and accessible markets made profitable their utilization.

Important as these resources were in determining the character of the region's economy, their influence on middle western attitudes toward wealth, its production and ownership, is equally striking. With the reality of abundance so inescapably impressed by experience, middle westerners have lived with ideas and habits deeply ingrained by a continuing oppor-

[2] Frederick Jackson Turner, "Contributions of the West to American Democracy," in *Frontier in American History* (New York, 1921), 261.

[3] David M. Potter, *People of Plenty* (Chicago, 1954), 144-60.

tunity to create new wealth. Even during years of widespread economic distress when this opportunity seemed severely limited, only a handful of radicals have challenged our inherited institutions of private ownership of property or of the individual's choice in its use. Middle western dissenters, except for a minority of doctrinaire socialists, anarchists and communists, have operated within a narrow spectrum, seldom demanding more than measures designed to preserve economic opportunity for small capitalists, rural or urban.

Middle western economic attitudes came first with the pioneers, who established capitalistic institutions in the image of those of their eastern or European homes. Thus the basic inheritance of our regional economy is that of a system using or investing capital for the production of income and possessing its own technology, organization, and spirit. But changes slowly transformed this extraregional inheritance as the Middle West's physical resources, technologies for their use, and social institutions shaped regional patterns of economic behavior.

American capitalism defies precise definition. A "mixed economy" pragmatically joining wide areas of individual freedom to government regulation and ownership, it dismays those seeking to measure fixed doctrines of economic theory against its performance. On the complex forces, ideas, habits, and customs composing this amalgam, we are content to place the label of "American Way."[4] Thus we pay tribute, however inadequate our terminology, to the uniqueness of the economic experiment in this country.

Important differences immediately explain this. The high rate of savings and reinvestment, the ready assumption of risk,

[4] Shepherd Clough, *The American Way: The Economic Basis of Our Civilization* (New York, 1953).

the emphasis upon efficiency, and the philanthropy of American capitalists distinguish their performance. Similarly, the conservatism of the American labor movement, its reluctance to assume a responsible political role, and its stubborn refusal to espouse socialist definitions of the workers' antagonism to capitalism are so characteristically American that it dismays doctrinaires, both foreign and domestic.

These differences, so much an accepted part of our heritage, can be explained only by understanding the social environment that nourished them. The unreserved commitment to progress of American society during the nineteenth century remains a stimulant to economic expansion. In a society that measures success by its economic growth, individual failure seemed less harsh, for it was never accepted as final. "We are creating a great city," an enthusiastic Chicago hotelkeeper told John L. Peyton in 1869, "building up all kinds of industrial establishments, and covering the lake with vessels—so that suffer who may when the inevitable hour of reckoning arrives, the country will be the gainer."[5] Not until 1929 did the American people seriously question this article of faith, and then only briefly.

With a mixture of idealism and practicality, we have always regarded our expansion as progress. New cities, greater productivity on farms and in factories, new industries and higher standards of living comprise a tangible and substantial record that middle westerners have viewed with satisfaction. By identifying economic well-being with progress, we have successfully fused private and public welfare. Thus from a people changing an underdeveloped continental heartland into high productivity to a people transforming underdeveloped

[5] Quoted in Warren S. Tryon, *A Mirror for Americans* (Chicago, 1952), III.

regions around the world with technology, industrialization, and higher living standards is something rather easy for middle western businessmen and farmers to understand and approve.

Middle westerners, from earliest settlement onward, have pursued economic goals with relentless energy, high optimism, and single-mindedness of purpose. This system of values, widely shared and practiced, encouraged economic growth and rewarded those who promoted it with social, as well as pecuniary, honors. Perceptive travelers visiting the Middle West, whether in this century or during the last, quickly identified a "go-ahead spirit" as a regional characteristic born of optimism and intellectual simplicity. "I recollect," wrote Captain William F. Butler in 1873 after visiting the Middle West, "a very earnest American once saying that he considered all religious, political, social and historical teaching could be reduced to three subjects—the Sermon on the Mount, the Declaration of American Independence, and the Chicago Republican Platform of 1860."[6] With but one change, and that a date, Butler's observation retains much of its validity to the present time.

Reinforcing this heritage of optimism and progress is the widely accepted view of the ideal society as one of fluid classes, open ended and constantly refreshed by new individuals and groups moving upward in the scale of social acceptance. Concepts of a classless society have not appealed to middle westerners, but traditions of a society offering opportunity for mobility and changing status are universally assumed. While this social mobility has created obvious tensions and psychological problems, few middle westerners would accept either of its alternatives—a classless or a rigid-status society. Economic

[6] William F. Butler, *Great Lone Land* (London, 1873), 16.

opportunity dictates these social views and keeps the image within the grasp of reality.

No development illustrates this more eloquently than the role of free public education. Middle western reformers arguing for government-owned-and-operated educational systems echoed the familiar arguments that American democracy depended upon an enlightened citizenry and that a wholesome public morality demanded universal education. They also emphasized the argument that a rising educational level promotes greater economic efficiency, higher earnings, higher standards of living, and a division of society into groups of specialists, each capable of greater productivity. Education meant the end of poverty, the beginning of wealth as well as of wisdom.

"The statistics of the penitentiaries and almshouses throughout the country abundantly show," declared James W. Grimes, Iowa's newly elected governor in 1854, "that education is the best preventive of pauperism and crime. They show, also, that the prevention of these evils is much less expensive than the punishment of the one, and the relief of the other."[7]

Public education would also guarantee social mobility by encouraging economic growth. The new states of the Middle West required engineers, mechanics, scientists, and professional men to lead their expanding economies. Governor Grimes again stated the case: "Education, too, is the great equalizer of human conditions. It places the poor on an equality with the rich. It subjects the appetites and passions of the rich to the restraints of reason and conscience, and thus prepares each for a career of usefulness and honor."

[7] Inaugural address, December 9, 1854. Quoted in Vernon Carstensen, "The University as Head of the Iowa School System," *Iowa Journal of History*, Vol. LIII, No. 3 (July, 1955), 218.

Regional influences reinforced and occasionally modified these essentially national traits. In middle western agriculture, for example, we first observe many of these regional changes in economic behavior and social attitudes. Here we see most clearly the pronounced shift among rural folk from an almost universal suspicion of change to an enthusiasm for improved techniques, crop and animal breeds, soil culture, and farm practices that promised increased efficiency and higher production. The mechanization of middle western farms, which paced the nation; the numerous experiments, called "crazes" in the early years, to find suitable crops for changing markets; and the widespread application of scientific knowledge to agricultural production illustrate this heritage. Middle western farmers shared with, if indeed they did not lead, their fellow Americans in the mechanical sophistication so characteristic of modern America.

In the well-watered, fertile prairies of the Middle West, moreover, the ancient dream of universal land ownership became a sufficient reality to create a region of small farms. To the economic utility of the owner-operated farm, middle westerners grafted the tradition of the social desirability and political necessity of preserving the family farm. Out of this widely accepted view, of course, came political action protecting the farmers' welfare with regulatory legislation and subsidizing agriculture with free lands; roads, canals, and railways providing access to markets; crop loans; agricultural experiment stations; extension services; and, eventually, price-support programs. Although the tactics shifted from generation to generation, the basic goals remained constant.

On top of this, the tradition of a restless, migratory agriculture marked the region's history for its first century. With the vision of fresh new soils always before them, middle western farmers joined the march across the continent, often deserting rich soils for poor and practicing a wasteful, slovenly husbandry. As late as 1913, this heritage of excessive mobility remained so powerful that *Wallace's Farmer* denounced it: "The farmers of the United States have been playing leapfrog over each other for over a hundred years, in fact, ever since the Revolution. . . . It is time for us to realize that the value of land depends more than anything else on the men who farm it."[8]

Agrarian protest movements figure prominently in middle western traditions during the years when farmers stopped playing leapfrog. From the Grange to the Farm Bureau or from the Populists to the Farmers' Union, farmers have sought through group action a better bargaining position in an increasingly complex economy. These movements represent changing tactics, not crusades for sweeping economic reforms.

Demands for government regulation rested upon pragmatic analysis and shrewd opportunism. The decline of agricultural prices and the consolidation of railways in the post Civil War years placed too much of a strain upon the tradition of individualism and *laissez faire* in the rural community. Thus farmers were among those who felt most keenly the stress of adjusting to a new economic environment. Frustrated by the rapidity of these changes and by their incapacity to halt the rush of forces destroying their secure position in the national economy, they demanded state and federal regulation in sectors of the economy affecting their welfare.

Self-interest, rather than ideological doctrine, led farmers to this desertion of faith in the natural laws of trade and dictated a defense of views strange and alien to many of their

[8] *Wallace's Farmer* (Des Moines, Iowa), October 31, 1913.

fellow Americans. Opportunism, rather than logic, determined the character of the solutions they proposed. Middle western farmers, indeed, small capitalists everywhere in the United States during those anxious years, insisted upon the maintenance of the same economic opportunity for themselves as for others. As entrepreneurs, they saw their competitive position in the struggle for economic rewards threatened by the rise of new groups wielding unprecedented powers.

Our historical interpretations of these protest movements have exaggerated the political panaceas espoused by colorful agrarian spokesmen orating in the idiom of the Old Testament with the fervor of religious conviction. The movement for economic reforms through agricultural education, systematic farm management, improved efficiency in production and marketing, crop diversification, soil conservation, and scientific agriculture created a more important tradition in middle western agriculture.

Agricultural rather than agrarian, these movements sought solutions to the farmers' problems with economic measures. Realistic rather than sentimental, they urged the continuing necessity of improved farm practices, crops, and business methods to create new markets and hold old ones. While their focus was economic reform, government assistance often figured in these plans, as for example the use of land grant colleges to provide scientific research and marketing information.

This emphasis upon efficient production led Wisconsin farmers in the post Civil War years to abandon wheat in favor of sorghum, hops, sheep, fat cattle, and finally dairying. Again, the emphasis upon efficient marketing through co-operatives following World War I provides further evidence of the continuing search for more effective economic mechanisms. Indeed, co-operative marketing for a brief period seemed to be an answer to low prices, for as Herbert Hoover explained in 1920: "There can be no question of the improvement in the position of both farmer and consumer in cases where co-operative marketing can be organized."[9]

When farmers resorted to group action, their programs often clashed with the older traditions of individualism in the Middle West. Thus they came under attack for subverting the American heritage and destroying the American way of life. The editor of the business journal *Industry* explained to his readers in 1921 that the American Farm Bureau Federation was conceived "under un-American policies" and was "a form of socialism or paternalism which has never before been extended into the economic realms in this country, and therefore is a subtle and direct attack at the roots of Democracy and individual freedom of initiative."[10] It seems quite clear that as different groups adjusted to the dynamic changes in our economy, their definitions of how the profits should be allocated inevitably collided, often in an atmosphere of hostility and acrimony.

To view these frequent collisions of self-interest as crusades, as challenges to the overweening powers of mammon by the embattled forces of righteousness, obscures two basic truths: the protests, opportunistic and pragmatic, did not challenge the system itself; nor did they come only from farmers.

As we have seen, few dissenters argued for more than an opportunity to share more fully in the rewards of the private enterprise system. Economic regulation was a pragmatic de-

[9] Address to Farmer's Co-operative Associations, Topeka, October 13, 1920.
[10] *Industry*, Vol. III, No. 7 (March 1, 1921), 3-4.

vice, not a logical system. It promoted opportunity to enlarge wealth, not diminish it by dividing only that which presently existed. The ultimate objective of the farmers' protest movements, so far as they were economic in character, was the improvement of the status of the individual.

Merchants, bankers, and workers also joined the chorus of protest against the evils of business consolidation unaccompanied by regulation when their profits or wages seemed threatened. The actions of several economic groups during the early years of this century illustrate this fact, but the role of lumbermen in the upper Middle West is particularly revealing.

Low transportation rates and adequate supplies of freight cars were so important to producers that one of the major functions of their trade associations was to protect them against the carriers. The complaints of lumbermen sound surprisingly like the farmers' grievances against the railroads. Spokesmen for the forest-products industries denounced the railways for their greed and indifference to the public welfare. The leading trade journal in the Middle West expressed these feelings when it wrote:

> *Behold the honest lumberman!*
> *Most ev'rybody tries to do him.*
> *The railroads seldom give him cars*
> *And when they do, they soak it to him.*

> *The railroads talk of raising rates,*
> *Although the times are blue*
> *The devil finds some mischief still*
> *For idle hands to do.*[11]

11 *American Lumberman* (Chicago), September 28, 1907.

BROADENING THE CULTURAL BASE: The Library at Ohio State University.

A TREASURE IN ART: Chicago Art Institute, Home of One of America's Great Collections, an Art School, a Theatre, and Art Libraries.

THE WIDER CULTURAL WORLD: A Panel of Parliamentarians from Various NATO Countries Meeting at Coe College, Cedar Rapids.

Lumber men would exercise this familiar devil through regulation, thus calling upon the same powers invoked by the farmers around them. In fact, some lumbermen spoke so vigorously for stricter regulation under the Interstate Commerce Commission that the nation watched the curious spectacle of substantial businessmen bitterly accusing each other of sponsoring "Socialism" with their pleas for regulation.[12]

Pleas for government assistance, whatever their source, sought to preserve the private-enterprise system, though no longer under conditions of unregulated, imperfect competition. Private property, economic individualism, the social benefits of the system, and profit motives they did not challenge; they simply transferred their loyalty to different tactics to preserve them.

Such appeals for government assistance were not unprecedented. On the contrary, as Robert Lively recently pointed out, "official vision and public resources have been associated so regularly with private skill and individual desire that the combination may be said to constitute a principal determinant of American economic growth."[13]

Shortage of capital during the early years of settlement prompted middle westerners to turn to the government for assistance, thus creating a pattern firmly established through continued practice. "In a country like this where the inducements for the investment of capital are so great in proportion to the amount of capital," argued the promoters of the Milwaukee and Rock River Canal in a memorial to Congress in

---

[12] *St. Louis Lumberman*, Vol. 41, No. 2 (January 15, 1908), 65.

[13] Robert A. Lively, "The American System: A Review Article," *Business History Review*, Vol. XXIX, No. 1 (March, 1955), 94. Professor Lively's article summarizes the current literature on this subject.

1838, "it is not to be expected that private capital can be obtained in sufficient amount."[14]

Financial aid from every unit of government, from local to national, provided much of the capital for business enterprises—from Ohio to Missouri—that promised to build the canals, railways, and internal improvements necessary to unlock the region's potential wealth. Often the timeliness, rather than the amount, of these subsidies was the important factor. Once the initial rush evaporated, private investors quickly moved in to take the profits and guide expansion.

State enterprise was seldom viewed as antagonistic to private enterprise. On the contrary, promoters generally welcomed it as complementary, offering an opportunity to put into use regional resources that would otherwise lie idle. But there was little enthusiasm for such projects on doctrinaire grounds of the desirability of state enterprise or its superiority to private ownership or operation.[15]

The disposal of the public domain in the post Civil War years is a familiar example of the pragmatic nature of government assistance to business enterprise. Government provided access to raw materials, such as coal, iron, copper, and timber, with a policy that placed these regional resources under private ownership as quickly and as cheaply as possible. And middle western entrepreneurs responded to this generosity by converting potential into actual wealth with a speed and prodigality that amazes the modern student.

[14] Increase A. Lapham (ed.), *A Documentary History of the Milwaukee and Rock River Canal* (Milwaukee, 1840), 33.

[15] The only book-length study of the role of state enterprise in the Middle West is James Neal Primm, *Economic Policy in the Development of a Western State: Missouri, 1820–1860* (Cambridge, 1954); see also Lively, "The American System: A Review Article," *Business History Review*, Vol. XXIX, No. 1 (March, 1955), 85.

The waste accompanying this assault upon the region's resources led ultimately to a public outcry demanding legal regulations to enforce conservative practices. Physical waste in the destruction of resources and economic waste through their poor utilization drew heavy criticism during the early years of this century. The conservation movement, so colorfully led by Theodore Roosevelt and Gifford Pinchot, effected a revolution in American minds that profoundly altered the heritage of "free lands, free timber and inexhaustible resources."

As pervasive as these changes in traditional attitudes seemed at the time, they were only the beginning. With the passage of years, the conservation movement came to emphasize comprehensive concepts of resource utilization that promoted soil conservation, wiser management, multiple-purpose programs, and by-products industries using waste materials. Through the years since 1900, middle westerners have sought new guideposts to replace the inadequate precedents left by a generation that could afford to take little thought of tomorrow in its haste to create wealth in a region of abundant resources.

Middle western attitudes toward the eastern metropolis also changed substantially after 1900. During the previous century, the eastern metropolis furnished the capital for economic expansion, organized communications and transportation for the region, and provided markets for its products. This interregional relationship, comprising an almost feudal chain of vassalage, kept the Middle West a debtor economy, relying upon the largess of outside metropolitan centers. The demand for interest payments accompanying this regional debt spurred production and stimulated heavy exports of agricultural products and industrial raw materials to Eastern and European markets.

Middle westerners at first welcomed this economic dependency as providing urgently needed credit accommodation and essential markets. The economic collapses in 1873 and 1893, however, turned enthusiasm into keen resentment and created a bitterness bordering upon regional paranoia. William Jennings Bryan expressed this feeling in his famous cross-of-gold speech: "Burn down your cities and leave our farms, and your cities will spring up again as if by magic; but destroy our farms and the grass will grow on the streets of every city in the country."

This colonial status gradually diminished, of course, as the region accumulated capital and raised its own centers of finance and industry. With these changes, the heritage of bitterness against eastern economic imperialism receded, conforming to what appears to be the behavior of debtors turned creditors through economic growth in underdeveloped areas, no matter where they exist.

The greatest changes in regional attitudes and economic behavior have accompanied industrialization and urbanization within the past half-century. From modest beginnings in agriculturally related industries such as food processing, meat packing, and farm machinery, as well as certain extractive industries, the middle western industrial picture has been transformed by the growth of large-scale steel, automobile, electrical-goods, chemical, pharmaceutical, machine-tool, rubber, and synthetic industries.

While this expansion was basically part of a westward movement of national industries already established in techniques and traditions, such names as Cyrus Hall McCormick, Henry Ford, Frederick Weyerhaeuser, and Marshall Field reminds us of important middle western contributions to American techniques of production and distribution. The world-wide association of Detroit with mass production, Akron with rubber, or Minneapolis with milling suggests regional predominance and leadership. Indeed, the names that make Milwaukee famous proclaim a regional leadership in the brewer's art, while the role of such cities as Canton, Cleveland, Cincinnati, Chicago, and Cedar Rapids suggests an alphabetical listing of industrially important communities that could continue almost endlessly.

Urbanization accompanied this industrialization so rapidly that by mid-century, nearly 70 per cent of the region's population lived in cities with populations exceeding 2,500. This concentration in the urban Middle West is further emphasized by the presence of seven of the nation's twenty-three cities claiming more than 500,000 inhabitants. Of the nineteen cities in the Middle West with more than 150,000 people in 1950, eight did not even appear in the census a century earlier!

Thus two Middle Wests, one urban and the other rural, grew side by side. Since the metropolis appeared after the region's heritage seemed well formed, its search for solutions to new economic and social problems challenged accepted traditions. The replacement of weak by strong labor unions during the past quarter-century, for example, is a central fact of recent economic history. This rise to power in the 1930's met vigorous opposition and frequent violence in a region where rural traditions of individualism strongly supported employers' contentions that collective bargaining was "compulsory unionism" involving an invasion of the individual's "right to work" and an intrusion into management's exclusive control over business.

Since World War II, however, middle western attitudes

appear to have undergone considerable change, with labor and management and big business leading the way. The successful negotiation of General Motors' contract with the UAW in 1950 and the signing of the guaranteed annual wage contract by Ford Motor Company with the same union five years later argue that in the large-scale industries at least, accommodations can be secured at the conference table. The acceptance of a 15 per cent wage reduction by Studebaker employees when management demonstrated that it was necessary to the company's survival indicates the the earlier hostility between labor and management has moderated considerably.

Serious tensions remain between the new and the old, between industrial and agrarian traditions. This is conspicuous at times in one-industry towns situated in rural environments throughout the Middle West. Labor-management disputes continue to flare up as rural-urban antagonisms and nineteenth- and twentieth-century views collide. In such communities, union leaders think of themselves as the last defenders of the American heritage.

Our economic heritage, however, is too rich to be the property of a single group, too diverse to nourish only a segment of our economy. Our inheritance is as varied as our many economic interests and social and political views. Thus we possess traditions that both clarify and obscure contemporary problems; both facilitate and impede their solution. Our generation, as indeed each succeeding one, must constantly choose and encourage those aspects of our heritage that best assist in fulfilling the promise of American life, a promise that began with the landing of the first settlers on the Atlantic Seaboard.

IV

※※※※※※※※※※※※※※※※※※※※※※※※※※※※※※※※※※※※

A POLITICAL WHIRLPOOL

John D. Hicks

To TALK ABOUT the political heritage of the Middle West some thirty or forty years ago seemed very simple. Turnerian pronouncements were then unchallenged, and historians were sure that they had found most of the important answers. The epic of the westward movement was still strong in our minds. It seemed fitting to liken the conquest of the continent by a race of pioneers to one of those large-scale military invasions with which, unfortunately, the twentieth century was making us so familiar.

The first landings along the Atlantic Seaboard were small and only feebly held, but as reinforcements appeared, the armies of settlers occupied all the principal ports of entry, made contact with each other everywhere along the coast, advanced up the rivers to the waterfalls, and consolidated the territory in between, preparatory to the coming attack on the foothills and the mountain barrier. Meanwhile, scouting parties had brought in news of the terrain ahead, had located the best ways through, had pointed out the paths that the next advance should take. And in about a third the time required to win the first great goal, the second also had fallen.

Then came a headlong rush into the unguarded Mississippi Valley, where in another fifty years the irresistible frontiersmen swept everything before them and finally halted on the edge of the western plains only because the Great American Desert, some of it real and some only legend, held them back. But an amphibious landing on the California coast, together with one thrust after another through the Desert (which proved to be not so much of a desert after all) soon carried the conquerors to, through, into, and all over the vast mountains and valleys of the Far West. And the deed was done.

A thousand years from now, if the United States remains intact as a nation that long, this conquest of the continent will still be chapter one in our country's history. Indeed, it was only when the people possessed the land that the foundations of the new nation could be laid. What went on behind the frontier battle line was, of course, of vast importance, but through all these years, the more settled East never lost track of the less settled West. The Revolution was fought in part to make sure that the trans-Appalachian West should not be closed to the eastern invaders; the War of 1812 and the Mexican War were both primarily episodes in the invasion itself; the Civil War might never have been fought but for the contest over the expansion of slavery. Great political issues tended to center on western themes. Who should oversee the growth of the West, a few large states or the nation as a whole? Should the western domain be used as a source of revenue or as a means of providing homes for the millions? Should France be permitted to hold Louisiana, or should the way to the farther West be opened at whatever cost? Should the nation or the states shoulder the burden of internal improvements? Should the creditor East or the debtor West have the greater voice in devising the nation's banking system? And so on.

In calling attention to the importance of the growing West

in the life of the nation, Frederick Jackson Turner made perhaps his most notable contribution to American history. But
neither Turner nor those of us who believed in him were content to let the matter rest merely with the peopling of the
wilderness. We all saw great significance in the pioneering
process itself—in the continual rebirth of civilization with each
new and unique experience—which at one time or another
every part of the nation had shared. We saw that it gave a remarkably equalitarian bent to American democracy; that it
promoted immeasurably the idea of individual freedom; that
in spite of such incidental sectionalism as developed with each
notable change in environment, it contributed mightily to the
growth of nationalism; that it served to accentuate certain
American traits—optimism based on an abundance of opportunity; open-mindedness toward new ideas; a restless, roving
mobility coupled with an ease of adaptation to new conditions;
an emphasis on practicality, materialism, and acquisitiveness;
a certain "coarseness and strength" that visitors mistook for
provincialism.

As a loyal son of the Middle West, I still find much that
is true and comforting in these ideas. But as time marches on
and the frontier recedes farther and farther into the background, I can no longer overlook the fact that much of our
middle western heritage, political and otherwise, stems from
the post-frontier period. For a long time the historians of the
West neglected these middle years and concentrated too much
on the beginnings. Of late they have begun to remedy this
defect, and for good reason. Nowadays we look to history for
an explanation of the present; we expect it to make the characteristics of our own times more intelligible; we ask it to
help us get a line on the direction in which we are moving and

even to throw some light on the course we should pursue in the future. The most cursory glance at the Middle West of today is sufficient to make clear that the frontier experience and the institutions of the frontier are quite inadequate to explain all that meets the eye. Later builders have extended the foundations laid during the early years to make possible a superstructure of which the original architects could never even have dreamed. Thanks to the work of our historians, our economists, our sociologists, and many others besides, we are increasingly able to re-create and evaluate what went on between the years that fascinated Turner and the years in which we must live our lives.

Parenthetically, one of the easiest of arguments to start almost anywhere in the United States concerns what really constituted the Middle West. I, for one, propose to go along with the census and to have no truck with those purists who would throw out parts of Missouri because of the Ozarks, or parts of the Dakotas, Nebraska, and Kansas because of the idiosyncracies of rainfall, or parts of northern Michigan, Wisconsin, and Minnesota on account of lakes, trees, and stumplands, or parts of the Old Northwest because it has gone so heavily industrial. The twelve North Central States are all Middle West and should know it. There's one thing you can say for Iowa, maybe two. Every definition of the Middle West I have ever seen or heard unfailingly includes all of Iowa, and every Iowan I have ever met makes haste to proclaim himself a middle westerner, even if he lives in Los Angeles.

I was never one to take much stock in the pedagogical device of unraveling history backwards. But if we expect history to explain the present, we can hardly avoid taking a close look at what the present is like. We note first the prodigious size to which our middle western population has grown: according to the Census of 1950, nearly 45,000,000 persons, some 5,000,000 less than live in the whole of the United Kingdom. Nor can we disregard the fact that ours has become an urban rather than a rural people. Shocked a little at what their figures told them, our latest census analysts came up with two new and badly needed definitions to supplement the old dividing line based on places of 2,500 inhabitants. They now recognize as "urbanized areas" each city of 50,000, plus the closely settled surrounding territory, whether or not it lies within any city, and any "county or group of contiguous counties which contains at least one city of 50,000 inhabitants or more." The result of these new definitions is a better picture of the extent to which urbanization has gone in the United States. As for the Middle West, the transformation of the last half-century is little short of revolutionary. The Census of 1900 found only one of the twelve middle western states, Illinois, to have more city dwellers than country dwellers; the Census of 1950 found only four states predominantly rural—Iowa, Nebraska, and the two Dakotas. For the Middle West as a whole, the city population outnumbers the country population nearly two to one. Even in the seven states that lie to the west of the Mississippi River, the population, taken together, is more urban that rural. As for those "standard metropolitan areas," of which in the entire United States there are now 168, nearly one-third of them lie in the Middle West, while Iowa, which still clings by a hair to its country majority, has within its borders all or parts of six of them. Middle westerners today not only live mainly in cities, but an astonishingly large number of them live in big cities.

It seems obvious that if we are to look for the political

heritage of the Middle West, we shall have to look for it in its cities no less than in the rural areas. And we shall have to have our eyes open for the conditions that produced the cities —manufacturing, merchandising, transportation, finance—as well as for conditions that produced the country, mainly agriculture. The trouble with the frontier approach is that it was geared so closely to an agricultural environment. Richard Hofstadter, in his arresting new book, *The Age of Reform* (1955), observes that "the United States was born in the country and has moved to the city." This is a little too sweeping; much of the United States has not yet moved to the city, and much of the city population never did live in the country —at least not on this side of the Atlantic. But there is no question that the rural heritage, taken by itself alone, is not the whole heritage and that the contributions made by city populations, city conditions, and city attitudes must also be taken into consideration.

Chronologically, however, the country came first and the city only later. The agricultural interest dominated every territory before it achieved statehood, wrote the new state constitutions, enacted the first basic laws. If Jefferson was right in his contention that "the proportion which the aggregate of the other classes of citizens bears in any state to that of its husbandmen, is the proportion of its unsound to its healthy parts," then the states of the Middle West started on their way in extremely good health.

To be sure, the western farmers were not great political scientists. When it came to forms of government, it never even occurred to them not to borrow extensively from the older states of the East. But in the application and interpretation of the old provisions there was a degree of equalitarianism that was sometimes lacking in the more settled regions. Of what hindrance to democracy were property qualifications for voting if every free white male over twenty-one was pretty sure to own property? Of what significance were the prerogatives of aristocracy if it turned out that everybody was somebody in the West? Of what importance was government, anyway, if opportunity lay equally open to all who had the wit to seize it, except possibly to register and defend land titles and to see to it that the game of getting ahead was fairly played? Individualism and equalitarianism went hand in hand as long as there was plenty of room for both.

The pioneer farmer resented being told what he could or could not do, wanted no interference from government, whether state or national, and asked only to be left to his own devices. He learned early, however, without noting any contradiction, that there was no percentage in putting an embargo on what a kind government, out of the goodness of its heart, wanted to do *for* him. On the land question, he progressed readily from acceptance of easy credit to insistence on low prices, pre-emption rights, and even free homesteads. On transportation improvements, the more help he could get from outside sources, the better. On defense against the Indians, if and when it was needed, he expected the national power to take the lead. On finance, he preferred easy money and so favored state banks rather than a national bank, but he gave a ready welcome to national deposits in western "pet" banks and to any other largess that the national government chose to dish out. Long before Franklin D. Roosevelt and the New Deal, the West was well conditioned to the idea of a benevolent Washington Santa Claus.

The way in which the West was settled also made for

nationalism. People came in from every section of the nation and from Europe, learned somehow to get along together, relaxed their earlier loyalties, and simply became Americans. It is worth noting that despite occasional outbursts of nativism, the absorption of immigrant groups in areas devoted to agriculture was accomplished with a minimum of difficulty. The immigrant problem was, and still remains, far more a matter of the city than of the country. In the country, there was no "other side of the tracks."

The painstaking studies which historians have made of our agricultural pioneering is only now beginning to be paralleled by studies of our urban pioneering. Bayrd Still's *Milwaukee* (1943) and Bessie L. Pierce's *Chicago* (1937–40) are cases in point. But as Graham Hutton has observed in his perspicacious book, *Midwest at Noon* (1946), we cannot much longer ignore the fact that there are two distinct Middle Wests, the older agricultural Middle West, with its scattered farms and villages, and the newer, but now much larger, industrial Middle West of growing towns and cities. Also, that which separates the urban from the rural Middle West is something far more fundamental than proceeds from a mere concentration of population. The difference is primarily occupational; the country people are engaged in agriculture, while the city people, nearly all of them, are, in some intimate way, connected with business.

Nor is the business of the later Middle West merely the business of ministering to the needs of the local farmers—buying their produce—and some of the smaller towns, towns that refuse to grow. However, this is not true of the cities, where population gains have been spectacular. The cities of the Middle West, like the cities of the East, the Far West, and the

South, are great industrial centers; their industrial beginnings
are sometimes recent, but many started off as industrial cities
as far back as the decade that preceded the Civil War. They
have become great mainly because of their devotion to manufacturing of one kind or another, whether of iron and steel,
machinery, transportation equipment, lumber and wood products, or any other of the infinite variety of durable and non-
durable, producer's or consumer's perishable or nonperishable
goods that our complicated civilization demands. No wonder
that business history is having a great vogue these days. It
should have. And if the historians of the Middle West are
to understand their section well, they should be in the forefront of it.

Whence came the people who made these cities? Speculators who dealt in real estate, merchants and middlemen who
helped the farmers, moneylenders and professional men of
every sort and kind, all were hard on the heels of each new
movement into the West, if indeed they were not actually an
intimate part of it. But the real makers of middle western cities
were the industrial pioneers; men with a vision of railroads,
such as James J. Hill; men who saw the possibilities of oil,
such as John D. Rockefeller; men who dealt in farm machinery,
such as Cyrus Hall McCormick.

You cannot have factories without customers and workers, so every industrial pioneer was also a great promoter of
settlement. Railroad men were particularly adept at this, and
they exerted themselves in every possible way in order to bring
the population in, whether farmers to live in the country or
industrial workers to live in the cities. And, especially in the
cities, the numbers came to be recruited more and more from
European immigrants. These city immigrants, unlike their

81

luckier relatives who went to the country, were not quickly caught up in the melting-pot, mixing-bowl, call-it-what-you-like, Americanization process that characterized the country. They lived apart from the native Americans and from other national groups, each in his own section of the city. They retained for a generation or longer the old-country language and customs, they accepted, because nothing better was offered, the most distressing living conditions, they fell easy prey to the city and state political machines, whose bosses were ready to exchange a crude sort of social security for votes. Middle western historians somehow fail to identify these urban characteristics with western, as well as eastern, cities and tend to assume that the cities of their section, with the possible exception of Chicago, were different from the rest. The fact is quite opposite. Nowhere in the whole nation was there more heartless exploitation, more ruthless intolerance, more bribery and corruption, more of what Lincoln Steffens describes in *The Shame of the Cities* (1904) than in our own Middle West.

Politically speaking, the Middle West fell under the sway of what we generally lump together as the business interests. The party boss, who takes his orders from the industrial leaders and exacts from those below him the same kind of fealty he gives to those above, is far more a city than a country phenomenon. The men who were making the West, and making it in a hurry, were unwilling to brook interference with their decisions from the public at large, and the party bosses saw to it that the will of the business leaders was done. Graham Hutton has suggested an analogy between the "forced savings" required of the Soviet peoples during the various five-year plans and the breakneck speed with which the Middle West achieved full settlement and industrialization. Had the leaders been will-

THE DUTCH INFLUENCE: Two Natives of Holland,
Michigan, Deep in Tulips.

KARLA MASARYK CHORUS of the Czechoslovak Society of America.

ing to proceed a little more slowly, they might not have found it necessary to charge such high freight rates, or to require so great an interest burden, or to insist on such handsome profits, or to corrupt so many legislatures. But they were unwilling to wait, and those who stood in their way had to take the consequences. Middle western spokesmen who saw in this chain of circumstances a kind of conspiracy may have been dreaming dreams and seeing visions, as some historians now say, but there was certainly a sufficient amount of agreement in business attitudes to make the charge seem plausible. Moreover, the tributary relationship that so often subordinated western to eastern business interests gave a sectional tint to the picture. Was not the agricultural Middle West suffering from exactions designed to benefit the industrial captains of the East?

It was this situation that prompted the farmers to revolt. In Granger times they found the exactions of the railroads more than they could bear, so they turned against the bosses, packed the legislatures with farmers, and demanded that the power of government be used to protect the agricultural interest, not to exploit it. They did not invent the Granger idea; it was as old as the English common law which held that all common carriers were quasi public and therefore subject to regulation. But they applied it with vigor to the railroads, who fought back bitterly against what seemed to the men who headed them a mere taking of property, or a usurpation of privilege, without due process of law.

Now there can be little doubt that the farmers were as much hurt by the world competition that had developed in farm produce as by railroad exactions, but the latter were a good deal more than a myth, and as they eased up, whether because of state regulation or because of reformed railroad

83

behavior, or both, the middle western farmers found themselves better off. Similarly, they discovered in the "trusts" a tendency toward monopoly that the common law seemed to condemn as conspiracy in restraint of trade, and here again they demanded and obtained, at least in faint degree, some redress. They resented also the appreciation in value of the dollar, which depressed prices and made the farmers' debts harder to pay. They were not very good economists, and at this point the English common law let them down, but whether it was railroad regulation, trust control, or monetary reform, they were determined to force the government, either state or national, to take their side against the business world, and they scored some notable successes. The Populist revolt, like most third-party movements, failed to produce a new party, but it contributed many important ideas to the older parties and to the main stream of American political history.

It was during these years that American businessmen laid down their definitions of conservatism and radicalism. Lexicographers, philosophers, and political scientists might regard the formulation of such definitions as difficult, but not our business leaders. Conservatism came to mean whatever they liked and believed in; radicalism, whatever they did not like and did not believe in. And to this day, at least among the hard-boiled old conservatives, whatever one may say for the soft-boiled new conservatives, one detects very little improvement in their pattern of thought. With nearly all of them, the central idea is that what's good for business is good for the United States. They regarded the revolt of the farmers as bad for business; hence it was branded as the work of radicals—socialists, communists, maybe even anarchists—who were bent on undermining the very foundations of American society.

Nation said of William Jennings Bryan in 1896: "Probably no man in civil life has succeeded in inspiring so much terror, without taking life." Actually, the farmers who voted for Bryan and for Populists were not radicals at all in the sense that they wished to make fundamental changes in the nature of the American political and economic order. They were devoted to the idea of ballot-box rule, they believed in the Constitution and the American way of life, and they were all either small capitalists or would-be small capitalists. What they wanted was a fairer share for themselves of the fruits of their labor, and they appealed to the power of government only because they thought that through governmental power alone could they hope for a restoration of at least some semblance of an economic balance. They believed that the extremes of individualism, as practiced by the great business leaders, must be restrained if the old American tradition of an equal chance for all was to stand. In fighting to obtain assistance from the government in time of need, the farmers were doing only what American businessmen had always regarded as fair and proper for the interests that they represented.

Self-appointed spokesmen for the farmers' point of view sometimes demanded more than the rank and file had in mind. In a day when party discipline was strong, irregulars were systematically dropped from positions of old-party prominence only to show up later in the forefront of whatever third-party movement might then be current. For this and perhaps other reasons, a substantial number of crackpots managed, during the later nineteenth century, to infiltrate reform circles, but it is grossly unfair to attribute to the reform movement as a whole the ideas expressed by these mere parasites. Indeed, it is unfair to think of the farmer protest as primarily a third-party affair. Within both of the older parties there was a spirit of insurgency that distressed and annoyed the bosses almost as much as did the activities of the Populists. And in the early years of the twentieth century, these intraparty reformers reached the climax of their strength, not in any third party at all, but actually within the Republican, rather than the Democratic, party. The head of a great middle western state university once told me that in dealing with the legislature, he found the regular Republicans to be the easiest to handle, the regular Democrats next, the liberal Democrats a good bit more difficult, and the liberal Republicans the real toughies. That same order of behavior held for many matters dear to the hearts of business executives as well.

When we get to the twentieth century, we must pay greater attention than formerly to what was actually going on within the cities. By this time population statistics had begun to roll, and the people who lived in urban places, like the farmers who lived in the country, were about ready to register their protest against being pushed around. Among the immigrant groups, who constituted a large part of each city's inhabitants, the tradition of equality and individual freedom that was so highly regarded in the country was at first almost lacking.

Gradations of society were a part of the European heritage, and they reappeared with a vengeance in the new American cities. Native Americans usually managed to monopolize the top rungs of the ladder, partly because of the unearned increment that came to those who retained their early holdings in real estate and partly because native Americans occupied most of the command posts in the new industrialism. But from there on down, class distinctions based on income, occupation, native origin, race, color, and creed were as marked as the hand of man could make them. They were emphasized by place of residence, if the country town had a right and a wrong side of the tracks; in the cities it was far more complicated. The least favored classes, mainly Negroes and recent immigrants, lived in the worst residential sections, usually close to the business center of the city, while those who had climbed higher in the social scale lived in better sections farther and farther out. Improved means of transportation, coupled with the steadily increasing population, resulted in the formation of one concentric circle of inhabitants after another, each new ring representing for those who lived in it a step upward in status. Like Holmes's chambered nautilus, the typical American suburbanite "stretched in his last-found home, and knew the old no more." As time went on, suburbs piled on suburbs and ex-urbs on ex-urbs, leaving at the center an area of dry rot into which, for business reasons, the outdweller might have to penetrate by day but from which he beat a hasty retreat each night.

There is room for more study of these city frontiers that contrast so markedly with the old agricultural frontiers of the early West. The city frontiers were created, in large part, by individuals who had worked their way up into middle-class status; they moved farther out because they were better off— the better off, the farther out. But the country frontiers were created by people who had left status behind and had begun all over again at the bottom of the ladder. Yet the two had something in common. Each had the vision of greater opportunity, of somehow building a new and better life. Each cherished as a principle the right to rise in the world and stood ready to oppose with vigor whatever forces barred the way. And as a matter of fact, it was only when the agricultural frontier had grown up, and had at least tasted prosperity, that it got around to registering really effective protests. The nineteenth-century revolt of the farmer was actually a small-capitalist, middle-class affair, and the twentieth-century Progressive movement, which got much of its momentum from the rising middle class of the cities, was not so vastly different.

The Progressive movement, with which we customarily associate such names as Theodore Roosevelt, Woodrow Wilson, and Robert M. La Follette, had its roots in both the country and the city. It was by no means exclusively a middle western affair, although it was most formidable in this area. Except for the free-silver heresy, it inherited virtually the whole Populistic creed, and it based its protests on the same resentment against the efforts of a greedy few to monopolize for themselves the principal profits of the new industrialism.

It is, of course, a fact that during these years there was not, in middle class circles—whether urban or rural—much real deprivation or want. But whatever one had, one wanted more, and the men at the top seemed bent on skimming all the cream for themselves. Resentment deepened against the steadily rising prices, the heavier mortgage exactions, the mounting burden of public-utility costs, and the increasing taxes, for all of which, it was generally assumed, the captains of industry were to blame.

Faced by these real, or fancied, oppressions, the Progressives were as ready to appeal to the power of government for redress as were the Populists. There was a growing concern, however, over the shortcomings of democracy and a fuller realization that if the government were to be of any aid, its techniques would have to be improved. Of what avail to expect help from a government that the vested interests themselves controlled? At this point, the experience of the white-collar city classes had something to contribute. They knew more about the seamy side of politics than their country cousins. Nearly everywhere the hold of the city machines was still strong, partly because so many of the new suburbs were not within the city boundaries and partly because so many of the city workers were still amenable to machine rule. The power of the city bosses was hard to break, although their alliance on one side with predatory business and on the other with crime and vice was a matter of common knowledge. The corruption that characterized city government also extended to the state level, where businessmen usually got what they wanted, regardless of how they got it. As for what went on in Washington, that, too, could stand a little face-washing.

For a time, the Progressive movement swept everything before it. Journalists who chose to wield the muckrake had a field day; humanitarians, including many Socialists and near-Socialists, all bent on the uplift of the lower classes, joined together in force; public-minded men of wealth who were not too deeply committed to the advancement of their own fortunes provided funds far in excess of anything the Populists had ever known; professional men and intelligentsia jumped on the band wagon. And the Progressives won some notable victories. They made a substantial beginning in the reform of city government, they instituted primary elections and other procedures that changed the whole character of state government, they invaded the national field under Roosevelt and Wilson, and they kept their banner aloft under LaFollette, even during the reactionary decade of the 1920's. They improved, too, on the Populistic formula for the use of the powers of government. They saw less and less virtue in the attempt to restore competition by an attack on big business as such, more and more in the extension of governmental regulation. Big business had come to stay; what the people needed was a fair-minded government that would lay down rules for its behavior, protect the interests of the public, and, to quote Jefferson again, restrain those who would "take from labor the bread it has earned." But, as a matter of fact, the working class as a whole did not participate extensively in the Progressive movement. From beginning to end it was primarily a middle-class affair, seeking only incidentally to better the interests of labor and often interesting the labor leaders, but with its eye fixed firmly on the goal of keeping business subordinate to government and middle-class opportunity alive.

It was not until after the Panic of 1929 and the darkening years of depression that the urban working classes really came into their own. The New Deal owed much to the course of Populist and Progressive thought; just as Progressivism was rooted in Populism, so was New Dealism rooted in Progressivism. But each went a step further than its predecessor. The Populist concern was mainly with the farmers, the Progressive interest included both the farmers and the urban middle classes, and the New Deal added to the list wage earners (or would-be wage earners) in all these movements, but each new manifestation of the reform spirit reached a greater distance beyond middle western boundaries. Populism had its significant southern manifestations, but its real home was in the Middle West. Progressivism, for all the contributions of such eastern leaders as Roosevelt and Wilson and such far westerners as Hiram Johnson, grew from the hard core of middle western insurgency. New Dealism, however, was essentially a national phenomenon, more urban than rural, and in a geographic sense not sectional at all.

As the decades roll by, it thus becomes more difficult to

nail down the precise political heritage of the Middle West. The old agricultural heritage, dating back to frontier days, still stands out most clearly. From the Populist era the middle western farmer emerged much less a political partisan than he had been before. To promote the agricultural interest, he stood ready at the drop of a hat to vote Democratic instead of Republican or even to abandon the old-party fold altogether. He also learned the pressure-group technique so common among business interests; a farm bloc of one kind or another has repeatedly held up, for what at the moment seemed to promise most for agriculture, first the Old Deal, then the New Deal, then the Fair Deal, and now the Eisenhower Deal. This demand for national assistance, whether it is called parity, or soil conservation, or the soil bank, or whatever else, has a strong middle western, bipartisan flavor, and it usually wins out. The farmers were in their day called poor politicians and on occasion were advised to go on home and slop the hogs, but they have managed to retain a vast overrepresentation in Congress and in the state legislatures, and their representatives rarely allow farmer demands to be overlooked. The farmer, however, is no more a socialist today than he ever was. He still believes earnestly in equality of opportunity, he cherishes the principle of individual freedom, and he demands that the national government shall somehow harness this unruly team and force it to pull together.

It is much harder to deal with urban heritage of the Middle West, for historians have not yet done the groundwork necessary to make its infinite complexities understandable. The cities of industrial America, wherever located, have much in common, and sectional distinctions are not readily apparent. That such differences exist, we cannot doubt; Chicago, for example, is no mere replica of New York. To point out a single developmental difference, many of the cities of the East were cities before the age of industrialization, whereas the cities of the Middle West were never cities at all until industry created them. Of one thing I think we may be certain. The cities of the Middle West provided in their industrial leaders and those who sought to do their will as convinced and immobile a group of conservatives as could be found anywhere in the nation. Graham Hutton goes a step further; in his judgment they were "more traditional, hidebound, and even reactionary in social outlook than any British Tory." These conservative businessmen and their servants met farmer demands with every variety of economic pressure and turned misrepresentation into a fine art. It was their tactics, rather than those of the rural reformers (as a current aberration now has it), that furnished the most impressive precedents for the blatant intolerance of our own extreme right-wingers. In dealing with labor, they exploited immigrant workers, resisted unionization, kept wages down, sought injunctions, employed strikebreakers, and held back history with all their might and main. In the political field, they operated almost totally without scruple; if they had any principle, when profits were involved, it was that the end justified the means. In the defense of property rights, they cheerfully switched their constitutional views. Time was when to be conservative was to favor building up the power of the national government, but of recent years the true conservative wishes to set close limits on the national power. It is almost axiomatic that when a business becomes big enough to need restraint, it is too big for a state to restrain it. So the modern conservative has gone back on Hamilton and Marshall and Webster and Lincoln and has become a firm advocate of States' rights.

The role of labor, like the role of business, is not easily separated, section by section, from the national whole, but few would deny to the activities of the city workers a place in the middle western heritage. Undoubtedly, the rapid spread of unionization during the last fifty years has done much for the wage earner, but it has also posed problems that will not be easily solved, such, for example, as the autocratic, rather than the democratic, control of labor unions, the prevalence of labor racketeering, and the misuse of union funds, whether for private or political purposes.

On the other side of the ledger, the labor unions themselves now provide many of the benefits that in times past the old city machines depended on to keep their voters faithful, while the social-security system, operated by government, goes even farther in the same direction. City machines still exist, but they are not quite what they used to be. Yet these things are as true of one section as of any other; in what particulars, if any, has middle western labor made a unique contribution? Some have said that a little of the old-frontier individualism has rubbed off on the middle western worker, that he is less *class* conscious and more *job* conscious than his eastern contemporary, and that he believes more firmly, and for better reason, in his chance to rise in the world. But any such generalizations, without more evidence than is now apparent, are hardly to be trusted. We do know, however, the middle western farmers and workers have had grave difficulty in understanding each other and that it was often easy for the business interests to set them at each other's throats. In isolated instances, as with the La Follette Progressives in Wisconsin and the Farmer-Laborites in Minnesota, they made some headway toward a common front, and under the New Deal they generally voted the same national ticket, whatever their animosities. But the mutual suspicions still exist and bid fair to remain as a part of our sectional heritage for many years to come.

One middle western characteristic seems to cut across all lines, city or country, business or labor. Throughout the twentieth century, the Middle West has been strongly isolationist in international affairs. As Professor Billington pointed out a decade ago, the "prejudices of alarmed business men, discontented farmers, immigrant voters, and pacifist churchgoers" tended to coincide at this point. Part of the reason for this state of mind undoubtedly lies in the very real geographic isolation of the Middle West. The great American cities that lie outside its borders are nearly all seaports, long conditioned to the coming and going of the ships and the trade of many nations, but middle western cities are from several hundred to as much as a thousand miles from the nearest ocean.

At least until recent years, middle western industrialists thought mainly in terms of American markets, and had no desire to risk the near and the known by interfering in European affairs. Middle western farmers were insulated even more against the outside world than middle western businessmen. A fraction of their produce might eventually find its way overseas and a few agricultural experts understood the significance of this "exportable surplus," but most middle westerners thought that if anything were wrong, strictly American legislation such as the McNary-Haugen bills, for example, could cure it. Furthermore, they were positive that involvement in foreign affairs would almost certainly get in the way of internal reforms.

Immigrants sometimes retained a degree of loyalty to the countries of their nativity, but their great concern was to get away from the quarrels of the Old World, neither to participate in them there nor transfer them to the New. Middle western workers, reflecting considerably the immigrant point of view, had little stomach for a foreign policy that might result in an exchange of peacetime pursuits for military service. And it may be that Christian pacifism was more pronounced in the Middle West than elsewhere in the nation. Whatever the reasons, the Middle West was slow to accept the necessity of war, whether in 1917, 1941, or 1950, and it still looks askance at the tremendous overseas commitments the United States has made. Many middle western Congressmen, when they vote funds for foreign aid, do it not with the idea of our country getting something back in return for what it gives, as most foreigners seem to think, but with the hope that American generosity will put the nations concerned on their feet again so that the United States can thereafter forget about them for all time.

And what of the future? It seems apparent that sectionalism is on the wane, particularly in the urban and industrial America of which the Middle West furnishes so large a part. Middle western agriculture, while still formidable, is of relatively less importance than it used to be, and as time goes on, the scales will probably tip still more against it. But neither the section nor the nation can ever afford to sacrifice the agricultural interest; too much depends on it. The nation must eat to live, and it cannot permit its principal source of food supply to be imperiled, whatever the cost may be. In a free economy, I suppose there is no escape from the clash of economic interests, not even in isolated community-living experiments, but one may at least hope that our dominant business leaders will remember that the price of freedom is a social conscience, that on occasion it may be better policy to allow competitive little business to live rather than to kill it off, and that both the farmers and the workers have fundamental rights that must be respected. If there is any one thing that the middle western political heritage emphasizes above all others, it is that the people generally have the right of appeal to government whenever justice is ignored and that the government, representing all the people and not merely some especially favored interest or interests, should use its power to correct the injustice. Only in this way can we hope to give more than lip service to those deeply cherished and long-remembered middle western ideals—individual freedom and equality of opportunity.

V

~~~~~~

THE SEARCH FOR UTOPIA

Arthur J. Bestor

IN THE YEAR 1875 a well-known newspaperman, Charles Nordhoff, published a volume which he entitled *The Communistic Societies of the United States, from Personal Visit and Observation.*[1] The book sent no shivers up and down the spines of its readers. Nordhoff had not got wind of a secret conspiracy against the Republic. He was not exposing a dangerously subversive movement into whose underground organization he had managed to penetrate. Quite the contrary, he had obtained his information by the simple expedient of entering the hospitable doors of one communistic society after another and quietly asking what he wanted to know.

Two of the societies Nordhoff visited were in Iowa. At Amana, in the villages of the Amana Society, he found "a remarkably quiet, industrious, and contented population; honest, of good repute among their neighbors, very kindly, and with religion so thoroughly and largely made a part of their lives that they may be called a religious people."[2] One hundred and

---

[1] New York, Harper & Brothers, 1875 (copyright 1874). The author, Charles Nordhoff (1830–1901), had just become Washington correspondent of the *New York Herald* after serving for many years on the *New York Evening Post*, latterly as managing editor.

[2] Nordhoff, *The Communistic Societies of the United States, from Personal Visit and Observation*, 43.

97

fifty miles to the west, near Corning, in Adams County, he visited the colony of Icaria, the "least prosperous" of all the communities he encountered. There he could admire the "courage and perseverance" of the colonists, but he could find little to cheer him in the life they had long been obliged to lead. "They have proved their faith in the communistic idea," he wrote, "by labors and sufferings which seem to me pitiful. In fact, communism is their religion."[3]

Nordhoff adhered rigorously to the limitations of his title and wrote only of the communities he could describe "from personal visit and observation." Had he delved into history, he could have given reports on at least four communistic societies in Iowa which antedated the founding of Amana and Icaria but which had long since perished. These will be discussed later. Before I go on, however, I feel obliged to answer an insistent and troublesome question: In what sense were all these various enterprises "communistic"?

Words are slippery things, and abstract words are especially deceptive. And when abstractions become involved with political and economic conflict, language is apt to play its most devious tricks. The fact of the matter is that only an accident of language connects the communism of Amana with the communism of today's headlines. But it is not enough merely to assert this lack of real connection. The ambiguities of existing terminology call for some explanation, and this can be given only by tracing the history of the usage of the word "communism."

The term "communism," with its various derivatives, is not, as commonly supposed, an ancient word. It was coined little more than a century ago—in 1840 to be exact. The period was one in which a large number of new terms of this kind

[3] *Ibid.,* 339.

were being invented because a large number of new social theories were being propounded and names were needed to describe them. The word "socialism," for example, came into being in 1827; "radicalism" seems to go back no farther than 1820; "collectivism" emerged as a word about 1850; even "industrialism" was a new word in the 1820's and 1830's, and it originally stood for the ideas that social reformers were preaching, not the things they were attacking.[4]

Although reformers were ingenious in word-making and although they produced some fairly bizarre neologisms, nevertheless, new theories came into existence faster than new words. Eventually there were not enough labels to go around. Social theorists had to double up, like the guests in a crowded inn. And the shortage of accommodations, linguistically speaking, produced some strange bedfellows. In particular, three groups of social reformers were in need of appropriate labels in the 1840's, and all three accepted for themselves the word "communism" when it finally made its appearance.

In the first place, there were reformers who believed (as had many of the early Christians) that the cure for selfishness and the social evils resulting therefrom lay in the equal sharing of all worldly possessions. Property, these men and women believed, ought to be held in common. "Communism," as applied to such beliefs, meant this and nothing more; it was merely a synonymn for the ancient phrase "community of goods." "Communism" was applied, retroactively but with perfect propriety, to all those social systems wherein (to quote the Biblical verse which such reformers especially revered) "the

---

[4] See Arthur Bestor, "The Evolution of the Socialist Vocabulary," *Journal of the History of Ideas*, Vol. IX (June, 1948), 259–302. This article furnishes detailed documentation for most of the points in the paragraphs that immediately follow.

multitude of them that believed were of one heart and of one soul: neither said any of them that aught of the things which he possessed was his own; but they had all things common."[5] Such, of course, was the communism of the Amana Society.

At the opposite pole among the social reformers of the mid-nineteenth century were those who preached a revolutionary overthrow of the existing order and a forcible establishment of economic equality through ownership by the community of the means of production. These men had some claim upon the word "communism," for it had actually been coined by quasi-revolutionary groups in Paris in 1840. This claim to the word was asserted in 1848 when Karl Marx and Friedrich Engels chose to call their revolutionary appeal the *Communist Manifesto*. Curiously enough, they did not adhere to the term for long. In the 1870's, when Charles Nordhoff wrote his book on the *Communistic Societies of the United States,* the Marxists were referring to themselves not as communists, but as socialists. At the time, and for fifty years thereafter, the term that Nordhoff used was quite devoid of revolutionary overtones.[6] The confusion which we experience today in connection with the word "communism" dates only from 1918, when the Bolsheviki of Russia deliberately revived the term that Marx and Engels had used in the *Communist Manifesto* and henceforth called themselves the Communist party. Since then, to think of communism has been to think of their program and their methods and to forget that programs quite different from theirs have in the past borne the same label.

[5] Acts 4:32.

[6] In 1880, "socialism" denoted the revolutionary movement and was authoritatively described as "far more imperious and widesweeping than communism." See Theodore D. Woolsey, *Communism and Socialism in Their History and Theory* (New York, 1880), 9.

This brief account should suffice to explain the major perplexity that arises in connection with the word "communism." But there is also a minor confusion to be cleared up. Other writers of Nordhoff's time described, under the heading of "early American communism,"[7] a large number of experimental communities that neither practiced community of property nor believed in revolution. Among these were the Fourierist associations—including the Iowa Pioneer Phalanx, earliest of all the communities to be planted on the soil of Iowa. Yet the founder of this particular movement, Charles Fourier, said categorically that community of goods was an idea "so pitiable that it does not deserve refutation."[8] How can the term "communistic" be applied to enterprises of this kind?

The answer is that these particular reformers were interested in community also, but not in the sense of community of property. They were giving to the word "community" what is actually its most familiar meaning. They were not using the abstract noun "community," but the collective noun. They were talking about *a* community—"a body of people organized into a political, municipal, or social unity"[9] or, to choose another dictionary definition, "a social group of any size whose members reside in a specific locality, share government, and have a cultural and historical heritage."[10] A great many social reformers in the first half of the nineteenth century traced the evils of their day to the disintegration of community life in this particular sense. The rural village—the basic, stable unit of social life throughout most of human history—was being de-

[7] See, for example, Richard T. Ely, *Labor Movement in America* (New York, 1886), chap. II.

[8] Charles Fourier, *Oeuvres complètes* (Paris, 1841–45), VI, 473.

[9] Oxford Universal English Dictionary on Historical Principles, article "community," definition II, 2.

[10] *American College Dictionary*, article "community," definition I.

stroyed or profoundly altered in the nineteenth century by the competition of agriculture in the New World, by manufacturing, by migration. The new factory towns and the great cities, which were becoming more crowded every day, seemed lacking in all the qualities that made a society healthy. They were places where masses of people resided rather than communities in which men and women lived.

If social life were to become sound again, the sense of belonging to a community would have to be restored to the people who had been uprooted. Reformers who felt this way put community at the center of their plans—not community of property, but simply *a community*; that is to say, a group of men and women few enough in number to know each other well, sympathetic enough to work together, idealistic enough to strive for a better world than the one stretching out before them.

This approach to social reform had as much right to the newly coined word "communism" as either of the other schools that adopted it. Confusion would have been less, of course, had a differentiated term come into use. One was, in fact, available, for the 1840's also produced the word "communitarian," which for a time was commonly applied to communities of the sort discussed here. Unfortunately, the term faded from use. It can, however, be revived. In this essay, as in earlier publications of mine, I propose to do so. I shall describe as communitarian all those colonies that were established for the definite purpose of creating a richer, nobler, more equitable social life by bringing men and women together to share their lives in closely knit communities. The term is broad enough to include those societies which adopted community of goods as well as those which did not. Indeed, the communitarian ideal—the ideal of

a shared community life—was actually more important than
the doctrine of community of goods, even in those colonies
that were both communistic and communitarian. As Mrs.
Bertha Shambaugh has perceptively said of Amana, "Communism had ever been incidental to the life and thought of the
Community." In all the inspired writings of the colony, she
observed, "there was no discussion of an economic, social, or
political philosophy—only the necessity of preserving 'the
faith which has love and the bond of peace for its essence and
foundation.' "[11]

The subject of this essay is the significance of the communitarian movement as part of the intellectual and social heritage of the American Middle West. I do not intend to offer
an extended narrative of events, although I shall look briefly
at certain communities in Iowa. These must, however, be
thought of as local representatives of a larger movement—a
movement with two hundred years of history behind it, one
which, during its flowering in the generation before the Civil
War, produced almost one hundred communitarian colonies,
two-thirds of them in the Middle West.[12]

This brings us to the first fact about the communitarian
movement: Although it achieved its greatest expansion in the
Middle West, it was not, in a real sense, indigenous to the region. The two communities that Nordhoff visited in Iowa—
Amana and Icaria—both spoke a foreign language. Both had
brought with them to America the ideas that so powerfully

[11] Bertha M. H. Shambaugh, *Amana That Was and Amana That Is*
(Iowa City, 1832), 351, 352.

[12] Arthur Bestor, "Checklist of Communitarian Experiments Initiated
in the United States before 1860," in *Backwoods Utopias* (Philadelphia, 1950),
231–43. This tabulation shows ninety-six communities founded during the
period 1825–1860, of which only nineteen were on the Atlantic Seaboard.

shaped their lives—in the one case German pietism, in the other the social theories of Étienne Cabet. Although the influence of ideas brought from a distance was less marked in certain other communities, the fact remains that the intellectual origins of communitarianism as a whole must be sought outside the United States.

Broadly speaking, three successive waves of communitarian enthusiasm swept in upon the shores of the United States. Through the accident of geography—that is to say, because the territory had not been open to settlement earlier—all three waves happened to reach Iowa at approximately the same time. In reality, however, the three waves belonged to quite different periods and manifested widely divergent intellectual characteristics. Let us examine the three and note briefly their manifestations in Iowa.

The first wave resulted from forces generated originally by the Protestant Reformation and remaining active over a period of at least three centuries. Within the Protestant areas of Europe, the Reformation did far more than substitute a group of established state churches for a single universal church. It created in the minds of many devout men and women a totally different conception of what a religious society should be. To them, a genuine church was a body of sincere believers, willing to strive mightily after holiness, anxious to separate themselves from worldlings and sinners, and happy to knit closer their ties with others of like religious mind and heart. This ideal appeared under hundreds of different sectarian guises, but in each instance it created a deeper sense of community among the believers. This was the soil from which communitarianism ultimately sprang and flowered.

It was largely in the New World that the flowering came.

A few sects practiced community of property in Europe. By and large, however, the classic examples of religious communitarian colonies were furnished by the United States. Members of a sect were apt to immigrate as a group, and the experience of being in a strange land drew even tighter the bonds of comradeship in faith. Lack of means pointed to the wisdom of pooling resources to make a start. One after another, small sectarian groups that had never bothered with economic and social theory found themselves drawn together into a communitarian organization that was uncustomary and yet at the same time reassuringly apostolic.

The Amana Community was one of the last of the important groups to experience the transformation from a religious society to a communitarian colony. By the time of their arrival, religious communitarianism in America had a history of nearly two centuries behind it. Several sectarian colonies had been established before the end of the seventeenth century, and the eighteenth century had seen the founding of Ephrata in Pennsylvania, the adoption of a "General Economy" by the Moravians for a score of years, and the establishment of the Shakers, who quickly planted their communistic villages from Maine to Kentucky. Early in the nineteenth century, Father Rapp shepherded his followers from Germany to Pennsylvania (where they established Harmonie in 1805), and Joseph Bäumler his to Ohio (where Zoar was planted in 1817). Religious communitarianism was thus a fairly familiar feature of the American scene when, in 1843, the Society or Congregation or Community of True Inspiration *(Wahre Inspirations-Gemeinde)* first established themselves in the United States at a spot they called Ebenezer, in western New York.

The Society of True Inspiration came into existence in

Hesse, Germany, in 1714, and embodied a pietistic reaction against the formalism of the established Lutheran church. The name reflected its special belief that the Holy Ghost "even now speaks and operates audibly through the instruments of true inspiration."[13] By the middle of the eighteenth century, a decline in spiritual fervor had occurred, but in 1817 it revived, and soon two new "instruments" *(Werkzeuge)*, endowed with the gift of true inspiration, arose to lead the Society: Barbara Heinemann and Christian Metz. In the 1820's and 1830's, persecution induced the Inspirationists to gather together in certain estates and ancient convents, which they leased and jointly occupied, but without adopting community of goods. Persecutions continued, however, and in 1842 the Society sent a group of members to the United States in search of a site to which they might remove. Five thousand acres of the former Seneca Indian Reservation near Buffalo, New York, were purchased, and between 1843 and 1846, some eight hundred members immigrated from Germany to the new village of Ebenezer. It was at this point that community of property was adopted, to remain the rule of the Society until 1932. In 1854, the decision was made to find a larger site, one farther removed from the carnal allurements of Buffalo. In 1855, the village of Amana was laid out in the valley of the Iowa River, and over a period of ten years, the Society gradually transferred its affairs and its members to the seven villages that now dot its twenty-six-thousand-acre domain.[14] It was here that Charles Nordhoff visited in 1875.

13 Confession of Faith of the Community of True Inspiration, printed in *A Brief History of the Amana Society or Community of True Inspiration, 1714–1930* (4th ed. [Amana], 1930), 28.

14 The standard history is that of Mrs. Shambaugh. See also William R. Perkins and Barthinius L. Wick, *History of the Amana Society or Community*

The sense of being a community is a precious thing. The fear that an industrialized society might lose it irretrievably was one of the powerful factors which produced the second great wave of communitarianism. To this I should like now to turn.

The end of the Napoleonic Wars in 1815 brought western Europe face to face with a host of critical problems engendered by the so-called Industrial Revolution and intensified by long years of war. Reformers began to urge upon the state a more forceful intervention in economic matters, but legislative mills ground exceedingly slowly. Revolutionary movements of a portentous kind were born during the same troubled years. There were reformers, however, who accepted neither the alternative of governmental action nor that of revolution. Their proposals are the ones that concern us here, for they offered a communitarian solution, secular in purpose but similar in pattern to that of the religious communities. They accepted the idea that drastic and immediate reform was necessary, but they repudiated the idea that revolution could produce a tolerable social order. They saw a way out through small communities, where totally new economic arrangements could be peacefully tried. And they had faith that if the world could but see a successful experiment, it would hasten to duplicate it and reduplicate it until whole nations were dotted with associations and a higher form of society would come into being.

Robert Owen was the first to win a hearing. His success in turning the mill town of New Lanark, Scotland, into a model village led him to propose a complete reconstruction of society

of *True Inspiration* (State University of Iowa Publications, Historical Monograph No. 1, Iowa City, 1891). The series of *Jahrbücher* of the Society and its other publications are many and substantial. A complete bibliography would be highly desirable.

into small co-operative communities combining agriculture and industry. From 1817 onward, he preached his doctrine up and down the British Isles, and finally, in 1825, he used his own fortune to inaugurate an experiment at New Harmony, in southern Indiana. The second wave of communitarian influence thus crossed the Atlantic with Owen.[15]

Of even greater appeal than Owen's program was that which was evolved almost contemporaneously by the French socialist Charles Fourier. The author himself never saw the New World, but an American disciple, Albert Brisbane, made Fourierism the most widely discussed of all communitarian programs by dint of earnest propaganda in the 1840's.[16] Almost thirty phalanxes (as the Fourierites called their communities) enjoyed a brief existence in this and the following decade. And one of these was located in Iowa, the earliest communitarian colony in the state.

The Iowa Pioneer Phalanx took up land on the Des Moines River, some nine miles from Oskaloosa, in the spring of 1844. The colony originated in Watertown, in northern New York, one of several upstate cities which had responded enthusiastically to Brisbane's propaganda. The Fourierites in Watertown launched not one project, but two. In their own immediate neighborhood they established, in 1843, a Jefferson County Industrial Association, which lasted about a year. Shortly thereafter, the Iowa Pioneer Phalanx was organized in the same city.

15 Although no Owenite community was established as far west as Iowa, the attenuated influence of Owenism can be detected in the settlement (hardly, however, a communitarian colony) of Salubria, in what is now Van Buren County, Iowa. This was founded by Abner Kneeland, who had been closely associated a few years earlier with the Owenite movement in the East. See Mary R. Whitcomb, "Abner Kneeland: His Relations to Early Iowa History," *Annals of Iowa*, Third Series, Vol. VI (April, 1904), 340–63.

16 Arthur Bestor, "Albert Brisbane—Propagandist for Socialism in the 1840's," New York History, Vol. XXVIII (April, 1947), 128–58.

Ambitiously it published one number of a periodical, *The Pioneer Phalanx, or Independent Magazine,* and then set out for Iowa. In April or May, 1844, the members established themselves on the north bank of the Des Moines River and erected the characteristic row of connected lodgings that Fourier's plans called for and that can still be seen in the Long House at Ripon, Wisconsin. Some fifty men, women, and children labored together on the domain for a year, but dissatisfactions arose and the phalanx was dissolved in May, 1845, to the pious satisfaction of certain home missionaries in the region who were distressed at the religious indifference of the community.[17]

The short life of the Iowa Pioneer Phalanx was characteristic of the experiments inspired by Fourier. So, too, was the wide geographical spread of interest in Fourierist ideas. Indeed, the diffused communitarian enthusiasm of the 1840's was responsible for a large number of projects that never came to fruition, such as a proposed Garden Grove Community in Iowa itself.[18] It entered also into many enterprises that acknowledged no particular interest in Fourierism as such—among them the Jasper Colony, which a group of German-speaking Swedenborgians established in 1851 shortly before the coming of the

[17] Philip D. Jordan, "The Iowa Pioneer Phalanx," *The Palimpsest,* Vol. XVI (July, 1935), 211-25, and "Fourierist Colony in Iowa," *Annals of Iowa,* Third Series, Vol. XVII (January, 1930), 233-36. On the antecedent movement in Jefferson County, New York, see the sources collected in John Humphrey Noyes, *History of American Socialism* (Philadelphia, 1870), 299-304, 409-10, and a series of three articles by David F. Lane in the *Watertown* (New York) *Daily Times,* January 29, 30, and 31, 1936.

[18] See A. J. Macdonald, "Manuscripts and Collections" (Yale University Library), 416, which cites the *Regenerator* (October, 1949); see also Noyes, *History of American Socialism,* 409. After reviewing the evidence, I am now of the opinion that Garden Grove should not have been included in my "Checklist of Communitarian Experiments," in *Backwoods Utopia,* 241 (where it appears as No. 101, under date of 1848). Its plan was hardly collectivist enough to label it communitarian, and the evidence is not sufficient to show that it ever passed beyond the stage of a project.

Amana Society and in the same neighborhood.[19] Even the Mormons betrayed communitarian tendencies on various occasions, and the colony called Preparation, founded in 1853 by a schismatic Mormon leader named Charles B. Thompson and located in what is now Monona County, was the counterpart in Iowa of experiments tried elsewhere.[20]

The third wave of communitarianism cannot be distinguished from its predecessor as sharply as the first two from each other. Nevertheless, the difference between them was fundamental, even though frequently overlooked. The communitarian plans of Owen and Fourier were complete and self-contained. The communities they proposed were not means to an end, they were not steppingstones to something else, they were ends in themselves. Society as a whole was to be transformed, it is true, but the transformation was nothing other than the reconstruction of society into communities.

The decline of Fourierism in the late 1840's and the 1850's was in reality the end of this particular concept of reform. The communities established thereafter, even though they might draw upon earlier ideas, were fundamentally different in purpose. The community itself was ancillary to some other program. It might be the place in which to nurture and marshal the forces that were expected ultimately to venture forth and remake the world. It might be the headquarters from which a greater movement would be directed. It might be a retreat to

[19] Charles A. Hawley, "A Communistic Swedenborgian Colony in Iowa," *Iowa Journal of History and Politics*, Vol. XXXIII (January, 1935), 3–26, and, by the same author, "Excelsior," *The Palimpsest*, Vol. XVI (June, 1935), 189–98.

[20] F. R. Aumann, "A Minor Prophet in Iowa," *The Palimpsest*, Vol. VIII (July, 1927), 253–60; Ralph Albertson, "A Survey of Mutualistic Communities in America," *Iowa Journal of History and Politics*, Vol. XXXIV (October, 1936), 383.

which the battlers in a larger cause might come to recruit their strength. It might even be an asylum of escape for those utterly weary of the struggle. But the community ceased to be what it had been for Owen and Fourier, the central mechanism of social reform itself, the unit which, indefinitely reduplicated, would constitute the society of the future.

Communitarianism can be observed in transition from its second to its third place in the history of the Communia Colony in Clayton County, some fifty miles from Dubuque. At its founding, in 1847 or 1848, Communia was simply another of the nonreligious communitarian experiments of the 1840's, in this instance undertaken by German-speaking Swiss-Americans. In 1851, however, the colony was brought into close connection with a movement of very different character and inspiration. The moving force in this change was Wilhelm Weitling (1808–1871).

Although indebted for some of his ideas to Owen and Fourier, Weitling was in reality one of the new social revolutionaries, who were beginning to preach a militant, class-conscious communism (in the mid-twentieth-century sense of the term) in the late 1830's. Driven from one country to another by the police, he finally came to America in 1847, only, however, to return to Germany the following year to fish in the waters troubled by the revolutions of 1848. He returned to the United States permanently in 1849 and organized an ambitious *Arbeiterbund* in New York with a periodical *Die Republik der Arbeiter*, a program for organizing the workers (especially German-speaking ones), and a plan for establishing local branches. To this scheme was annexed the idea of communitarian colonies. In 1851, Weitling visited Communia and swept the colony into his program. Funds from the *Arbeiterbund* were channeled to the Iowa community, but resistance developed to Weitling's imperious demands that Communia be fully integrated into the *Arbeiterbund.* By 1854, the community was torn by factions, some demanding dissolution. The experiment came to an end in a welter of litigation which dragged on until 1864. Long before this date, the *Arbeiterbund* had disintegrated, and Weitling himself had completely abandoned his career as a social reformer.[21]

Somewhere midway between Fourier and Weitling in his ideas was Étienne Cabet (1788–1856), founder of the Icarian movement which Nordhoff observed in one of its final stages at the colony of Icaria, in Adams County near Corning, in 1875. Cabet had also belonged to the radical group of social reformers of the 1830's and 1840's—more like Weitling than like Fourier. His book, *Voyage en Icarie,* published in 1839, pictured a transformation of society that was essentially national in scope, not communitarian.[22] In 1847, however, he determined to attempt the realization of his plans through a colony in America, and thereafter his program conformed more and more to the communitarian pattern characteristic of Owen and Fourier.

Nevertheless, Cabet and his followers brought with them much of the doctrinaire rigidity and the bitter factionalism that

[21] Carl Wittke, *The Utopian Communist: A Biography of Wilhelm Weitling, Nineteenth-Century Reformer* (Baton Rouge, 1950); George Schulz-Behrend, "Communia, Iowa, a Nineteenth-Century German-American Utopia," *Iowa Journal of History,* Vol. 48 (January, 1950), 27–54.

[22] The standard work on Cabet and the Icarian experiments in America is Jules Prudhommeaux, *Icarie et son Fondateur Étienne Cabet* (Paris, 1907); the extensive literature of the movement, published both in France and America, is fully listed in the bibliography, pp. xiii–xl. See also Albert Shaw, *Icaria: A Chapter in the History of Communism* (New York, 1884), and William A. Hinds, *American Communities and Co-operative Colonies* (2nd revision [i. e., 3rd ed.], Chicago, 1908), 361–96.

characterized the revolutionaries as a group.[23] After a disastrous attempt in Texas in 1848, Cabet brought his followers to the abandoned Mormon town of Nauvoo in Illinois. There a moderately successful working community developed. It was torn, however, by almost continuous factional strife, culminating in the actual withdrawal of Cabet and a group of his followers to St. Louis. The departure took place in October, 1856. On the eighth of November, Cabet died.

The subsequent history of Icaria is filled with disputes and schisms. Two communities existed in bitter enmity for a time, one at St. Louis (or Cheltenham) and one at Nauvoo. Eventually, the Nauvoo group transferred its activities to lands already acquired in Iowa. Even after Nordhoff's visit to Icaria in 1875, splits continued to occur, resulting in two rival colonies side by side at Corning, Iowa, and even an offshoot in California.[24] The last remnant dragged the experiment on until 1895, when the affairs of Icaria were finally wound up.

There have been new experiments of many sorts in the century since the decline of Fourierism in the 1850's, although none of consequence have had a foothold in Iowa. All of these have belonged to what I have called the third wave of com-

[23] Striking manifestations of this spirit are to be found not only in the pamphlet wars of the Icarians after their arrival, but also in records of the voyages to America, such as those edited by Fernand Rude, *Voyage en Icarie: Deux Ouvriers Viennois aux États-unis en 1855* (Paris, 1952). See also my review in *American Historical Review*, Vol. LIX (January, 1954), 449–50.

[24] Two parties developed in the Iowa colony. After a split in 1878, one party, *la jeune Icarie*, retained the old property and name, Icarian Community; the other party, *les vieux Icariens* moved to a site a mile away and established the New Icarian Community. The latter did not disband until 1895. Prior to that, however, the members of *la jeune Icarie* had joined other Icarians in California at Cloverdale, where the Icaria Speranza Community existed until 1886. See, in addition to the works already cited, Charles Gray, "The Icarian Community," *Annals of Iowa*, Third Series, Vol. VI (July, 1903), 107–14, and Robert V. Hine, *California's Utopian Colonies* (San Marino, Calif., 1953), chap. 4, "The Icaria Speranza Commune."

munitarianism. Perhaps a wave is not a proper metaphor, for these experiments were, unlike their predecessors, more like ripples and eddies. After 1860, in other words, experimental communities were appendices or footnotes to other and more powerful movements of reform. They were rarely proposed as possessing in themselves the key to a transformation of society. They were, to most socially conscious observers, escapist and backward looking. No longer, as in the hopeful days of Owen and Fourier, were they looked upon as harbingers of a completely communitarian future.

The three waves of communitarian influence that I have undertaken to sketch belong, all alike, to the past. The colonies at Amana are the most substantial vestige remaining in America of three hundred years of sectarian community life, and a quarter of a century has already passed since the communistic system was abandoned by the True Inspirationists. The Shakers number only a handful of believers today, and the sect itself will shortly be extinct. Ephrata, Harmonie, and Zoar are now museums.

The second wave of communitarianism spent its force even more quickly than the first. The experiments inspired by Robert Owen were short lived in the extreme. Two or three of the Fourierist phalanxes survived long enough to be called more than mere episodes, but all had disappeared by the time of the Civil War. If Icaria is considered a part of the second wave rather than the third, its tenacious hold on life until 1895 prolonged this phase of communitarianism to the end of the nineteenth century, but not beyond.

The third wave has produced sporadic experiments in communitarian life in the twentieth century, but I know of none of consequence in existence today. In other countries—

notably contemporary Israel—communitarianism may be accounted a living force. But the special circumstances that make it alive are so evidently absent in the United States that it seems safe to treat communitarianism as a closed chapter in American social and intellectual history.

Did the communitarian movement actually bequeath anything to the people of today? It is risky to ask this question of one who, like myself, has immersed himself in the history of a particular movement, for he is always tempted, lawyer like, to make out a case when there really is none.

Let us then honestly admit, at the outset, that the influence cannot have been great. Communitarianism was not a vast, overwhelming fact. Neither was it a recurrent activity engrossing the attention of millions. And it was certainly not a necessary part of the life of every man and woman. At the height of its influence, communitarianism won the lively attention of only a few thousand persons at most. Only a hundred or so widely scattered localities ever witnessed even an attempt to put its principles into practice. A single day's editorials in the newspapers of the nation on one great issue of public policy probably reach more people than were ever made conscious of communitarian ideas during two or more centuries of discussion.

Moreover, the various communitarian groups did not convert the nation, or even any continuing minority within it, to the principles they considered important. None of the communitarian sects succeeded in propagating their religious ideas very much beyond the original circle of adherents. Community of goods exerted no discoverable appeal. The reconstruction of society into self-sufficient co-operative communities never came about. And to realize the extent of the failure, we must remember that the secular communitarians promised themselves that even a single successful trial would be enough to set the whole earth on a new course. "If," wrote Fourier's most influential American disciple in 1843, "one Association be established, and *it is of little consequence* where, which will prove practically to the world the immense advantages of the system . . . it will spread with a rapidity which the most sanguine cannot anticipate."[25] The Fourierites might argue, it is true, that no trial ever met the conditions they laid down. So be it. History can afford to be magnanimous in granting excuses, but history is nevertheless obliged to write off unfulfilled promises as unfulfilled.

Let all this be said, but let it not end our quest for the heritage of communitarianism. We are mistaken if we look for a spreading banyan tree; we may not be mistaken to look for a lily of the valley.

Whatever influence the communitarian movement possessed was obviously indirect, for its direct objectives were never realized. The importance of such indirect influence, however, is illustrated by the best known of all the communitarian theorists, Robert Owen. A whole lifetime and a sizable fortune went into his attempt to establish a self-supporting co-operative community combining industry and agriculture. Every attempt ended in failure, and since his death no one has undertaken to revive his particular plan. Nevertheless, Owen is recognized in Britain today—and, I think it is correct to say, increasingly recognized—as the precursor of many movements and many achievements that were derived only indirectly from his principal effort. Co-operation, in the sense in which that term is used by the co-operative movement, was only one ele-

25 Albert Brisbane, *A Concise Exposition of the Doctrine of Association* (2nd ed., New York, 1843), 73. Italics are Brisbane's.

ment in Owen's program—and not a carefully formulated element—yet the co-operative movement honors him as one of its principal founders. In the broader realms of social and economic reform, Owen's influence stems not from the specific things he proposed or even the specific things he did, but from the direction in which all his efforts pointed, a direction opposite to that of his time but concurrent with that of subsequent generations.

All this provides a clue, I believe, to the ultimate influence of the communitarian movement in America. Its significance lay in the fact that it moved against the tide and that the tide ultimately turned. It must be conceded that communitarianism was only one force—and perhaps a minor force—among the many that gradually reversed the current of social thought, but in the beginning, such forces were few, and communitarianism was one to be reckoned with.

Let us briefly note some of the forces in American society which communitarianism opposed. One, most obviously, was individualism. Today this is the name of a virtue; it was coined, however, as the name for a vice. Alexis de Tocqueville was the first to use the term, and the passage on the subject in his *Democracy in America* should perhaps be briefly excerpted:

> *Individualism* is a novel expression, to which a novel idea has given birth. Our fathers were only acquainted with egoism. Egoism is a passionate and exaggerated love of self, which leads a man to . . . prefer himself to everything in the world. Individualism is a mature and calm feeling, which disposes each member of the community to sever himself from the mass of his fellows and to draw apart with his family and his friends, so that . . . he willingly leaves society at large to itself. . . . Egoism blights the germ of all virtue; individualism, at first,

only saps the virtues of public life; but in the long run it attacks and destroys all others and is at length absorbed in downright egoism.[26]

Tocqueville, it should be noted, believed that democratic institutions themselves provided important correctives to individualism, but he did not cease to believe that individualism (as he defined it) was an evil.

Now it was precisely this kind of individualism to which communitarianism offered a direct antithesis, and explicitly so. The constitution of the Amana Society spoke of "this bond of union tied by God amongst ourselves."[27] On the title-page of Cabet's *Voyage en Icarie*, the first of the mottoes was: *Tous pour chacun, chacun pour tous*.[28] In the most influential American statement of Fourierist doctrine, Albert Brisbane condemned existing society as "based upon the principle of isolation, of separation of man from his fellow-man, upon individual effort, and envious strife and anarchical competition." He urged instead "a Social Order based upon the principle of Association —of Union between Man and his fellow-man—upon Unity and Harmony of interests."[29] If these expressions fall dull and heavy on our ears, we must remember that the battle cries of one generation are the platitudes of the next.

Communitarians believed, in the second place, that many things should belong to the community and should be for the use of all. The holding of goods in common is the extreme of

[26] Alexis de Tocqueville, *Democracy in America* (revised translation by Phillips Bradley, New York, 1945), II, 98. (Part II was first published in 1840.) This translation renders the original *égoïsme* as "selfishness." I have substituted the literal equivalent, "egoism."

[27] Constitution of the Amana Society (1859), Art. II, in Shambaugh, *Amana That Was and Amana That Is*, 284.

[28] See the facsimile in Shaw, *Icaria*, 17.

[29] Brisbane, *A Concise Exposition of the Doctrine of Association*, 2.

this belief, but there are many intermediate stages. Most communitarians held to a middle ground, and I think their influence contributed something to the gradual retreat from the view, so characteristic of nineteenth-century *laissez faire*, that good social policy called for the placing of all things in unequivocally private hands. To illustrate the extreme form in which this doctrine was often stated, let me quote from the most influential textbook of the period, *The Elements of Political Economy*, published in 1837 by the Reverend Francis Wayland, president of Brown University:

> When property is held in common, every individual of the society to which it belongs, has an equal, but an undivided and indetermined, right to his portion of the revenue. Hence, every one is at liberty to take what he will, and as much as he will, and to labor as much or as little as he pleases. There is therefore, under such an arrangement, no *connexion* between *labor* and the *rewards* of labor. . . .
>
> On the contrary, as soon as land with all other property is divided, a motive exists for regular and voluntary labor, inasmuch as the individual knows that he, and not his indolent neighbor, will reap the fruit of his toil. . . .[30]
>
> When property is perfectly divided, and every thing is owned by some one, and every one knows what is his own, nothing is left in common. Of course, no man can then obtain any thing more than he has, unless he obtain it by labor. . . .[31]
>
> And thus we see, that division of property, or the appropriation to each, of his particular portion of that which God has given to all, lays [*sic*] at the foundation of all accumulation of wealth, and of all progress in civilization.

[30] Francis Wayland, *The Elements of Political Economy* (New York, 1837), 111–12.
[31] *Ibid.*, 123.

Hence, we see the reason why property held in common, is so generally prejudicial to the best interests of a society. A common, where every one, at will, may pasture his cattle; and a forest, from which every inhabitant may procure his fuel; are severally encouragements to indolence, and serve to keep a community poor. Thus, also, funds left at large for the support of the poor, on which every one is supposed to have an equal right to draw, have generally been found to foster indolence.[32]

There are few today who would try to defend Wayland's view that property owned by the community for public use impoverishes that community or that funds set aside for social security intensify the very evils they are designed to relieve, but at the time Wayland wrote, there were few to defend any other view. Among those few were the communitarians.

I have said enough, perhaps, to suggest the direction in which the communitarian movement exerted its influence. To measure influence in anything like quantitative terms is a matter of extreme difficulty even when a force of major importance is at work. When the influence is that of a minor current of thought, the difficulties become immeasurably greater. When, finally, that force is exerted against the prevailing trend, measurement virtually becomes an impossibility.

Perhaps, of course, a counterforce is actually more powerful than it appears to be. It may be worth our while, at least, to meditate upon a paradoxical statement by Henry David Thoreau: "A minority is powerless while it conforms to the majority; it is not even a minority then; but it is irresistible when it clogs by its whole weight."[33]

[32] *Ibid.,* 113.
[33] Henry David Thoreau, *Walden and Other Writings* (ed. by Brooks Atkinson, New York, 1937), 647.

VI

LAND OF THE FREE

Václav L. Beneš

THE PROBLEMS of the refugee—racial, religious, or political—is one of the perennial curses of mankind. History is full of involuntary human migrations, resulting at first from the crude instincts of the primitive man and later from the maladjustments and tensions of organized society. Intellectual growth and technological progress, as well as an increased consciousness of moral and social responsibility, did very little to relieve mankind of the refugee problem. In fact, the liberation of man's mind from the bonds of medieval oppression, the greater complexity and refinement of social life, and the immense growth of social relations revealed new areas of conflict and friction, thus adding to causes which may bring about involuntary human migrations.

There are two periods in modern history which stand out as having brought unheard-of misery and suffering to millions of people, casting them outside the pale of organized societies. One is that of the religious wars of the sixteenth and seventeenth centuries; the other began after World War I—within the lifetime of the present generation. Like the period of religious wars, our age is marked by a fundamental and irreconcilable conflict of beliefs and ideas—a conflict which almost inevitably must result in the expulsion of both individuals and whole groups from the body politic of the individual national societies. The struggle for a total control over man's mind and soul leaves no place for the nonconformist, whose only choice —if he can make use of it at all—is exile.

The modern refugee problem can be regarded as primarily European. It can be traced back to the nineteenth-century revolutions in central and eastern Europe, all of which caused a considerable movement of political refugees to the West, yet its scope and nature were limited by the relatively tolerant and humane practices of that period. Thus the sudden emergence of mass flights of refugees after 1917 came as a shock to the Western world. Not realizing the true significance of Soviet Communism, the first modern totalitarian system, many people were inclined to interpret the problem of the White Russian refugees in the rather narrow terms of Russian history. The advent of fascism and naziism, however, proved clearly that involuntary migrations and mass expulsions—far from being accidental phenomena—represented a basic characteristic of an age of ideological conflict. The development after World War II, which was marked by a mass flight of refugees from the Communist-dominated areas, made the refugee problem one of the most painful and difficult problems of our time.

Unlike their predecessors of the period of religious wars, modern refugees are faced with a world which is less responsive to their plight and needs. The hundreds of thousands of refugees from totalitarianism who, since 1918, poured over the European frontiers in search of asylum and livelihood created a crisis for which Western society was both morally and materially unprepared. Of course, the world was by no means overpopulated, and many countries needed to augment their population. But the structure of the modern society of states, with its rigidness and its political, as well as economic, insecurities, precluded an imaginative and daring solution of the problem. Very often, especially after the outbreak of the world economic crisis, refugees were regarded as intruders and dangerous competitors; in many countries they were considered as persons of "ambiguous political loyalties" likely to endanger relations with other states.[1]

It was clear from the outset that the chaotic onslaught of the refugee masses, which represented a serious cause of world unrest, could be dealt with only by international action. Yet the post–1918 international refugee movement, rather than being a conscious action of the members of the League of Nations, was primarily a result of the endeavors of one man, the great humanitarian Fridtjof Nansen. However commendable the activities of the League of Nations might have been, they proved to be insufficient to cope with the refugee problem.[2]

Even before the end of World War II it became clear that after the termination of hostilities, the problem of refugees would be as urgent as it was before. More than one and one-half million persons, almost entirely from central and eastern Europe, refused to return to the countries of their origin, declaring themselves political exiles and seeking asylum in the West.[3] Their number was swelled by the tens of thousands of postwar refugees escaping from behind the Iron Curtain to avoid the cruelty and persecutions under Communist regimes.

The gigantic proportions of the refugee problem made

[1] Jaques Vernant, *The Refugee in the Post-War World* (New Haven, 1953), 18.

[2] Dorothy Thompson, *Refugees: Anarchy or Organization* (New York, 1938), 54–55.

[3] Vernant, *The Refugee in the Post-War World*, 31.

immediate international action imperative. At first, UNRRA (and later the International Refugee Organization), created as a temporary specialized agency of the United Nations, aided hundreds of thousands of these new victims of modern totalitarianism. In 1950, a special United Nations High Commissioner for Refugees was entrusted with the task.[4] This, perhaps the most successful activity of the United Nations, was made possible by the generous support of the member states of the organization, the United States, above all. America became the haven of several hundred thousand refugees.

The origin and development of the United States have been inextricably connected with the problem of the refugee. Early in its history, America gave refuge to victims of religious persecution—the Pilgrim Fathers, the Huguenots, and Protestant minorities from the continent of Europe. Of course, the great majority of the original settlers were refugees only in the broadest sense of the term. Rather than escaping direct persecution, they left their homes in Europe because of their dissatisfaction with the social and economic conditions of the Continent. Many, however, were genuine refugees, as for instance William Penn or the grandfather of George Washington.

The successive waves of immigrants who, after 1820, began to flow into America could not, in their great majority, be regarded as refugees. However important they might have been for the cultural and political development of American life, the Forty-eighters and other groups of political exiles—such as the Polish or Hungarian revolutionaries—represented only a small fraction of the immigrant stream. Yet the principle

[4] The mandate of the UN High Commissioner for Refugees does not include refugees in Korea and those from Palestine.

that the United States would become "more and more a safe
and propitious asylum for the unfortunate of other countries"[5]
became an important part of American consciousness. Beginning with George Washington, American presidents emphasized the principle of the right of asylum; as a political issue,
it figured in the program of both parties.[6]

Although extolled as the oldest and most honored of
American traditions, the policy of asylum for the oppressed
was never written into American public law. No distinction
was made between refugees and other immigrants. As long as
the gates of America stood open to virtually all comers, those
who sought admission in order to escape racial, religious, or
political persecution and discrimination were welcomed. The
radical restrictions of immigration by the so-called Quota Acts
of 1921 and 1924, however, brought about, if not a total abandonment, then at least a serious curtailment of the traditional
policy of asylum. Refugees could be admitted for permanent
residence only as immigrants. As such, they had to meet the
requirements of the immigration laws and regulations, and their
number was strictly limited by fixed national quotas. Consequently, only a relatively small proportion of the post-1918
political, religious, and racial refugees were able to find asylum
in the United States.[7]

The new great wave of refugees caused by the victory
of naziism in Germany and, later, on the European continent
soon reached American shores. In the period between 1933

[5] Louis Adamic, *America and the Refugees* (New York, 1939), 4.
[6] *Ibid.*, 5.
[7] See Read Lewis and Marion Schibsby, "Status of the Refugee under
American Immigration Laws," *The Annals of the American Academy of
Political and Social Science*, Vol. CCIII (May, 1939), 74–82.

and the end of World War II about 250,000 victims of Nazi totalitarianism found new homes in the United States.[8]

Although political considerations prevented a change in the existing legislation which would alleviate the tragic plight of the refugee, both the American government and the American public displayed an ever increasing interest in the refugee problem. Before and during World War II, administrative arrangements to facilitate the admission of refugees were adopted,[9] and in 1938, the President of the United States gave the initiative to the convening of the Évian Conference, at which the Intergovernmental Committee for Refugees was established. After the termination of the war, further special measures to expedite and facilitate immigration from Europe to the United States were taken, and the American government became the chief sponsor of the International Refugee Organization, whose function was to cope with the problem of refugees and displaced persons. By means of the Displaced Persons acts passed between August, 1948, and July, 1952,[10] more than 400,000 refugees and displaced persons were admitted to the United States. In no case, however, did a basic modification of the quota provisions take place. Finally, in the Refugee Relief Act of 1953,[11] the Congress provided for the admission of 214,000 refugees above and beyond the regular quotas.

It is almost impossible to ascertain, with any degree of accuracy, the total number of refugees who, since the begin-

[8] William S. Bernard (ed.), *American Immigration Policy—A Reappraisal* (New York, 1950), 33.

[9] Harold Fields, *The Refugee in the United States* (New York, 1938), 10–12.

[10] Act of 25 June 1948, Public Law No. 774, 80th Congress, as amended by Act of 16 June 1950, Public Law No. 555, 80th Congress, and by Act of 28 June 1951, Public Law No. 60, 81st Congress.

[11] Act of 7 August 1953, Public Law No. 400, 82nd Congress.

ning of the nineteenth century, found asylum in the United States. Prior to World War I, refugees represented only a very small segment of the total number of immigrants. The age of ideological conflict, which started with the Bolshevik Revolution in Russia and culminated in the present "Cold War" between the East and the West, greatly increased their numbers. All in all, perhaps one million people have come to the American shores as fugitives from oppression in their home countries.

To be able to understand the role and contribution of the refugee in the United States, it is necessary to distinguish him from the immigrant. This distinction, while difficult and at times almost impossible, is of fundamental importance. Of course, legally, both are regarded as immigrants, and the immediate problems which they face after their arrival in America are essentially the same. But apart from that, the immigrant differs substantially from the refugee.

There was no single motive which caused the monumental movement of immigrants, the "ragged millions of Europe," to America. In their great majority, however, the immigrants were lured by the prospects of better life and material gain.[12] In many cases, immigration was the only opportunity offered to the lowest strata of the social spectrum of the European countries to escape conditions of social and economic misery. The millions of landless peasants and manual workers regarded immigration to America as the fulfillment of their lifelong aspirations, the beginning of their social and material growth. Psychologically, they were well prepared for the hard struggle awaiting them in the New World. They had nothing to lose

[12] Marcus Lee Hansen, *The Immigrant in American History* (Cambridge, 1940), 79–80.

in Europe; in America, they eagerly seized the equality of opportunity which was offered to them.

How different were the circumstances of the refugees! Unlike the immigrants, who voluntarily left their own land and chose a new one, the refugees were individuals or groups of individuals uprooted by fundamental political changes and expelled from their homes by the persecutions of tyrannical regimes, often only after a desperate struggle.[13] For them, immigration to America, rather than being the beginning of a new life, was the tragic end of the old one. In their homelands they lost everything—wealth, power, and social prestige. In America they had to start anew, facing the uncertainties and difficulties of immigrant life.

From the psychological point of view, most of the refugees were less prepared for life in the New World than the immigrant masses. Although thankful to America for granting him asylum, many a refugee regarded himself more as an exile than an immigrant. For long years, he hoped and, more often than not, worked for a reversal of political affairs in his home country which would enable him to return. In many cases he did not fit into the circumstances of life in America. This was especially true of the intellectuals, who traditionally represented a large percentage of the refugees. For them, exile was a doubly painful experience. It was much more than the loss of a profession, or property, or status. They were cut off from their cultural heritage and historical traditions and thrust into

---

13 The definition of the refugee in international law contains two elements:

(a) Persons or categories of persons qualifying for refugee status must have left the territory of the state of which they were nationals.

(b) The events which are the root-cause of a man's becoming a refugee derive from the relations between the state and its nationals.

Vernant, *The Refugee in the Post-War World,* 4–5.

an entirely alien cultural environment.[14] Only a few proved to be completely able to adjust themselves to their new lives. Many, perhaps the majority—despite their intellectual background—could be described as persons "who learned everything except what would be useful to them in America."

Such were the characteristics of all the waves of refugees who, since the beginning of the last century, found asylum in the United States. Yet there is a fundamental difference between those who escaped the tyranny of the old type of absolutism and the refugees from modern totalitarianism. The victims of the nineteenth- and early twentieth-century struggle for constitutionalism, democracy, and national liberation, were in most cases young revolutionaries who were defeated in their bid for power. Defeat and the harsh treatment which they received at the hands of the victorious tyrants failed to destroy their will power, life energy, and youthful enthusiasm.

Unlike the refugees of the past, the victims of totalitarian persecution who, after 1918, and particularly 1934, began to pour into America represent a mass movement of hundreds of thousands of persons. Among them, especially in the more recent years, there are not only intellectuals, but also the rank and file of the citizenry of central and eastern Europe, including farmers as well as industrial workers. Not all can be regarded as political refugees in a strict sense. The overwhelming majority are passive victims of the totalitarian regime—members of those races and social classes which were condemned to death and destruction.

This last wave of refugees, especially those who fled from

[14] For an elaboration of this theme, see Franz L. Neumann, "The Social Sciences," in *The Cultural Migration: The European Scholar in America* (Philadelphia, 1953), 4-26.

Communism after 1945, are escapees from a tyranny which through its methods and total impact on human personality is much more destructive than the autocracies of the past. Some have gone through horrible experiences and arrive in the United States with anxieties and fear. The active struggle against the Communist menace, the hopeless attempts at compromise, and the final defeat left an indelible mark on the minds of political refugees. The passive victims of Communism show the effects of flight and persecution, and only gradually are they able to shake off the nightmare of life under tyranny. Unlike the immigrants, or even the political refugees of the past, many victims of modern totalitarianism lack the vitality and optimism which are the main ingredients of success in their new lives.

What, if any, was the contribution of the refugee to the formulation of the social, cultural, and political patterns of American life? To what extent did he help to mold those great ideals which our present generation regards as the spiritual and intellectual heritage of the American people? What was the nature of the complex processes of action and interaction through which the refugees became integrated with American society?

Such and similar questions cannot be easily answered. It is even more difficult to undertake a study of the impact of the refugee element on a particular region of the United States, such as the Middle West. Yet there are reasons which appear to justify such an attempt. Lord Bryce observed: "The West is the most American part of America . . . the part where those features which distinguish America from Europe come out in strongest relief."[15] For this, the most important single region

[15] James Bryce, *The American Commonwealth* (New York, 1895), II, 830.

of the New World—more than any other part of the United States—possesses those qualities which are generally regarded as typically American: individualism, competitive spirit, self-reliance, firm belief in the democratic way, and independence of thought. The Middle West was the main scene of the miraculous and essentially American process in which millions of people of different racial, cultural, and social backgrounds have grown into one nation. More than one third of the people in the Middle West are either foreign born or first or second generation Americans. For many decades, the Middle West attracted not only the immigrants, but also the refugees. When, after 1945, America opened its gates to the new, predominantly refugee immigration, almost 30 per cent of the newcomers settled in the Middle West.[16]

It is true that the majority of the nineteenth-century refugees, hoping for a change of political conditions in their old countries which would allow them to return, at first preferred to stay on the eastern seaboard, particularly in New York. There they could better maintain contacts with the refugee revolutionary movements in western Europe. As the hopes for an early return waned, they began to move westward. Without a doubt, their decision was influenced by material considerations and many succumbed to the exaggerated reports about the riches of the "promised land" in the West. But there was still another, perhaps more important reason why the Old West attracted the rebels of European revolutions. Disillusioned by the failure of their endeavors in the Old World, they sought opportunities of a freer and wider life in the new one. But the more settled and rigid society of the East could hardly fulfill their hopes and expectations. They struck westward, looking for the "prom-

[16] Vernant, *The Refugee in the Post-War World*, 503.

ised land" in the immense region beyond the mountains. In the more primitive, less stratified, and more equalitarian society of the West, they hoped to acquire a new status which would help them to forget the misfortunes of their lives. The quality of men, the lack of restraints, and the spiritual climate of the West, so different from what they had experienced in their homes, greatly appealed to the victims of European tyrannies. Some dreamed of building utopias, others wanted to establish communities and compact settlements "under their national flags" on American soil. The Middle West proved to be equally attractive to the twentieth-century refugees, including those who fled from the horrors of modern totalitarianism. They settled in this region because of the existence of large and very often prosperous colonies of their compatriots, still speaking their native tongue and sympathizing with their old countries.

In the Middle West, the refugees found not only a means of livelihood, but also a keen understanding for their political and national aspirations. The intense feeling of Americanism which soon developed among the immigrant groups could not destroy their ties with their original homelands. Thus the immigrants maintained their interest in Europe and reacted strongly to all its political developments. In the early 1850's, the middle western German communities, inspired by the refugees of the 1848 revolution, followed with great interest the progress of the liberal movement in Germany. In 1871, however, their liberal enthusiasm was replaced by an unreserved admiration for the achievements of imperial Germany.[17] Until the American entry into World War I, the Americans of German origin living in the Middle West acted as guardians of the interests of

---

[17] Carl Wittke, *Refugees of Revolution: The German Forty-Eighters in America* (Philadelphia, 1952), 345–64.

their old country on American soil. By then, another element of the middle western population, equally strong and active, had focused its interest on the European scene. The central and eastern European immigrants declared themselves in favor of the activities of the Polish, Czechoslovakian, Yugoslavian, and Baltic exiles working for the liberation and unification of their nations. Again, during World War II, Americans of central and eastern European origin became protagonists of the national cause of their old countries. This attitude was perhaps best expressed by the motto of Vojta Náprstek, one of the Czech Forty-eighters: "That which the heart unites, the sea shall not divide."[18]

Thus on several occasions the Middle West became the center of feverish activities in which hundreds of thousands of Americans of European descent took a very active part. But the impetus for such movements and actions invariably came from the political refugees who—during the time of crisis—found asylum on American soil. The exiled political leaders were quick to realize the importance of the Middle West to their national cause. It served them not only as a source of generous financial aid for their political activities, but also as an important means by which they could influence the policies of the American government. The hundreds of thousands of foreign-born voters who embraced the cause of their old countries represented a factor which no middle western politician could afford to disregard. In order to gain and maintain their votes, the candidates for Congress and even for the presidency of the United States had to make concessions to the demands of their foreign-born electorate. In fact, there is ample evidence of the influence and power of the immigrant voters. Writing—

[18] Thomas Čapek, *The Czechs in America* (Boston, 1920), 127.

at the height of the Congressional election campaign of 1946
—to the owner of a Polish newspaper in Detroit, Senator Arthur
H. Vandenberg observed:

> The votes are of no personal consequence to me because the
> outcome of my personal campaign is a matter of substantial
> indifference to me. But these same "votes" are, in my humble
> opinion, a matter of very great importance to the true Polish
> cause because, no matter how little I may deserve the repu-
> tation, I believe I am considered Poland's "first friend" in this
> and every other capital on earth.[19]

Although thoroughly Americanized and fully aware of
their indebtedness to the United States, which helped them to
increase their material and social status, the immigrants combined their loyalty to America with an intensive love for their
old countries, which gave them so little. Indeed, the behavior of
the middle westerners of foreign birth is perhaps one of the most
peculiar of the many paradoxes which characterize middle
western life. It was mainly because of their influence that the
Middle West—the most American part of the Union—which
had been secluded from the main trends of world affairs and
had lived a life of its own, could combine its essentially isolationist tendencies with a genuine concern for the cause of
freedom on the European continent.

The troubled political conditions of western and central
Europe provided the main motive for the nineteenth-century
movement of refugees. The first wave came after 1817 when
the reactionary regimes in Austria and Germany launched an
attack against the adherents of the liberal ideas of the French

19 Arthur H. Vandenberg, Jr., *The Private Papers of Senator Vandenberg* (Boston, 1952), 314.

Revolution. The unsuccessful uprisings of 1830 and 1848, as well as the tragic Polish revolt of 1863, were followed by a mass exodus of the leaders of the European liberal, democratic, and nationalistic movements. Many of them were given asylum in the United States, and they eventually found their way into the Middle West. This was true of a group of exiles of the Polish insurrection of 1830, of the Hungarian and Czech Forty-eighters who settled in Iowa, and of the refugees of the Warsaw uprising of 1863 who found new homes in the West Side of Chicago.

The most important influx of political refugees, however, came from Germany and Austria. Almost every middle western state received a number of outstanding personalities who had taken an active part in the struggle for constitutional government and democracy in Germany. Gustav Körner and Friedrich Hecker settled in Illinois, Bernard Stallo and Franz Hasaurek in Ohio, Franz Münch and Franz Sigel in Missouri. The most famous of the German Forty-eighters, Carl Schurz, who settled in Wisconsin, became the recognized leader of the entire German community in the United States.[20] The revolutionary immigration was by no means entirely German. Substantial groups of refugees came, especially after 1848, from Poland, Bohemia, and Hungary.

The most colorful of the Czech Forty-eighters was Vojta Náprstek, who remained in the United States for almost ten years and became the founder of Czech settlements in Wisconsin and Iowa. Jan Herman and A. L. Schlesinger, former members of the Bohemian diet, found new homes in Nebraska. Refu-

---

[20] For a list of prominent German political refugees of the nineteenth century, see Carl Wittke, *We Who Built America: The Saga of the Immigrant* (New York, 1940), 191–94.

gees from Prussian Poland settled in Wisconsin, and Laszlo Ujhazy, a Hungarian "Forty-eighter," founded the colony of New Buda, Iowa. Another group were the Jewish refugees who participated in the mid-century revolutions in central Europe. Their immigration to the United States was motivated not only by the defeat of the revolutionists, but also by the realization that the liberal movements, especially in Germany and Hungary, were tainted by anti-Semitic overtones. While the majority of the Jewish refugees settled in the East, some also came to the Middle West.[21]

Despite their relative youth, the refugees of the European liberal revolutions assumed an important position in the political and cultural life of the Middle West. Many of them were university graduates, writers, journalists, and professional men. At first their influence was limited to their compatriots who came to the Middle West in the previous decades. Thus the German refugees gave the rank and file of the German element a political and cultural leadership. In Cincinnati, St. Louis, Milwaukee, Indianapolis, and other centers of German population, a flowering of German culture took place. The refugees published newspapers, started orchestras and singing societies, and carried on other cultural and communal activities.[22] Of similar significance were the activities of the Polish and Czech exiles who assumed leading roles in the cultural life of the growing colonies of their compatriots. Perhaps most important was the transplanting of gymnastic movements, such as the German *Turnverein* and the Czech *Sokol*, in American soil.

No doubt, the problem of the integration of refugees of European revolutions into middle western society was not an easy one. Many regarded their stay in the United States as only

[21] Wittke, *Refugees of Revolution*, 85–89.
[22] *Ibid.*, 262–320.

temporary, believing that soon they would be able to return to their homelands to participate in the final struggle against tyranny and oppression. Others—and this was especially true of many German Forty-eighters—did not fit into middle western society and its conservative habits. These were the radical reformers, rationalists, freethinkers, and atheists, who were shocked to find slavery and nativism in a free republic and who opposed Puritanism as "an invasion of their personal liberty."[23]

Yet as a group, the mid-century refugees from Europe represented an important element in the making of the spiritual image of the Middle West. All of them were genuine republicans and liberals. Their main characteristic was their passionate hatred of all oppression—political, religious, or intellectual —their devotion to liberty, and their intense patriotism. When their expectations of revolution in their homelands remained unfulfilled, they settled down and became American citizens. Many of them devoted their knowledge, energy, and zeal, which they originally reserved for the struggle against the European despots, to public service in their new homeland.

Of course, it is easy to overestimate the importance and general influence of the nineteenth-century political immigrant on life in the Middle West. In one respect, at least, his decisive role appears to be definitely established. Most of the mid-century refugees came to the Middle West as great admirers of Jefferson and Jackson. Unlike the majority of the middle western immigrants, however, they were violently opposed to slavery. As early as 1834, Gustav Körner of Illinois observed: "Negro slavery is the only rope by which the devil holds the American people."[24] Hence the passing of the Kansas-Nebraska

23 Wittke, *We Who Built America*, 195.
24 Quoted in Wittke, *Refugees of Revolution*, 191.

Act had an immediate influence on the refugees' political orientation. Accustomed to fight for a "cause," they eagerly seized the opportunity to take up the struggle for "liberty" which they were forced to abandon in their homelands. When the controversy over slavery flared up, the German Forty-eighters used their influence on their compatriots in favor of abolition. They entered the campaign on behalf of John C. Frémont, addressing meetings and exhorting their compatriots to enter into the new Republican party. Men like Gustav Struve, Franz Hasaurek, George Schneider, and Carl Schurz battled for the Republican cause.[25] Their enthusiam was shared by the Forty-eighters of other nationalities, such at Vojta Náprstek, who became an agent for Frémont.[26]

In 1860, the efforts of refugee leaders were crowned with success. They produced a political revolt among the midwestern Germans which contributed, perhaps decisively, to the election of Abraham Lincoln. By their active participation in the Civil War, the German Forty-eighters, as well as a number of prominent Poles, assumed a relatively important role among those who helped to preserve the Union.

What was the contribution of the European refugees to the molding of the middle western cultural and spiritual heritage? It can be best understood if it is considered as a part of the general contribution of the individual national groups of immigrants, for the refugees have greatly influenced and enriched the life of their compatriots. In their efforts to perpetuate the culture of their motherland and to reproduce its main institutions, they brought elements of higher culture to the less advanced immigrants and aroused their intellectual

[25] *Ibid.*, 206–207.
[26] *Ottův slovník naučný* (Prague, 1901), XVII, 1037.

interests. The great centers of German civilization in the Middle West, with their libraries, dramatic clubs, reading circles, and musical bodies, would hardly have risen without the relentless efforts and devoted work of the German exiles. As individuals, many refugees became prominent in the fields of science, art, and, particularly, education.

Above all, the nineteenth-century political refugees helped to strengthen middle western democracy. Through their devotion to freedom, they set an example, not only to their own compatriots, but also to native Americans. They displayed a great psychological asset which enabled others to understand and appreciate the meaning of American freedom. The activities and, in fact, the mere presence of fighters against tyranny reminded middle westerners of the spiritual foundations of their own civilization, which arose from the struggle against oppressive authority and vested interests. Only thus can it be explained why the American Middle West—the West as it was then—reacted so strongly to the arrival of European refugees and to their cause. Perhaps most indicative of this attitude, which, of course, was also supported by the concepts of Jacksonian democracy, was the rousing welcome given to Lajos Kossuth on his almost triumphal tour of the Middle West.

The great masses of immigrants which flooded the middle western cities and countryside in the period following the 1880's lacked the motivation, the ardor, and the intellectual vigor of the mid-century political refugees. No doubt their contribution to the development of the Middle West was immense; without the work of their hands, it would not have changed into what may perhaps be the most industrialized region of the world.

Although the population pressure of the rural areas of

central and eastern Europe provided the immediate impulse to immigration, many of the newcomers arrived in America with definite political convictions. This was especially true of the Slavic immigrants from Austria-Hungary, Germany, and Congress Poland, as well as of the immigration from the Baltic territories of Russia. In their great majority, they were imbued with a feeling of intense nationalism and hatred for the autocratic regimes of their old countries.

Thus it was not surprising that they reacted at once, and spontaneously, to the outbreak of World War I realizing its significance for the very existence of their compatriots in Europe. Even before the outbreak of hostilities the dramatic events in the Balkans were reflected on the middle western scene. On July 27, 1914, Americans of Czech and Yugoslavian origin staged a mass sympathy demonstration in the Czech district of Chicago for their "Serbian brothers." The meeting culminated in the trampling down of the Austro-Hungarian coat of arms, the two-headed eagle, an event which was noted by the entire Chicago press.[27] The Czech example was emulated, but in a different way, by the Chicago Poles. At a meeting on August 4, they tore up the picture of the Czar and demonstrated against Russian despotism.[28] Also, the American Lithuanians, at their congress in Chicago on September 22, 1914, demanded political autonomy for their native land and expressed their solidarity with the other nations oppressed by Russia, particularly the Poles, White Russians, and Ukranians.[29]

American neutrality during the first stages of the war im-

[27] Vojta Beneš, *Československá Amerika v odboji* (Prague, 1931), I, 68–71.
[28] *Ibid.*, 73.
[29] T. Norus and J. Zilius, *Lithuania's Case For Independence* (Washington, 1918), 71.

posed legal, as well as moral, restrictions on the activities of Americans of central and eastern European origin. Although incensed at the autocratic governments of Europe which plunged their compatriots into a senseless and fratricidal war, the new Americans remained intensely loyal to their adopted country. They did not want to be regarded as "hyphenated" citizens, but as genuine Americans, albeit of foreign origin. After the proclamation of American neutrality and President Wilson's appeal "that the United States must be neutral in fact as well as in name, they limited their activities to the organization of relief to alleviate the suffering of their old countries and the defense of the legitimate interests of their former nations, especially against German propaganda in the United States. But the new Americans could not remain indifferent to the basic issues involved in the European struggle. Accepting President Wilson's appeal to impartiality, the Czech-American Press Bureau in Chicago declared:

> Peace in Europe will be impossible so long as certain nations will be dominated by others. America abolished slavery of individual human beings fifty years ago. Undoubtedly, this country will, at an appropriate moment, help Europe to abolish slavery of whole nations.[30]

This statement expressed the feelings of the great majority of middle western immigrants from central and eastern Europe. They knew well that even in case of permanent neutrality, the United States would assume an important position at the peace conference. Thus to gain American friendship and sympathy for the cause of freedom of their old countries was regarded as a sacred duty. No opportunity to address American

[30] Beneš, *Československá Amerika v odboji*, 92.

audiences was overlooked; books, pamphlets, and posters were issued to remind the American public of the terrible plight of central and eastern Europe suffering under the yoke of tyrannical despots. The middle western immigrants eagerly listened to the emotional appeals of the exiled leaders of their old countries, who regarded the war as an opportunity for the liberation of their peoples. To carry on their wartime activities, the political leaders needed money, and this they received in ever increasing volume from their American compatriots in the Middle West.

When America declared war, the organizations of Czechs, Slovaks, Poles, Yugoslavs, and the Baltic peoples enthusiastically joined the movements of the political refugees, openly recognizing and fully backing the efforts of such exiled national leaders as Ignace Paderewski, Milan R. Štefánik, and Tomáš G. Masaryk. The propaganda and other activities of the immigrant "colonies" increased in force and volume. Toward the end of the war, when the American government gave official recognition to the individual liberation movements, their activities fused with the general effort of the Allies.

Perhaps most effective was the work of the Czechs and Slovaks whose main organizations were centered in the Middle West. Their success was due mainly to the achievement of absolute unity among the existing Czech and Slovak organizations—the Bohemian National Alliance, the Slovak League of America, and the National Union of Czech Catholics. These three organizations, with a membership of several hundred thousand, created in 1918 the American Branch of the Czechoslovak National Council in Paris.[31]

Of special significance was the work of the Bohemian Na-

[31] Vojta Beneš, *Revoluční hnutí v severní Americe* (Prague, 1923), 56.

tional Alliance, which replaced the former Czech relief organizations and established its headquarters in Chicago. Soon after the outbreak of the war, the leading members of the Alliance established contacts with Professor Tomáš Masaryk, who informed them of his intention to start a revolutionary movement against Austria. From the beginning it was understood that the Czech and Slovak community in the Middle West would devote itself to the task of raising funds for the financing of the revolutionary movement. The first financial aid was sent in October, 1914, and in January of the next year, a conference of the Bohemian National Alliance recognized Tomáš Masaryk as "leader of the Czechoslovak revolution." It was also agreed that "all collected funds should be sent only to him without any conditions or reservations."[32] When, on July 6, 1915, the quincentenary of the death of Jan Hus, the Czech national hero and martyr, Masaryk made his "declaration of war" against the Central Powers, he found in the American Middle West the rudiments of an organization with a definite purpose—to help the cause of Czechoslovakian independence. From that time on, Chicago—then the largest "Czech" city in the world— became a center of a well-organized and co-ordinated effort of the entire Czech and Slovak community. The Bohemian National Alliance spread a network of branches throughout the whole country, and by the end of the war, it had almost four hundred local groups. Some, especially those in the cities of the Middle West, such as Chicago, St. Louis, Milwaukee, and Cedar Rapids, had many thousands of members.

The Bohemian National Alliance carried on a variety of activities. It supported financially and morally the cultural and political efforts of the Czech nation; it informed the American

[32] Beneš, *Československá Amerika v odboji,* 265.

public through lectures and articles of the Czechoslovakian national aspirations; it published Czech and English reviews and provided funds for the publication of periodicals and other propaganda materials in Europe. By far the most important, however, was the collection of funds to be used for the financing of the political activities of Tomáš Masaryk. It was mainly because of the financial aid of the Bohemian National Alliance in the Middle West that at the end of the war, Masaryk could declare with pride that not a dollar was asked for or accepted from any foreign source.

Even before the American entry into the war, the Alliance organized a small force of men who had not yet acquired American citizenship, sending them to Canada to join the Canadian army. In June, 1917, General Milan R. Štefánik arrived in America to organize, with the help of the Alliance, the recruitment of volunteers for the Czechoslovak Legion in France. A large part of those who entered the Legion came from the Middle West.[33]

The enthusiasm of Americans of Czech and Slovak origin reached its highest point in May, 1918, when Masaryk arrived in America. His ties to this country were especially close; his wife, Charlotte Garrigue, whose name he added to his own, was American. Before 1914, he made three visits to the United States, and these brought him into close contact with the Middle West. In 1902, under an endowment by Charles Crane, well-known Chicago industrialist, the University of Chicago brought him to its campus for a series of lectures on the problems of small Slavic nations.[34] Masaryk established close ties of

[33] The action resulted in only about 2,500 volunteers, since the majority of the Czechoslovaks entered the American army. See Tomáš Masaryk, *The Making of a State* (London, 1927), 262, and Beneš, *Revoluční hnutí v severní Americe*, 80.

friendship with Crane, and in the university circles and among its intellectuals, he found a host of admirers who held him in high esteem. During his visit, Masaryk also studied the conditions of the middle western Czech and Slovak immigrants, giving a number of lectures on the cultural and political problems of the old country. In 1907, he paid another visit to the Middle West, this time devoting his interest almost entirely to his countrymen, and before World War I, he was regarded by the majority of American Czechs and Slovaks as the most capable and promising of all the Czech political leaders.

Thus the magnificent reception which he was given in Chicago, on May 5, 1918, when he arrived there on his way from Siberia across the North American continent, was of symbolic significance. He was welcomed by the Chicago press, representatives of the University of Chicago, led by its president, Harry Pratt Judson, leaders of the central and eastern European immigrant groups, and, above all, by his own compatriots. The thousands who greeted him—perhaps 200,000 people were assembled on Michigan Avenue—were mainly Czechs and Slovaks. Most of them, however, were American citizens, and their behavior reflected very accurately the feeling of the major part of the middle western public. These sentiments found their expression in a number of acts which, in a concrete and practical way, helped to promote the Czechoslovakian cause. After the American entry nito the war, middle western Congressmen Adolph J. Sabath and W. S. Kenyon presented the Czechoslovakian problem to their colleagues on several occasions.[35] Of the twenty-seven members of the House

[34] G. B. Carson, Jr., "Masaryk the Scholar," in *Thomas G. Masaryk and His Country* (Chicago, 1955), 60.

[35] Charles Pergler, *America in the Struggle for Czechoslovak Independence* (Philadelphia, 1926), 58–76.

and Senate who welcomed Thomas Masaryk on his arrival in Washington, seven were from the Middle West.[36] Another middle westerner, Charles Crane, helped the Czech statesman to establish contact with President Wilson. Crane's son, Richard (who during the war served as private secretary to Robert Lansing) acted as liaison with the Secretary of State. In *The Making of a State*, Masaryk recalls a memorandum from his work at that time, favorable to the Czechoslovakian point of view, prepared by A. Hutchinson Putney, chief of the Near Eastern Division of the Department of State and former dean of the Illinois College of Law in Chicago.[37]

Masaryk was a keen student of America; in many respects he regarded it as a model for his own country. He believed that the historical experience of the Czechs and Slovaks was basically similar to that of the Americans. Both were opposed to aristocratic privilege and a foreign dynasty, and both lacked militaristic traditions.[38] Masaryk's judgment of the United States was greatly influenced by his contacts with the Middle West, to which he was attracted because of its large settlements of Czechs and Slovaks. Their love of freedom and their devotion to the principles of democracy strengthened his faith in the fundamentally democratic character of the Czech and Slovak nation. Thus the Middle West played an important role in the emergence of independent Czechoslovakia. If there is any truth in the statement that Czechoslovakian freedom was, in some ways, made in America, then one may say with full justification that to the Middle West belongs more than a lion's share.

Equally important was the middle western contribution

[36] *Ibid.*, 76.
[37] For the contents of Putney's memorandum, see Pergler, *America in the Struggle for Czechoslovak Independence*, 78–90.
[38] Masaryk, *The Making of a State*, 213.

Photograph by Chicago Park District.

HUB OF THE MIDDLE WEST: Chicago Skyline at Night.

INDUSTRIAL GIANT: The Rouge Plant of the Ford Motor Company Near Detroit.

MAKING MILWAUKEE FAMOUS: The Schlitz Brewery Parent Plant In Wisconsin.

to the liberation and unification of other central and eastern European peoples. Although the Americans of Polish origin failed to achieve unity comparable to that of the Czechs and Slovaks, their organizations, particularly the Polish Roman Catholic Union of America and the Polish National Alliance, worked relentlessly for the rebirth of Poland. Influential Polish refugees from Russia, Austria, and Germany came to the Middle West to remind the Polish Americans, "the fourth part of Poland," of their duty to the old country. Foremost among them was Ignace Paderewski, world-famous pianist who became a statesman in order to promote the cause of his nation.

The Middle West also participated in the unification of the Yugoslavs. At a congress of Croatian, Serbo-Croatian, and Slovene organizations held in Chicago in March, 1915, delegates of more than five hundred American-Yugoslav organizations declared themselves unanimously in favor of a union of Croatia and other southern Slavic lands with Serbia as a single state.[39] The middle western Croats and Serbs helped to finance the activities of the revolutionary Yugoslav Committee in Rome and carried on propaganda and publicity work in the United States.

The struggle for freedom and democracy in faraway central and eastern Europe became one of the symbols of the American participation in World War I. To the immigrant groups in the Middle West, it was much more than a mere symbol—it was a reality with which they were intimately connected and which was an important part of their every-day life. The arrival of the indomitable fighters against tyranny, exiled from their homelands, fired the imagination of the middle westerners, both immigrants and native Americans. What is

[39] P. D. Ostovič, *The Truth About Yugoslavia* (New York, 1952), 57.

more, it provided them with an opportunity to rededicate themselves to the great ideals which were the very basis of their own freedom.

Only a relatively small part of the victims of the Bolshevik Revolution found their way into the United States. After 1933, the large size of the German immigration quota enabled America to receive a much greater number of fugitives from Nazi Germany. The bulk of refugees from modern totalitarianism, however, entered America after World War II as a result of the Sovietization of eastern and much of central Europe. In fact, the influx of refugees from this area has not yet been terminated and will continue for a long period of time.

In many respects, the new refugees—both the political exiles and the passive victims of totalitarianism—resemble the political refugees of the nineteenth century. Many of them are intellectuals and men who in their own countries occupied leading positions in government and society. The great majority are men dedicated to freedom, some of whom had been actively engaged in the struggle for its preservation.

Many, perhaps one-third of those who come to the United States, settle in the Middle West. This is especially true of the passive victims of totalitarian terror, who are less interested in the refugee political movements centered in New York and Washington and are more prepared to accept their exile as permanent. The diversity of the economic structure and the wealth of the Middle West offer them greater opportunities of securing a livelihood.

Despite the multiplicity of its attitudes, the Middle West provides for the refugee an atmosphere which is conducive to both his adjustment and his gradual Americanization. Middle westerners have been described as "the kindest, most generous, and most hospitable people in a country famed for these great virtues."[40] The traditions of the pioneer community—with its vast distances, technical inefficiency, and constant struggle against the harshness of nature—which emphasized the need of mutual aid and Christian charity, have not disappeared in the age of modern technology. It may well be that the spirit of mutual aid and comfort which characterized the pioneers has been turned into sympathetic consideration of all men.[41]

Thus the middle westerner regards the refugee as a new neighbor and is eager to help him in his first steps in the new surroundings. In the big centers, the difficulties of this first transitional period are also mitigated by the help which the refugees may receive from the immigrant communities and their organizations. In the smaller towns and countryside, where there are still traces of the "old school" of courtesy, gallantry, and friendliness of the Old West, the people show understanding for the plight of the refugee and readily accept him into society. Paradoxically enough, in an area which in the past has acquired the label of isolationism, there is no xenophobia similar to the nativism of the 1850's.

In their sympathy and consideration for the refugee, however, middle westerners are very realistic. A society of great social mobility, in which the American competitive spirit is perhaps most developed, expects the newcomer to be able to make full use of the opportunities offered him.

The heritage of the Old West—of the old world of pre-industrial America—has a tremendous appeal to the refugee from totalitarian oppression. The spiritual foundations of middle western civilization, emphasizing the idea of dissent and

[40] Graham Hutton, *Midwest at Noon* (Chicago, 1946), 168.
[41] *Ibid.*, 175.

the concept of individualism, are well understood by those who escaped from the regimentation of collectivism and a society in which the state has devoured everything, including the soul of man. Reacting to his past experience, the refugee soon discovers the virtues of a tradition based on belief in man and his ability to build up society from below without the constraining elements of constant state control and supervision.

The new Middle West, with its tremendous wealth and industrial activity, typifies to the new refugees the image of modern America. In its cities and countryside he comes into a more intimate contact with the older immigrant groups from his own country. At first he may be unable to adjust himself to their ways and outlook. This is especially true of the many refugee intellectuals whom the old immigrants reproach—and often with full justification—for an unwillingness to take up manual occupations and work themselves up in the hard way, as is customary in America. Not infrequently, friction arises from the fact that the new refugee, who is often engaged in political activities of the exiled groups in the free world, tries to impose himself on people whose loyalties belong to the United States.[42] Although they may be sympathetic with the cause of freedom in their old countries and prepared to make sacrifices on its behalf, the old immigrants are Americans whose center of interest is in first place on this continent.

Sooner or later, the new immigrant learns to appreciate the contribution of his own national group to middle western civilization. He realizes with a feeling of pride that at least a part of middle western freedom, wealth, and prosperity has resulted from the endeavors of men and women of his own

[42] For a discussion of the psychology of political refugees, see Jiří Kolaja, "A Sociological Note on the Czechoslovak Anti-Communist Refugees," *American Journal of Sociology*, Vol. LVIII (November, 1952), 289–91.

blood and language. Gradually, this realization becomes a source of internal strength which helps the new refugees to restore their self-confidence and life optimism. Comparing the misery, both spiritual and material, into which Communist totalitarianism has thrown his own nation with American freedom, the refugee suddenly recognizes that some of the finest ideals, for which he fought at home, have been put into effect by his own nationals on the free soil of America.

It is perhaps too early to attempt to pass a final judgment on the total effect of the great influx of refugees from totalitarianism into the Middle West. Nor is it possible to consider, with any degree of accuracy, their contribution, if any, to the middle western heritage. No doubt, as a whole, America has profited greatly from the arrival of the members of the European elite, to which many of the refugees from totalitarianism belonged. Also, the Middle West has received its share of the eminent artists, musicians, and scientists who have come to America since 1934.

One conclusion, however, appears to be justified. The nineteenth-century political refugees came into the Middle West in its formative period, in time to be able to participate in the molding of its spiritual and intellectual image. Young as it may be, the Middle West of our days has firmly established its own moral, cultural, and political patterns. This, of course, greatly limits the scope of action of the new refugees, who represent only a small fraction of the total middle western population. But it does not limit their opportunity to lead a life that is free of the terror and destitution of totalitarian regimes. The Middle West welcomes the refugees, for many of its builders also came from distant lands. Perhaps this is why it has so often been called "the crossroad of Western civilization."

VII

<hr/>

IN SEARCH OF GOD

Sidney E. Mead

SINCE ITS discovery by Europeans, the Middle West has always been a crossroad of Western civilization. Before the end of the eighteenth century, the French, the Spanish, and the English had crossed and recrossed each other's paths through the western wilderness many times, and soon thereafter came the deluge of peoples from all over the world. Hence from the beginning there has been a great mixture of peoples of different racial, national, and religious backgrounds—many of them in continual motion, seeking profits in the fur trade, fertile lands, the Northwest Passage, or the mythical "passage to India." At times, their differences led to head-on collisions, but more commonly, with each concentrating on his own goal in an orgy of individualism, they flowed past each other in the great stream of ever increasing prosperity. Thus as Graham Hutton has noted, the Middle West is still characterized by great intolerances, but it is also characterized by an equally great and even more amazing tolerance of intolerance itself.[1] This thought provides the setting and suggests the basic motif for our discussion of the religious heritage of the Middle West.

By the time the extensive movement into the Middle West got underway during the years following the War of 1812,

[1] Graham Hutton, *Midwest at Noon* (Chicago, 1946).

the great organizational revolution which marked the passage from the ideal of religious uniformity enforced by the civil power to the ideal of religious freedom and separation of church and state had already taken place. Thomas Jefferson's conception of a church prevailed almost universally: *"A voluntary* society of men, joining themselves together of their own accord, in order to perform the public worshipping of God in such a manner as they judge acceptable to him and effectual to the salvation of their souls."

This meant that the conception of "churches" and "sects" or "dissenters" traditional in European Christendom had been supplanted by the conception of a "denomination." A denomination is a voluntary association of like-minded and/or likehearted individuals for the purpose of accomplishing tangible objectives, usually defined in terms of its missionary thrust. Its basis is not primarily creedal and/or territorial consideration, but purposive action—namely, the propagation of its point of view. The church as such has no legal existence in the United States, being represented in all civil matters by a legally recognized board or corporation. Hence all religious bodies are "free churches"; that is, they are independent of the state and autonomous in relation to it. Thus Roger Williams' prophetic ideal came to prevail in America. A church, he said,

> (whether true or false) is like unto a Body or College of Physicians in a City; like unto a Corporation, Society, or Company of East-Indie or Turkie-merchants, or any other Society or Company in London; which Companies may hold their Courts, keep their Records, hold disputations; and in matters concerning their Society, may dissent, divide, break into Schisms and Factions, sue and implead each other at the Law, yea, wholly break up and dissolve into pieces and nothing

without any interference whatsoever. The suggestion is that the internal peculiarities of a religious group are of no relevance to or the concern of the commonwealth in which it lives.

Nevertheless, with the acceptance of religious freedom, these "free" churches had assumed a grave responsibility in relation to the civil government of the new Republic. Traditionally in Christendom, the church-state relationship described as "establishment" rested upon two basic assumptions. The first was that the being and continued well-being of a civil commonwealth depended upon the existence in the population of commonly shared, essentially religious beliefs regarding the nature and destiny of man. The second was that the only way to guarantee that these beliefs would be widely enough inculcated in the people to provide this foundation for the commonwealth, was to put the coercive power of the government behind the institution responsible for the definition, dissemination and inculcation of them—at least enough coercive power to compel the people to attend upon the teachings.

Religious freedom did not mean giving up the first assumption, only the second. Hence the "free" churches assumed the responsibility of disseminating and inculcating these beliefs in the population while armed only with persuasive power. Inherent in this view of things was the devastating implication that only that which all the free churches held and taught in common was relevant to the general welfare. The obverse side of this implication was that whatever any group held and taught as peculiar to itself must be irrelevant. But it was only these matters that excused a group's continued separate and independent existence. Therefore, the more successful the denominations have been in making people peculiarly Methodist,

Baptist, Roman Catholic, Presbyterian, etc.—as the competition between the groups inherent in the voluntary system
pressed them to do—the more successful they have been in
inculcating a freedom of irrelevance to the general welfare of
the commonwealth. All the tremendous expansion and growth
of the denominations in America has taken place within the
shadow of this fact.[2]

The Christmas present which the young United States
received with the Treaty of Ghent at the close of the War of
1812 was a century of relative peace and freedom from em-
broilment in the affairs of the European countries. Immediately
following that treaty—which a Frenchman thought embodied
"the peace that passeth understanding"—during President Monroe's "era of good feelings," the country turned its back on
Europe and faced toward its own great West. Monroe, in his
message to Congress in December, 1823, let the world know
that America now wanted to be left alone to work out its
own problems.

By this time, the various denominations had adjusted themselves to the new situation existing under religious freedom.
Each had stabilized its organization and was more or less prepared to face the problem of survival and expansion under the
American conditions. The common problems which all faced
were set in motion toward the West by the now rapidly growing heterogeneous population. All denominations shared the
desire to Christianize the nation; however, as voluntary associations, they had only persuasive power, and the work was
urgent because at most only about 10 per cent of the people
were church members.

---

[2] I have described this view at length in "Thomas Jefferson's 'Fair Experiment'—Religious Freedom," *Religion in Life,* Vol. XXIII (Autumn, 1954),
566–79.

Meanwhile, a broad ideological context was provided by the prevailing myth of America's destiny, under God, to benefit all mankind by demonstrating in practice the feasibility of democratic or free institutions. Religious leaders caught up and amplified this theme, mingling the traditional millennial hope of Christians with the more secular ideas of destiny. With the rise of America, said Lyman Beecher, "the trumpet of jubilee will sound, and earth's debased millions will leap from the dust, and shake off their chains, and cry, 'Hosanna to the Son of David!' "[3] Francis Wayland, Jr., a distinguished Baptist leader, proclaimed in 1825 that "our power resides in the force of our example," that already "our country has given to the world the first ocular demonstration, not only of the practicability but also of the unrivalled superiority of a popular form of government" until, while we cannot be sure "what nation will be second in the new order of things . . . the providence of God has already announced, that, if true to ourselves, we shall be inevitably first."[4]

But the momentous decision to gather the territories into federal hands and to carve from them new states which would be equal to the original thirteen had been made, and the rapid admission of new states thereafter clearly indicated that the West would soon hold and wield determinative power in the land. "It is . . . plain," wrote Lyman Beecher in 1835,

> that the religious and political destiny of our nation is to be decided in the West. There is the territory, and there soon will be the population, the wealth, and the political power.

[3] Quoted in Alice Felt Tyler, *Freedom's Ferment* (Minneapolis, 1944), 1.
[4] *The Duties of an American Citizen: Two Discourses Delivered in the First Baptist Meeting House in Boston, on Thursday, April 7, 1825* (Boston, 1825), 27, 29, 35-36.

The Atlantic commerce and manufactures may confer always some peculiar advantages on the East. But the West is destined to be the great central power of the nation, and under heaven, must affect powerfully the cause of free institutions and the liberty of the world.[5]

In 1829, when Abraham Lincoln was twenty years old, the Reverend J. Van Vecten told a meeting of the American Home Missionary Society:

The strength of the nation lies beyond the Alleghany. The centre of dominion is fast moving in that direction. The ruler of this country is growing up in the great valley: leave him without the gospel, and he will be a ruffian giant, who will regard neither the decencies of civilization, nor the charities of religion.[6]

At the same time, a people imbued with the conception of "stages" of civilization easily came to the conclusion that the farther west one moved, the lower the state of civilization must be.[7] This view was reinforced by such observations of the actual effects of frontier living as those portrayed by St. John de Crèvecoeur. The actions of men "living in or near the woods," he argued, "are regulated by the wilderness of the neighborhood." Intending to be farmers, they find themselves in conflict with marauding animals. This "puts the gun into their hands . . . and thus by defending their property, they soon become professed hunters," and "once hunters, farewell to

[5] *Plea for the West* (2nd ed., Cincinnati, 1835), 11–12.
[6] Quoted in Walter B. Posey, *The Presbyterian Church in the Old Southwest, 1778–1838* (Richmond, 1952), 111.
[7] See Henry Nash Smith's brilliant treatment of this theme in *Virgin Land: The American West as Symbol and Myth* (Cambridge, 1950), 218ff.

the plough." "Our bad people," he concluded, "are those who are half cultivators and half hunters; and the worst of them are those who have degenerated altogether into the hunting state."[8] Later, easterners evolved the theory that there were selective factors at work which resulted in the worst people going west in the first place. Timothy Dwight, president of Yale College and commonly known as the Congregational Pope of Connecticut, argued in *Travels in New England and New York,* that at least the first settlers on a new frontier are "men who cannot live in regular society" because "they are too idle; too talkative; too passionate; too prodigal; and shiftless to acquire either property or character" and so "are impatient of the restraints of law, religion, and morality." These people, he said, "under the pressure of poverty, the fear of gaol, and the consciousness of public contempt, leave their native places, and betake themselves to the wilderness."

Methodists especially, Baptists,[9] and, after 1830, the Disciples, the Christians, and the Cumberland Presbyterians most fully developed and represented the western attitude toward

[8] St. John de Crèvecoeur, *Letters from an American Farmer* (New York, 1904), 66, 69.
[9] Actually, the Baptist denomination was divided in outlook between those in the North, centering in New England and the Philadelphia area, and those in the South, who were already moving into Tennessee and Kentucky. The former, like their powerful eastern rivals, had a long tradition of educated leadership extending back to Roger Williams and John Clarke and the English Baptists. By and large, they frowned upon the more "enthusiastic" revival manifestations. In the South, however, the Baptist thrust had begun during the great colonial revivals, and their appeal, in the context of the dominant Anglican Establishment, was to the lower, less educated class of people. Thus from the beginning, the southern wing of Baptists were closer to the general level of westward-moving people, and their ministers were largely of the "farmer–preacher" type which Professor W. W. Sweet stressed so much in his writings. While northern Baptists were generally "eastern minded," those from the South were generally "western minded," and in the Middle West, where the two streams met, the denomination was divided.

religion. These groups literally "lived on the land," making converts out of the raw materials and developing a leadership in local churches and on the circuits which was trained in what they liked to call "brush college." These dedicated men pursued the souls of the settlers like hounds of heaven. "As a general rule," wrote Alfred Brunson, "the itinerant was there . . . as soon as the curling smoke ascended from a new settlement."[10] Peter Cartwright tells of the "high-strung Predestinarian" who had moved beyond the edge of settlement "especially to get rid of those wretched people called Methodists." But, adds Cartwright, "he had scarcely got into his rude cabin before here was the Methodist preacher, preaching hell fire and damnation, as they always did."[11]

Leaders of these groups not only felt a proprietary interest in the Republic, they tended to think that they and their people *were* the Republic. Hence there early developed among them a widespread suspicion of "easterners," whose efforts to further education and culture in the West were widely interpreted as "a Crusade to Extend Yankee Culture."[12] Their suspicion was enhanced by the continuation of establishment among the New England Congregationalists. Freeborn Garrettson pithily summed up this aspect of the western attitude in an open letter to Lyman Beecher in 1816:

The glimmering light beaming through your performance, leads us to suppose, that as you are the privileged order in

[10] *A Western Pioneer: Or, Incidents in the Life and Times of Rev. Alfred Brunson, A.M., D.D. . . . Written by Himself* (Cincinnati, 1879), II, 398.
[11] W. P. Strickland (ed.), *Autobiography of Peter Cartwright, the Backwoods Preacher* (New York, 1856), 330–32.
[12] See Richard Lyle Power, "A Crusade to Extend Yankee Culture, 1820–1865," *New England Quarterly*, Vol. XIII (December, 1940), 638–53.

the eastern states, so you wish to be through the whole union; and then, as in your own state [Connecticut], so through the union, you can sit at free-cost near the sessions of legislative bodies.[13]

Peter Cartwright's autobiography is the classic expression of the western outlook in Methodist dress. Cartwright's idea was the old-fashioned Methodist preacher who,

> when he felt that God had called him to preach, instead of hunting up a college or Biblical institute, hunted up a hardy pony of a horse, and some traveling apparatus, and with his library always at hand, namely, Bible, Hymn Book, and Discipline, he started, and with a text that never wore out nor grew stale, he cried, "Behold the Lamb of God, that taketh away the sin of the world."[14]

Such a minister, he thought, could meet the demands "of our Western people," who "wanted a preacher that could mount a stump, a block, or old log, or stand in the bed of a wagon, and without note or manuscript, quote, expound, and apply the word of God to the hearts and consciences of the people.[15]

Cartwright was very suspicious of eastern people, who "brought on their learned preachers with them . . . and were always criticizing us poor back woods preachers."[16] To him, they were personified in the "thin-faced, Roman nosed, loqua-

[13] *A Letter to the Rev. Lyman Beecher Containing Strictures and Animadversions on a Pamphlet Entitled An Address of the Charitable Society for the Education of Indigent Pious Young Men for the Ministry of the Gospel* (New York, 1816), 18.

[14] Strickland, *Autobiography of Peter Cartwright, the Backwoods Preacher,* 243.

[15] *Ibid.,* 358.

[16] *Ibid.,* 98.

cious Yankee [woman], glib on the tongue," and, being "generally educated . . . they jumped into Deism, Universalism, Unitarianism," and "all the isms that I ever heard of."[17] Their ministers came with "a smattering knowledge of the old Calvinistic system of theology" and "tolerably well furnished with old manuscript sermons, that had been preached or written, perhaps a hundred years before."[18] These men were sent West "to evangelize and Christianize us poor heathen."[19] One of them, whom Cartwright describes as "a pious, good man, much devoted to prayer," he attempted to instruct in the ways of the "out-spoken and off-hand people" of the West and the kind of preaching adapted to their needs. But he soon gave up, telling the Presbyterian that "if he did not adapt this manner of preaching, the Methodists would set the whole Western world on fire before he would light his match."[20]

Western suspicions were not alleviated by some of the letters sent home by the missionaries. In 1851, for example, a Presbyterian wrote of "the way they 'get religion' as they call it!"

> After a passionate appeal (which is evidently intended to reach the weaker part of the congregation first) . . . and a vindication of shouting, the mourners are called for. And then the singing and shouting commences, and the mourners are brought in and required to kneel down. In this . . . position, they are sometimes kept for hours at a time, until wearied out, they sink down and stretch themselves upon the floor. This is considered a favorable symptom. . . . After awhile, through suffocation and exhaustion, a profuse sweat breaks out upon them, and they are made to feel as they "never felt

[17] *Ibid.*, 99.
[18] *Ibid.*, 358.
[19] *Ibid.*, 308.
[20] *Ibid.*

before." This they conclude is the "witness of the Spirit," and then as it is expected they relieve themselves from their procumbent situation, by springing upon their feet, and hopping about, and clapping their hands, and screaming with loud percussive emphasis, "Glory, glory, glory hallelujah, I've got it" &c.[21]

Such letters, said Cartwright, containing "wailings and lamentations over the moral wastes and destitute condition of the West... would be printed, and come back among us as published facts in some of their periodicals."[22] What hurt was the missionaries' tendency to completely ignore the Methodist classes and churches scattered all over the West under the care of circuit riders. "On a certain occasion," says Cartwright,

> when these reports came back known to contain false statements, the citizens of Quincy called a meeting, mostly out of the Church, and after discussing the subject, pledged themselves to give me a thousand dollars per annum, and bear all my traveling expenses, if I would go as a missionary to the New-England States, and enlighten them on this and other subjects, of which they considered them profoundly ignorant.[23]

But, he adds, "owing to circumstances beyond my control, I was obliged to decline the acceptance of their generous offer."[24] Hence what might have been one of the most interesting experiments of the nineteenth century was nipped in the bud.

It should be noted the western-minded religious groups

[21] Quoted in Colin B. Goodykoontz, *Home Missions on the American Frontier* (Caldwell, Idaho, 1939), 33.
[22] Strickland, *Autobiography of Peter Cartwright, the Backwoods Preacher*, 359.
[23] *Ibid.*, 359–60.
[24] *Ibid.*

KANSAS CITY SIRLOIN ON THE HOOF: The Stock-
yards Which Rank as the Nation's Largest Stocker and Feeder
Market.

AIR TRANSPORTATION: Far-sighted Planning Gave the Middle West an Early Lead in This Field, Now Enhanced by Extensions of Its Facilities.

swept into the Middle West originally and largely with the great crescent-shaped movement of population exemplified in the life of Cartwright. Born in Virginia and moving in westward successive steps through Kentucky and southern Indiana, he concluded his pilgrimage in northwestern Illinois. His typical "easterner" was a "Yankee," not a Virginian or a Carolinian.

Finally, at a time when New Orleans and St. Louis constituted ports of entry from abroad, there was notable direct immigration into the Middle West. Outstanding among the immigrants were the Saxon Germans, who came in the forties and, after some internal difficulties, emerged as Missouri Synod Lutherans. For these, as for the later German and Scandinavian Lutherans, the primary problems were survival on the physical frontier and in the American denominational wilderness and resistance to "Americanization." More sober and dogmatic in orientation than the acclimated American groups and insulated by the difference in language, they tended to form about their churches religious and cultural islands, which have remained fairly intact to the present.

Looking back upon the religious situation that existed in the Middle West before the Civil War in the interest of what we may have inherited from it, we are first struck with the general success of the various denominations in triumphing over barbarism, infidelity, superstition, and tremendous physical obstacles to effect a general Christianizing of the land. However, the triumph presents a paradox; namely, it was effected by intense competition between implicitly absolutistic groups, and it seems to have resulted in a general washout of real belief in the matters which divided them.[25]

---

[25] L. W. Bacon notes: "In the existence of any Christian sect the presumption is of course implied, if not asserted . . . that it is holding the absolute

Revivalism, of course, was the almost universally accepted and used technique. Theodore Parker noted that even the Boston Unitarians tried it, but "nothing came of that" because these men "were so cold in their religious temperament that any one of them would chill a whole garden of cucumbers in dog days" and they could not "force Christians under the Unitarian glass."[26] However that may be, from beginning to end, revivalists defended all their ways on the grounds that they produced "results." Their common theme was stated by J. B. Finley: In the West, "infidelity was triumphant, and religion on the point of expiring"; therefore, "something of an extraordinary nature was necessary to arrest the attention of a wicked and skeptical people."[27] Thus in spite of the competition between the sects, the general evangelical outlook and the use of revivalistic techniques tended to undermine distinctive standards of doctrine and polity.[28]

Two residual effects of revivalism are a part of the middle western heritage. First, the almost universal use of revivalistic techniques in the church inculcated a general belief in their efficacy which was far beyond the boundaries of the churches. Just as the ever ready answer to a decline in membership or the appearance of religious apathy in a local church was to bring in a forceful evangelist to "revive us again," so, too, are many people today inclined to believe that the answer

---

right and truth, or at least more nearly that than other sects; and the inference to a religious mind, is that right and trust must, in the long run, prevail." *History of American Christianity* (New York, 1900), 404.

[26] Theodore Parker, *Works* (Centenary ed., Boston, 1908), IV, 384.

[27] W. P. Strickland (ed.), *Autobiography of Rev. James B. Finley: Or, Pioneer Life in the West* (Cincinnati, 1855), 299.

[28] For a general treatment of this theme, see Sidney E. Mead, "Denominationalism: The Shape of Protestantism in America," *Church History*, Vol. XXIII (December, 1954), 291–320.

to troublesome national problems is to bring in a morally impeccable plumed knight to lead a great moral and spiritual crusade in politics. Second, many members of new and respectable denominations whose people have generally risen on the economic and social scale are embarrassed by the revivalistic noise and crudities of their spiritual forebears, just as many a second-generation immigrant child has been embarrassed by the "foreign" ways and crudities of his parents. I have had respectable middle-class Methodists, who could by no means conceive of shouting in church, chide me for telling young peoples' groups about the common practices of nineteenth-century Methodists in camp meetings and revivals. This kind of estrangement from one's spiritual tradition is a part of our heritage, and it tends to undermine the sense of historical continuity which has always been such a potent force in Christendom.

In 1865, denominationalism was generally accepted in the United States and was assumed to be the proper organizational form for the free churches. Evangelical Protestant Christianity largely dominated the American culture, setting the prevailing moral standards by which both personal and group conduct was judged.[29] This was a source of pride and self-approbation in the denominations, for it demonstrated their success in defining and inculcating in the people the basic beliefs necessary for the being and well-being of democratic society. It was not yet clear, as it later became to denominational leaders that they were the "victims of their own success." For, as Professor W. S. Hudson has so convincingly argued, the very "strength and

---

[29] Cf. H. Paul Douglass, "The Protestant Faiths," in Harold E. Stearns (ed.), *America Now: An Inquiry into Civilization in the United States* (New York, 1928), 514: "Despite multiplying sectarian differences, Protestantism's prevalence tended to create a Protestant cultural type. . . . It was a triumph of religion still on a communal level."

vigor of the culture which the churches had brought into being
led men to discount the importance of the churches," while the
churches, "proud of their achievements and pleased that their
mission had been so largely accomplished . . . relaxed and made
peace with the world."[30]

All the necessary elements for a great Evangelical Protestant American-way-of-life synthesis were present at the time
Lincoln was assassinated, and the road was cleared for what
Hudson calls "a culture religion," distinguished by "its lack of
normative content."[31] It was already obvious that real religious
belief, in the traditional sectarian sense, had been relinquished
by the intellectuals and that the views of no single religious
group—or even the peculiar collective views of Evangelical
Protestantism—could win complete dominance in the heterogeneous population. These tendencies have not been diverted,
and what has happened since has merely augmented and hastened to their logical conclusions the tendencies already present.
The only new thing about developments since 1865—which is
only now becoming clear—is that the religious-cultural synthesis has come to include Roman Catholics and Jews.

A new Middle West emerged very rapidly after the Civil
War, being ushered in not with a whimper, but with a bang.
Its physical assets were raw materials—notably iron ore, coal,
lumber, corn, wheat, and cattle—improved means of transportation—steamships on the lakes, railroads on the land; faster
communication; and the host of immigrants. These assets embodied the trinitarian bases of the new Middle West (i.e., three
for purposes of analysis, actually only one): industrialization,

[30] Winthrop S. Hudson, *The Great Tradition of the American Churches*
(New York, 1953), 109, 201.
[31] *Ibid.,* 161.

urbanization, and immigration. Industrialization and the closely related influx of immigrants were the twin components of the terrifying new urban centers that mushroomed overnight. Sprawling urban communities, with their strange culture—if such a fortuitous concatenation can be distinguished by such an honorable name—were established amidst the existing relatively peaceful trading and distribution centers, taking the land with much noise and violence. Chicago is pre-eminently the city of the new Middle West a spreading, amorphous, violent bastard city, without acknowledged father or mother, which "growed up" into a heartless Frankenstein monster.[32]

The first great thrust was carried on an optimistic wave of belief in "progress" and the prevailing sense of the essential soundness of the existing religious, social, political, and economic systems which had produced such phenomenal wonders in so short a time. People were awed by this "brave new world" which they had somehow created and were reverently pleased that it had "such people in it" as themselves.

Then, quite unexpectedly as far as people that mattered were concerned, their "brave new world" exploded in violence, bloodshed, smoke, and flame all along the rails from Baltimore and Philadelphia to Chicago and St. Louis. The great strikes during the years following 1870 bespoke the growing pains— or was it the essential sickness?—of the systems which had spawned such a monster. This, plus the less spectacular revolt of the farmers, brought the first shock of recognition to the heretofore complacently happy middle-class denizens of the new urban Edens.

[32] Bessie Louise Pierce, "Changing Urban Patterns in the Mississippi Valley," *Journal of the Illinois State Historical Society,* Vol. XLIII (Spring, 1950), 46–57.

From 1885 to 1890, representative spokesmen nurtured in the old Middle West were near hysteria, screaming about what Augustus Strong, in *Our Country: Its Possible Future and Present Crisis* (a very popular book that went through many editions), called the great "perils" to the American way of life. He made it clear that America was "Christian," by which he meant, with all the aplomb of Fielding's Parson Thwackum, "Protestant"; the perils were immigration, Romanism, Mormonism, intemperance, socialism, materialism and the concentration of wealth, and the cities. Finally he argued that "the West," wherein America's destiny lies, because of "the plastic and formative" nature of its society, "is peculiarly exposed" to these dangers.[33]

This assessment of the situation indicates that the general ideological equipment with which Protestant leaders confronted the problems of the new day was essentially that which had been formed and sanctified in the old, simple, agrarian, trading Protestant Middle West. There are several pertinent elements of this ideological constellation which form a part of our heritage.

First, the United States is a Christian country. Strong quoted Chief Justice Shea with approval: "Our own government, and the laws by which it is administered, are in every part—legislative, judicial, and executive—Christian in nature, form and purpose."[34] So prevalent was this view that it led some to a strange interpretation of religious freedom. The Reverend J. M. Foster of Cincinnati argued in 1887 that "America does not belong to us, it belongs to God." Therefore, "all men who

[33] Augustus Strong, *Our Country: Its Possible Future and Present Crisis* (rev. ed., New York, 1891), 200.
[34] *Ibid.,* 101.

may choose should be allowed to come here without let or hindrance." But because the "country was settled by Christian men with Christian ends in view," there is one stern condition— all who come must "conform to our Christian civilization." For example, "the Chinamen are just as much God's creatures as Americans, and have the same inalienable right to dwell here that we have." But, he added, "they have no right to bring their idols here, or to pursue their idolatrous customs. That is a violation of the Divine law. And our government was derelict in her duty when she allowed them to bring their idols to San Francisco . . . and follow their heathenish practices, until a portion of that city became absolutely leprous." Hence, he concluded, "there was a show of reason in the hoodlum cry that was raised, 'the Chinese must go.' "[35]

Second, the United States is a Protestant country, in the sense that only Protestant Christianity is compatible with "our free institutions" and "our republican prosperity." Lyman Beecher, in his *Plea for the West,* published in 1835, struck the keynote in going out of his way to argue that "the Catholics have just as good a right to their religion as other denominations have to theirs," and this includes the *"perfect right to proselyte the nation to their faith if they are able to do it."* Hence the only question is, not "whether Catholics are pious or learned," but "what are the republican tendencies of their system?" Indeed, he argued, all we are concerned about is "the tendency upon our republican institutions" of "the Catholic religion, and its church and state alliance with the political and ecclesiastical governments of Europe" which are "hostile to

[35] J. M. Foster, "Immigration," in *National Perils and Opportunities: The Discussions of the General Christian Conference Held in Washington, D. C., December 7th, 8th, and 9th, 1887, under the Auspices and Direction of the Evangelical Alliance for the United States* (New York, 1887), 78–79.

liberty." For, he argued, "the opinions of the Protestant clergy are congenial to liberty" because "they are chosen by the people who have been educated as freemen, and they are dependent on them for patronage and support." On the other hand, the Roman Catholic clergy, who "have almost unlimited power over the conscience of their people as it respects the performance of every civil or social duty," are "to a great extent . . . dependent on foreigners opposed to the principles of our government, for patronage and support." Therefore, he said, "the Catholic system is adverse to our liberty."[36]

This is the basic line of argument followed from Lyman Beecher in 1835 to Augustus Strong in 1885—the latter concluding, after an extensive show of arguments, that "manifestly there is an irreconcilable difference between papal principles and the fundamental principles of our free institutions."[37] This feeling is a part of our heritage which is still with us. In 1951, Thomas Sugrue, a Roman Catholic of Irish descent, noted that "old suspicions stir easily, and there has never been any evidence that the papacy looked with even mild approval on democracy as a political idea" until even some Catholics fear that the Pope's "rule in religious matters, will spill over, as it has in the past, into secular matters." This also "worries Protestants, and it should."[38]

Third, this complex conception of the Christian and Protestant character of the American way of life, plus the traditional sense of the destiny of America, plus awareness of its increasing might as a world power, plus the tidal wave of im-

[36] Beecher, *Plea for the West*. The quotations in this paragraph are, in order, from pp. 91, 90, 69, 60, and 61.
[37] Strong, *Our Country*, 77.
[38] Thomas Sugrue, *A Catholic Speaks His Mind on America's Religious Conflict* (New York, 1951), 24, 30, 59.

migrants from southern and eastern Europe, helped to accentuate the fear of the "foreigner" and to produce a Christian–
Anglo-Saxon racism which is most clearly articulated by Augustus Strong in *Our Country*.[39]

The Protestant–Anglo-Saxon view of American institutions is a part of our complex religious heritage, and the con-
sequent attitude of suspicion and fear toward the peoples of
the "new immigration"—like some old soldiers—does not die,
but seems to be fading away.

By 1885, Protestantism, ideologically, was almost universally identified with and hence sanctified the complex conception of the American way of life exemplified in the existing religious, social, political and economic institutions. I have summarized the situation in a recent article:

> While the Protestant denominations remained very conscious
> of the evils due to a formal connection between church and
> state demonstrated in history, they were rendered by cir-
> cumstances . . . less critically conscious of the equally grave
> evils contingent upon ideological amalgamation with a par-
> ticular way of life. Hence while abhorring Erastianism, and
> being skeptical of theocracy—in their overt forms—the free
> churches eventually found themselves entangled in a more
> subtle form of identification of Christianity, nationalism, and
> economic system than Christendom had ever before known.[40]

I trust that enough has been said to suggest that the religious
heritage of the Middle West has many facets, contains not a
few paradoxical elements, and is, in brief, very complex. Per-

[39] For a full discussion of this point, see the chapter entitled "The
Anglo-Saxon and the World's Future," in *Our Country*, 77.

[40] "American Protestantism since the Civil War: II. From Americanism
to Christianity," *Journal of Religion*, Vol. XXXVI (April, 1956).

haps, however, the central theme is the "trying out" of religions in America. Into the pot has gone every sect and sectarian view of Christendom, plus Judaism, and representatives of all the world's religions. The "melting pot" was the great Republic of "free institutions," which provided the fact that in spite of their sectarian differences and absolutistic claims, the various groups did live and work together side by side in peace, each contributing its bit to the great chorus of the Union. This situation tended continually to undermine real belief in the peculiar views of any group.

Thomas Sugrue's story of his personal religious pilgrimage through his "booming, aggressive, materialistic, socially ambitious" church institution in America to its "mystical core" is persuasively typical. For, he says, it was the Protestants who introduced him to the mystics who "are the heart of Catholicism," while "among Catholics, lay and cleric, I never heard of them." In college, he says, he, a southern Baptist preministerial student and a Presbyterian "ran a bull session on God which lasted without interruption for two years," with the result that

> We are friends yet, we three, and we belong still to the same denominations, probably because we discovered then, together, that no man is truly religious until he takes up within himself the burden of his redemption, and that when this happens all denominations fall away and the soul is alone with God.

Hence, he concluded, the sum of our American religious experience is this:

> All religious roads lead in the end to God, just as all rivers, eventually reach the sea; pilgrims on these highways know

that this is so, and realize that many roads are necessary for the many kinds of people, who begin their spiritual journeys from a multitude of points of view. It is the commanders of the highways who will not have it so; each wants preferential rating for his thoroughfare, and longs to reduce all other turnpikes to the status of tributary.

And it is this which "marks the defeat of religion and the perversion of its purpose as an aid to man in his search for inner and outer peace, in his desire to be known well by others and feel well with God."[41] Thus Sugrue articulates clearly the widespread feeling in America among lay people in all religious groups—that somehow, the division into sects which still grope in the shadow of absolutistic sectarian claims stands in the way of individuals who are trying to be truly religious.

Even Augustus Strong (of all people!) noted with approval that the Christianity of America must, in the long run, be Justice Story's "general, tolerant Christianity, independent of sects and parties," and he argued, as a host of others had before him, that finally,

> the teaching of the three great fundamental doctrines which are common to all monotheistic religions is essential to the perpetuity of free institutions, while the inculcation of sectarian dogmas is not. These three doctrines are that of *the existence of God, the immortality of man*, and *man's accountability*. These doctrines are held in common by all Protestants, Catholics and Jews.[42]

Strong's view—that it is only the perpetuation of the doc-

[41] Sugrue, *A Catholic Speaks His Mind on America's Religious Conflict,* 20, 49-50.
[42] Strong, *Our Country,* 101-102.

trines common to all the dominant religious families in America which "is essential to the perpetuity of free institutions"—suggests the two closely related strands in our heritage which today struggle for dominance.

The first is revealed in a statement attributed to President Eisenhower in the *Chicago Daily News* of January 12, 1952: "I am the most intensely religious man I know," *but* "that doesn't mean I adhere to any sect. A democracy cannot exist without a religious base. I believe in democracy."[43] The conclusion of the implied syllogism is obvious—*therefore* I believe in religion. Whether or not this comment was a putting of the foot into the mouth, it was certainly a putting of the cart before the horse. It suggests the widespread tendency to believe in religion because it is necessary or useful to peace of mind, to peace of soul, to confident living, to prosperity, to republican government, to popularity, or what not. Reviewing this tendency, one wit has remarked that America's religious pilgrimage is illustrated by the movement from Jonathan Edwards' conception of "Sinners in the Hands of an Angry God" to the present conception of God in the hands of fearful, unpeaceful, unconfident, unprosperous, unpopular men and women who think He might make a good and powerful ally. This is a much more present danger to high religion in America than the "secularism"—that current "latest form of infidelity" —which is so much railed against today, even by some thoroughly secularized ministers and denominational leaders.

But there is another strand in our tradition which is equally a part—and I think the more profound part—of our religious heritage. It is exemplified outstandingly in Abraham Lincoln, the spiritual center of our American history.

[43] Quoted in Daniel J. Boorstin, *The Genius of American Politics* (Chicago, 1953), 146.

Lincoln can be called the flower and culmination of the old Middle West, representing, with peculiar persuasiveness, an integration of the most profound elements of religious and democratic experience to his time. He proved to be Van Vecten's "ruler of this country growing up in the great valley" in 1829; in a new and cruder western way, he incarnated both "the decencies of civilization" and "the charities of religion" because he had not been left "without the gospel." Because the denominations did their missionary work so well—indeed better than they perhaps imagined—Lincoln absorbed the most profound relevant meanings of Christianity in the new *West* of the Great Republic and, in the way he used them, indicated that he clearly saw how they gave the necessary religious and metaphysical sanctions to the democratic way of fulfilling America's historical destiny under God. He spoke out of the folk process itself, and, gifted with unusual powers of articulation, he wove the strands of mystical piety and calculating logicality, of intense idealism and cold practicality, into one luminous whole that expressed the real meaning of America.

Lincoln believed in democracy as "the last, best hope of earth" *because* he believed in God—the God who created the world and still governs it, who stands in judgment over all the works of men—even Americans—and whose judgments are "true and righteous altogether."

Although commonly recognized by all parties as exemplifying the deepest currents of religious and political meaning in the United States,[44] Lincoln joined no existing denomination, and down to the present, he is claimed by no existing religious group without grave misgivings from within or the valid charge

[44] See, for example, Herbert Croly, "Lincoln," *The New Republic* (40th Anniversary Issue, 1914-1954), 69-71.

of presumption from without. This kind of understanding of Lincoln as the legitimate expression and culmination of what was implicit in the heterogeneous religious situation in America has seldom been grasped, least of all by ardent sectarian denominationalists—Sugrue's "commanders of the highways"—who continue to talk and act as if they thought the perpetuation of their group's peculiarities is the basis of ultimate hope for the country and "the last, best hope of earth." But, to paraphrase Emerson somewhat—as who does not?—the facts of our history "have always suggested" to us "the sublime creed that the world is . . . the product . . . of one will, of one mind . . . and whatever opposes that will is everywhere balked and baffled, because things are made so, and not otherwise."

This seems to be the thrust of the complex religious heritage which our history brings to us, and, as Lincoln said, "we cannot escape history." Or, as Franklin put it in the vernacular: "he who spits against the wind spits in his own face."

VIII

~~~~~~

FOOD FOR
MIDDLE WESTERN THOUGHT

Joseph L. Blau

DIONY HALL, the courageous heroine of Elizabeth Madox
Roberts' novel *The Great Meadow*,[1] is first described by
her creator as a young girl in the home of her parents in the
western part of Virginia at the time of the American Revolution. The few books in the possession of her father included
Bishop Berkeley's *The Principles of Human Knowledge*.
Thomas Hall returned to this book continually, for Berkeley
was "his philosopher."[2] Diony herself, despite her youth, had
read Berkeley with an intensity of concentration that we today
find difficult to realize. Passages from the philosopher echoed
and re-echoed in her mind as she helped her mother in the
unending round of women's work. "Stepping back and forth
in the dance of spinning, she would recall words from her
father's books, from one book: 'It is evident to anyone who
takes a survey of the objects of human knowledge, that they
are either ideas actually imprinted on the senses or else such as
are perceived by attending to the passions and operations of the
mind.' "[3] As she reflected on the words so well remembered,

[1] New York, The Viking Press, 1930.
[2] *The Great Meadow*, 6.
[3] *Ibid.*, 21. Cf. Berkeley, *The Principles of Human Knowledge* (Chicago, 1920), 29.

she rephrased them in a mixture of the elegant eighteenth-century phrasing of the author and her own coarse speech. "They, these things, or any small part of the whole mighty frame of the world, are withouten any kind or sort or shape until somebody's mind is there to know. Consequently, all the ways you wouldn't know, all you forgot or never yet remembered, mought have a place to be in Mind, in some Mind far off, and he calls this Eternal Spirit."[4] When, after her marriage to Berk Jarvis and their pioneering journey westward into Kentucky, Diony was living through danger and hardship, the words remembered, perhaps with understanding or perhaps merely with the force of an incantation, brought solace to her in moments of distress.[5]

This, you may say, is but fiction. Were there, actually, among the westering pioneers in the late eighteenth century some who, like this imaginary Diony Hall Jarvis, carried with them into the new country such philosophic furnishings for the minds of their children? Doubtless there were, though they were very few. Certain it is that within a few short years after the first pioneer settlements had been established at Boone's Fort and Harrod's Fort, there was established the pioneer institution of learning beyond the mountains, Transylvania Seminary. Further evidence of intellectual interests is to be found in the number of bookstores that sprang up in Kentucky, and the direction of these interests is indicated by the titles advertised for sale in these stores. In John Bradford's bookstore in Lexington, as early as 1795, philosophic and theological works included Butler's *Analogy of Religion,*

---

[4] *The Great Meadow,* 24. Cf. Berkeley, *The Principles of Human Knowledge,* 32–33.
[5] *The Great Meadow,* 198, *passim.*

Hume's *Essays* and his *Dialogues on Natural Religion*, Paley's *Natural Philosophy*, Jonathan Edwards' *Treatise on the Religious Affections*, and many others—a mixed bag indeed. William Leavy, bookseller in the same town, advertised, also in 1795, many of these works and some others. Trotter and Scott, in the same year and town, advertised Montesquieu's *Spirit of Laws* and Adam Smith's *Theory of the Moral Sentiments*. In 1795, too, the Transylvania Library was founded; its catalogue of 1804 includes works by Condorcet, Voltaire, Adam Smith, Richard Price, Rousseau, Godwin, Locke, Priestley, Wollaston, Bolingbroke, Lord Kames, Hume (again the *Dialogues on Natural Religion*), as well as Edwards, Reid, Stewart, and Paley, among more conservative authors. This library was founded originally as an adjunct to the work of Transylvania Seminary.[6]

Transylvania Seminary came into existence in 1785 under terms of an enabling act of 1783. During the first few years of its existence, it was most unstable and conceivably did not function at all between 1786 and 1789. At no time before 1794 did it house more than sixteen students, and despite its bold assertion of teaching logic, metaphysics, and moral philosophy, there is no evidence that it was actually teaching these subjects. By 1799, the Seminary had combined with the Kentucky Academy under the name of Transylvania University. The Reverend James Moore became president and professor of logic, metaphysics, moral philosophy, and belles-lettres. Moore was an orthodox Presbyterian who uncovered a surprising tinge of liberality in recommending to the students, in 1800, intellectual curiosity and independence of judgment. After his

[6] All this information is in Niels Henry Sonne, *Liberal Kentucky, 1780–1828* (New York, 1939), 24-26.

forced resignation, there was considerable difficulty in filling the chair he had vacated.[7]

If Moore at Transylvania be regarded as the first middle western teacher of philosophy, another Kentuckian, Dr. Joseph Buchanan, must be given credit for being the first middle western philosopher. Buchanan was born in Virginia in 1785; at ten he was taken to Tennessee, where he had only a smattering of education before entering Transylvania University in 1804. We may assume that he studied with Moore, for he was one of the student signers of a petition to keep Moore at Transylvania. Buchanan did not remain at the University long enough to receive a degree; he left to study medicine privately. In 1809 he was elected professor of the "Institutes of Medicine," but the medical school in anticipation of which he was named to this position did not materialize. In 1812, Buchanan published *The Philosophy of Human Nature* (Richmond, Kentucky), a book based upon the lectures he had planned to give in the medical school. Buchanan's philosophy, a materialistic monism, rested largely and avowedly on the ideas of Locke, David Hartley, Hume, and Erasmus Darwin. From Hartley, Buchanan derived an emphasis on association of ideas that led to his stress on the early formation of habits. From Hume, he took over the general outlines of his theory of knowledge; he used this skeptical theory to establish a presumption in favor of materialism and monism by showing that the more usual dualism, of material body and immaterial mind, does not rest on direct perception but on inference. Directly, we cannot gain complete knowledge of either mind or matter; without this

[7] *Ibid.*, 46–77, where full details of the early years of Transylvania are summarized from records of the University and contemporary newspapers, as well as from secondary literature.

knowledge, we are not in a position to assert either that mind and matter are the same or that they are different. With respect to matter, however, Buchanan asserted that the then recent discoveries of Sir Humphrey Davy tended to show that every material particle is sufficiently active to account for all the effects that had generally been regarded as probative of mind. Further details of Buchanan's philosophic position are not germane to this summary treatment.[8] What is important here is to recognize that the first original philosophic work to be written in the American Middle West was continuous in temper with the generally sensationalistic and materialistic thought of Virginians of the late eighteenth century and that its more remote sources are to be found in the Lockeian tradition. The surprising feature is that the French continuers of this tradition—Helvétius, Condillac, Condorcet and the philosophs—who were read in Virginia and some of whose names appear in the early book catalogues to which I have made reference, played no discernible part in the background of Buchanan's ideas.

In the very next year after the publication of Buchanan's book, a reply came from the pen of another Kentuckian, James Fishback. Fishback's book was entitled *The Philosophy of the Human Mind, in Respect to Religion; or, A Demonstration from the Necessity of Things that Religion Entered the World by Revelation* (Lexington, Kentucky, 1813). Fishback's original inspiration came directly from Locke, as well as from the developments of Locke's epistemology by Hume. He argued that Locke had shown man's cognitive powers to be inadequate

[8] There is a full summary in I. Woodbridge Riley, *American Philosophy: The Early Schools* (New York, 1907), 373–95, as well as a brief discussion in Sonne, *Liberal Kentucky, 1780–1828*, 78–107. Buchanan's *Philosophy of Human Nature* is not easy to come by; a reprint edition is a desideratum.

for the acquisition of transempirical knowledge and that, therefore, knowledge of matters of religion required revelation.
Both Locke and Hume had pointed out that the natural operations of the human mind are limited to reflection upon simple
ideas gained from sensory perception or from an introspective
consideration of its own operations. These limitations exclude
the possibility that the mind might arrive at conceptions of
spiritual truths, since these are simple ideas that cannot arise out
of sensory perceptions. For this reason (disregarding Locke's
own view that our idea of God is a complex idea, derived from
combining simple ideas of existence and duration, knowledge
and power, pleasure and happiness, and other such qualities
"enlarged" with our idea of infinite),[9] Fishback denied the
possibility of natural religion. Furthermore, in his discussion
of revelation as that which man must have had in order to have
the spiritual knowledge that he has, Fishback argued that the
revelation must have been verbal: "Upon subjects whose objects, and qualities are insensible, or lie beyond the reach of
sense, man *could not think*, till he had language given; and of
course could not upon those subjects be a rational creature.
Upon them he can no more think than speak without words;
words are as necessarily prior to both . . . as causes to their
effects. The mind cannot think upon nothing."[10] On the question of whether revelation can convey simple ideas, Fishback
explicitly dissented from the Lockeian view that "no man, inspired by God, can by any revelation, communicate to others
any new simple ideas, which they had not before from sensa-

[9] John Locke, *An Essay Concerning Human Understanding*, Book II,
Chap. 23, No. 33.
[10] Fishback, *The Philosophy of the Human Mind*, 39, as quoted in
Sonne, *Liberal Kentucky*, 237.

tion or reflection . . . because words, by their immediate operation on us, cause no other ideas but of their natural sounds."[11]

Middle western philosophy may be said to have begun,
then, in two works giving different and opposed interpretations to the Lockeian tradition, one supporting a materialistic
position, the other a conservative and conventional Christian
theism. Inasmuch as Berkeley falls into the same tradition,
using it for religious ends, there is at the very least poetic truth
in the fictional account of early Kentucky given by Elizabeth
Madox Roberts. Moreover, our brief examination suggests the
correctness for the earliest Middle West of Merle Curti's description of Locke as "America's Philosopher."[12]

The middle western lands did not long remain exclusively
overflow reservoirs for the eastern seaboard. The early years
of the nineteenth century brought a small but significant flow
of immigration from Continental Europe, particularly from
the German states. New York was the port of entry for some
of these new arrivals, but in those days, when ships of lesser
draught were used for trans-Atlantic voyages, Philadelphia,
Baltimore, Norfolk, Charleston and Savannah on the Atlantic
Coast admitted a large number of immigrants. Many of the
newcomers, after a short stay in the eastern city in which they
landed, moved westward into the more open country beyond
the Appalachians. In many cases, they settled near the natural
lanes of transportation, especially the waterways, in Kentucky,
Ohio, Indiana, Illinois, and Missouri.

To the newcomers from Germany especially, the Middle

[11] Locke, *An Essay Concerning Human Understanding*, Book IV,
Chap. 18, No. 3.
[12] See Merle Curti, "The Great Mr. Locke, America's Philosopher,
1783–1861," *The Huntington Library Bulletin*, No. 11 (April, 1937), 107–51.

West was a second homeland. Within a few years after its first settlement, Cincinnati acquired a German character that it retained until well into the twentieth century. The German language was spoken as widely as English, if not more widely. Newspapers, magazines, and books were published in German in Cincinnati and other Ohio towns. If these new Americans could not live in Germany, they could at least live in the most nearly German cultural environment that they could re-create. It must be remembered, too, that this migration was not that of a famine-ridden peasantry, eager for bare subsistence. Although the causes of German migration were partly economic, they were political, too. Many were of the middle class, supporters of democratic ideas who had to leave their homes either during the Napoleonic conquest or during the still more reactionary era that followed the defeat of Napoleon. These middle-class political exiles were literate and, in some cases, even well-educated folk who brought into American life a knowledge of German philosophy even before the New England transcendentalists gained their hard-won, chiefly second-hand acquaintance with it.

Unfortunately, there has, as yet, been no adequate study of this early German-American culture. It is probable, too, that when it is thoroughly investigated, it will prove to have had little influence on the development of philosophy in the Middle West, for the German group at this time kept to themselves, forming an enclave within the country. It was some time later before there arose an interpreter who chose for himself the double role of apostle of German philosophy to America and enunciator of American tradition to the Germans of the Middle West. This man was Johann Bernard Stallo, who, though by no means merely a publicist (as his late work, *The Concepts*

and Theories of Modern Physics, reveals), chose deliberately
to serve as a bridge between the two cultures he loved.

Stallo came to America, a fugitive for political reasons, at
an early age. He taught briefly at Fordham and St. John's colleges in New York and then followed the sun to the west; he
settled in Cincinnati, became a lawyer, entered political life,
and was rewarded with a judgeship. In many speeches before
German-speaking audiences, Judge Stallo expounded the democratic ideas of the American heritage, showing particular interest in the ideas of Thomas Jefferson. In a book entitled *General Principles of the Philosophy of Nature, with an outline of
some of its recent developments among the Germans, embracing the philosophical systems of Schelling and Hegel, and
Oken's System of Nature* (Boston, 1848), Stallo fulfilled his
role as apostle to the Americans. The book was deliberately
conceived as a mission. "I shall think myself happy," Stallo
wrote, "if I have in any manner contributed to introduce more
distinct ideas respecting German philosophy among the American public."[13] He regarded it as the peculiar province of German philosophy to support and justify an alliance between
theistic philosophy and scientific investigation. This alliance
had been revoked by British-American thought "under color
of a misconceived Baconism."[14] Despite what he considered
the concrete mission of German philosophy, Stallo asserted
that it had been presented to English readers, even in the writings of "the excellent Carlyle," as if it were "a medley of vague
abstractions, or a series of distractive day-dreams." The reason
for this is that "certain pre-established English criteria have
been applied to German philosophy."[15] He distinguished the

[13] *Philosophy of Nature*, viii.
[14] *Ibid.*, vii.
[15] *Ibid.*, ix.

national characteristics of German philosophy as aprioristic and deductive and those of English and French philosophy as empiricistic and inductive.[16]

Although Stallo asserted in the preface his obligation to Hegel, the first part of his *Philosophy of Nature*, setting forth a general point of view from which he conceived that a philosophical study of natural science was possible, is largely dependent upon the philosophic views of Goethe.[17] It is notable for its explicit (and, of course, pre-Darwinian) evolutionism. In the second part, there is a summary statement of Kant's *Critique of Pure Reason* which serves as the epistemological starting point for the nature philosophies of Schelling, Oken, and Hegel. Of these three, Schelling's philosophy is presented quite summarily, Oken's in more detail, and Hegel's *in extenso*. Stallo's abstracts are far more accurate representations of these thinkers than those by J. Gostwick, a later popularizer.[18] Furthermore, quite aside from the second part, the first, or programmatic, section of Stallo's book can stand by itself as a thoroughly competent piece of philosophic writing in the nineteenth century German tradition.

[16] *Ibid.* "The Germans . . . always set out from *themselves*, from a few axiomatic notions relating to *being, thought, ideas, the Deity*, &c., and upon these synthetically constructed their system of science; whereas the English and French began with objective nature, analyzed it, and then by generalizations sought to arrive at absolute conclusions. The Germans could not descend to the material world; hence they became idealists;—the English and French were unable to ascend to the summits of the Absolute; on that account they remained materialists."

[17] This point is thoroughly and carefully documented in an unpublished Ph.D. dissertation on Stallo by George Wilkinson (Columbia University Library).

[18] It was Gostwick's abstract on which Walt Whitman relied for his scant knowledge of Hegelian philosophy (cf. *Specimen Days*, yet Whitman claimed Hegel as the philosopher for Americans. It is interesting to speculate whether, had he known more of Hegel in a more accurate version, Whitman would have been more or less firmly of this opinion.

Less well known and far less worthy of being remembered than this work, but probably more typical of philosophic writing among the German-Americans of Ohio, is Peter Kaufmann's *The Temple of Truth, or the Science of Ever-Progressive Knowledge; containing the foundation and elements of a system for arriving at absolute certainty in all things* (Cincinnati, 1858). This remarkable book was published by its author in both English and German. It presents, in something less than 300 pages, a complete philosophy, beginning with a "preliminary survey of materials and methods," followed by a discussion of terminology and definition. Then in rapid succession, we have Kaufmann's psychology and epistemology, including a discussion of language and its relation to thought, his theory of man, logic, dialectics, metaphysics, and a hint of theology on which depends his social philosophy of a "saviour nation."

Kaufmann's assurance is worthy of note. We feel great gratification in the possession of the immovable conviction, that we have neither lived, suffered, nor labored *in vain*, but have at last, in their *fullness, found* the foundation, *elements*, and *skeleton theory* of a *system of absolute and* Unassailable *TRUTH*.[19] The sources and conditions of both knowledge and existence are three in number: Nature, Reason, and Religion. Man lives his physical life surrounded on all sides by Nature; he exists in it. Whatever he knows of Nature or or himself he knows by means of Reason. And since he knows that both Nature and himself coexist and that other beings exist with them, he knows that he exists in a physical and intellectual Infinity. Only in terms of this all-surrounding Infinity can he know his own true being or that of nature because only in these terms can he know the "absolute relation" of each indi-

[19] Kaufman, *The Temple of Truth*, iii.

vidual being to the inclusive totality and to its laws. This knowledge is Religion. Nature, Reason, and Religion are all derived by emanation from God, and constitute His voice, or revelation. The character of Nature, Reason, and Religion is all goodness, even as their source is the All-Good.

Kaufmann, during his "interior and exterior *experience,* infinitely copious and multiform in *variegation,* in extent, and amount, of *nearly half a century* in duration,"[20] had read widely if not too wisely. He quotes Emerson to refute Hume, discusses Plato, Aristotle, Leibniz, Kant, Descartes, Rousseau, and Holbach. The name of Hegel is mentioned only once, and yet there is much in Kaufmann's book to suggest that the basic source of his enterprise was Hegel's *History of Philosophy.* Perhaps the most noteworthy feature of the book is the chauvinistic note on which it closes. America is to be the "*saviour nation* of the whole race," divinely appointed to that redemptive mission, "*the realization of the ultimate perfection and happiness of all mankind.*"[21] The proof is in its history. "If ever there was a country, led 'onward' by a 'manifest destiny,' that country is America,—the States of this Union. Hence 'Young America' is ambitious, which is right and proper, that it should be, as it feels itself '*beaconed onward*' by a grand though as yet not clearly understood, destination."[22] He foresaw the ultimate achievement of everlasting peace by a gradual annexation of state after state, nation after nation, until the United States of America should have become "the *United States* of the *whole Earth.*"[23] His vision of the future seems to combine Henry

[20] *Ibid.*
[21] *Ibid.,* 285.
[22] *Ibid.,* 284.
[23] *Ibid.,* 290.

Clay's "American System" and the Jacksonian "manifest destiny" with the Kantian *ewige Frieden*.

In the German population of the Middle West, then, as these samples attest, there was philosophic activity of varying quality being carried on. This activity had the virtue of introducing the great German philosophers of the nineteenth century to the American audience and may have prepared the soil for the later, flourishing, German-inspired thought of the St. Louis Philosophical Society.

Private church-related colleges and state universities burgeoned in the Middle West. The original provisions for education contained in the Northwest Ordinance were taken over and added to by the states as they came into being. In these institutions of learning, philosophy was taught, much as it was in the colleges of the east, as an adjunct to religion. Original thinking on philosophic questions was not encouraged, and the conventional system of instruction was a dogmatic version of the Scottish philosophy of common sense, a system that was satisfactory because it led to no conflict with the Calvinistic theologies that were preached by most of the middle western denominations. By and large, those teachers on whom fell the responsibility for instruction in philosophy in the middle western colleges were content to use textbooks prepared by professors at the eastern colleges. The one notable exception was the Reverend Leicester A. Sawyer, president of Central College, in Ohio, Sawyer's *Elements of Mental Philosophy* (New York, 1846) was a very dull textbook which spiced the bare bones of common sense with pinches of Kantian criticism. Interspersed in this "excessively academic analysis" was an occasional "outburst of faith, hope, and rhetoric,"[24] giving expres-

[24] The descriptive phrases are quoted from Herbert W. Schneider's

sion to Sawyer's millenarian apocalyptic belief in the imminent coming of the Kingdom of God on earth. On the whole, however, philosophic productivity was at a low ebb in the colleges of the Middle West in the first seventy-five years of the nineteenth century.

Another source of philosophic stimulation came as the lyceum movement spread from New England into the Middle West. In later years, distinguished lecturers like Emerson and Bronson Alcott found it profitable to tour middle western lyceums. Before their time, however, the lyceums of the Central States had to depend upon local talent. The lack of philosophic perspective in the available lecturers prevented the managers from placing much emphasis on this field of interest. To this generalization, one large exception may be taken. Early in its history, the Middle West came within an ace of developing its own Emerson in the person of Alexander Kinmont. Kinmont was born in Scotland and came to the United States as a young man of twenty-four who had been educated in St. Andrews and Edinburgh universities in his native land. Some four years later, after entering on a teaching career in Pennsylvania, he shifted to Cincinnati, where he established a successful private school and acted as a minister in the Swedenborgian church. From the year 1833, he was in great demand as a lecturer in Cincinnati, and it was in that city, during the winter of 1837–38, that he delivered his series of lectures on *The Natural History of Man, and the Rise and Progress of Philosophy* (Cincinnati, 1839). Unfortunately, while he was engaged in preparing these lectures for publication, Kinmont

---

discussion of Sawyer in "A Century of Romantic Imagination in America," *The Philosophical Review*, Vol. LVI (1946–47), 352.

died; he had not yet reached his fortieth birthday. The lectures show him to have been a man of a daring and original cast of mind who utilized for his speculations in philosophical anthropology his wide readings in both classical and modern literature and in philosophy and theology. Kinmont's twelfth and final lecture, "On the Elements of American Civilization," develops his erratic and idiosyncratic notion that the American people were the spiritual heirs of the ancient Phoenicians, "the peaceful cultivators of . . . mechanical and economical arts, and the type of the industrious races of this western continent. . . . The second Phoenicia now rises under the auspices of the Christian religion, and will be sheltered beneath its shade."[25] Apart from this eccentricity, what Kinmont has to say on the nature of civilization and the way in which earlier influences act upon the national life of any people, on language, on religion and science, and on art is well worthy of being remembered.

The heart of the philosophic heritage of the Middle West, is found, however, in a small group of devoted students who came together by chance in St. Louis. In the 1850's, this cosmopolitan city, with a preponderantly German population, counted more than 150,000 inhabitants. It was a center of trade, filled with zest and enthusiasm and the conviction that it was to become the greatest city in the Middle West. To St. Louis, in 1857, came Henry Brokmeyer, who had left Germany for political reasons at the age of seventeen, had drifted about America, had attended Brown University briefly. Brokmeyer was an eccentric who rose as high as the acting governorship of Missouri and then retired into the Indian country to live out the rest of his life as a trapper. Somewhere, Brokmeyer had

[25] Kinmont, *The Natural History of Man*, 322.

conceived the notion that the philosophy of Hegel contained the seed for the understanding of the political situation in America. Somehow, he was able to convince others that this was so and to lead them to join him in studying the German philosopher.

Most important of those who were persuaded by Brokmeyer was William Torrey Harris, a young graduate of Yale, who came to St. Louis as a teacher of stenography in the public schools and remained to become, in a matter of eleven years, the city's superintendent of schools. As early as 1858, Brokmeyer and Harris collected a group of friends for the study of philosophy. The Civil War put a temporary stop to the activities of this group, but in 1866, they came together again, with whatever recruits they had been able to attract, as the St. Louis Philosophical Society. In addition to Brokmeyer, the prophet, and Harris, the organizer, early members of the group included Denton J. Snider, G. Stanley Hall, George Holmes Howison, Anna C. Brackett, Thomas Davidson, Adolph E. Kroeger, and a number of others. They were devoted to the study of "speculative philosophy," a field which the editors of the German philosophic journal *Zeitschrift für Philosophie und philosophische Kritik,* interpreted as meaning German philosophy from Kant to Hegel.[26] Harris denied that so narrow an interpretation

---

[26] *Zeitschrift für Philosophie und philosophische Kritik* (ed. by J. H. von Fichte, Hermann Ulrici, and J. V. Wirth, Halle, 1866), Neue Folge, Vol. XLIX, 191. "*Zu St. Louis in Missouri besteht seit einiger Zeit eine philosophische Gesellschaft, gestiftet zu dem Zwecke, das Studium und das Verständnis der Deutschen Philosophie von Kant bis Hegel nicht nur unter ihren Mitgliedern (durch Discussionen, Vorträge, u.s.w.) zu fördern, sondern auch in weiteren Kreisen unter den Gebildeten der Vereinigten Staaten zu verbreiten.*" The editors picked up this information from a notice in the *Missouri Republican,* where an editorial commendation of the group had appeared. "*Der Missouri-Republican, dem wir diese Mittheilung entnehmen, wünscht der Gesellschaft einen gedeihlichen Fortgang, und hält ihre Grün-*

of the group's interest was justified, but there is no doubt that this was the core of the Society's activities.

Soon after the rebirth of the St. Louis Philosophical Society, Harris submitted to the *North American Review* an article on Herbert Spencer. The editor of the *Review* asked Chauncey Wright, who was himself sharply critical of Spencer's work, for a reader's opinion of Harris' article. Wright's report was decidedly against the publication of the article, and the article was accordingly rejected.[27] Harris and his friends decided that the rejection had been an expression of a general eastern prejudice against thinkers from the provinces and that the only way to be sure that repetitions could not occur was to publish their own journal. In 1867, then, with Harris as editor, the *Journal of Speculative Philosophy* was born; it published twenty-two volumes of four numbers each in the next quarter of a century, ceasing publication in 1892. The *Journal of Speculative Philosophy* was the first regularly issued philosophic periodical to be published in the English language, antedating by several years the British journal, *Mind*.

Throughout its history, the *Journal of Speculative Philosophy* published a great many translations of German and French philosophic writings. In many cases, these are still the only available English versions. Although at first the emphasis was almost equally divided between works in metaphysics and in esthetics, Harris' concern with educational problems gradually led to an increase in the number of translations and paraphrases of treatises on the philosophy and psychology of edu-

dung für ein Zeichen der Zeit, das die Regung eines neuen freieren, tieferdringenden Geistes Wissenschaftlicher Forschung in den Vereinigten Staaten ankündigt."

[27] See James Bradley Thayer (ed.), *Letters of Chauncey Wright* (Cambridge, 1878), 87.

cation. Among the authors translated were Descartes, Fichte, Eduard von Hartman, Hegel, Herbart, Kant, Leibniz, Lotze, Michelet, Rosenkranz, Schelling, Schopenhauer, Trendelenburg and Zeller.

Original articles came to the *Journal* from members of the St. Louis Philosophical Society and, as time went on, from other parts of the United States, Canada, England, Germany, and Italy. The very first number of the *Journal*, after a prefatory note "to the Reader" and a brief discussion of "The Speculative," both by Harris, continued with Harris' article on Herbert Spencer, the first chapter of Harris' "Introduction to Philosophy," a paper on "Goethe's Theory of Colors" that Harris had presented before the St. Louis Philosophical Society, and several translations. Never thereafter was so large a part of any issue devoted to Harris' own writing. A. Bronson Alcott, Denton J. Snider, Thomas Davidson, Charles Sanders Peirce, William James, George Holmes Howison, Josiah Royce, George Sylvester Morris, and John Dewey, as well as many other Americans whose names would be less well known, contributed one or more articles to the *Journal*. John Watson, a Canadian, was a frequent contributor. T. Collyns Simon, a British writer whose career was devoted to the exposition of Berkeley, was one of the earliest non-Americans to write for the *Journal*. J. Hutchison Stirling, the British student of Kant and Hegel, had several articles published and in one instance, he and Edward Caird conducted a controversy over Kant in the pages of the *Journal*. Of the Germans, both Franz Hoffman and Karl Rosenkranz wrote directly for the *Journal*, as did Karl Theodore Bayrhoffer.

One of the occasional American contributors who deserves special notice was Dr. Hiram K. Jones of Jacksonville, Illinois.

Dr. Jones was the founder and moving spirit of an enterprise similar to that of the St. Louis Philosophical Society. The group he led in Jacksonville was called the Plato Club, in tribute to the influence that Plato had on Jones's thought. In his published articles, Jones reveals the Platonic sources of his ideas throughout, and in the reports of his lectures at the Concord Summer School of Philosophy, we can see that he limited himself almost entirely to discussions of Plato. In addition to the St. Louis and Jacksonville clubs, there were similar groups in other middle western cities and towns, including Quincy and Chicago, both in Illinois.

Regional chauvinism has led to an overvaluation of the philosophic worth of the contributions made by the St. Louis group. It is only a just corrective to emphasize here that whatever his merits as an educator, William Torrey Harris was but a mediocre philosopher; that the name of Denton J. Snider lives because of his effectiveness as a teacher, not because of any great worth in his original ideas; and that, except for those like Howison and Davidson, who left St. Louis and found themselves on a broader stage, the members of the St. Louis Philosophical society and its fellow societies in other towns were earnest, but scarcely competent, students of philosophy. But to have said this is to reflect all the more credit on them for what they attempted and for what they achieved. If some chance had brought together in St. Louis, shortly after the Civil War, a round dozen philosophic geniuses, it would scarcely be surprising to find an important influence emanating from that city and interest from other major philosophic centers in what was going on there. Chance did not bring together these geniuses; it brought together, instead, a group of rather humdrum minds with a great organizer at their head. With little talent, this group nevertheless wielded a large influence and made themselves of interest to the philosophic world.[28]

Indeed, when Harris wrote, after completing the *Journal's* first volume, a preface for the gathered volume, he offered what can still stand as a just apology for the amount of space given to translations and a reply to a complaint about what certain people were "pleased to call the Un-American character of the contents of the Journal." Where, he asked, was the true American type of speculative philosophy to be found? The popular philosophers in America were not Americans: "We, as a people, buy immense editions of John Stuart Mill, Herbert Spencer, Comte, Hamilton, Cousin, and others. . . . If this is American philosophy, the editor thinks that it may be very much elevated by absorbing and digesting more refined aliment . . . like Plato and Aristotle, Schelling and Hegel." If these philosophers were to be carefully and thoroughly studied and absorbed, Harris believed, we should have a "phalanx of American thinkers . . . to boast of."

> For after all it is not "American *thought*" so much as American *thinkers* that we want. To think, in the highest sense, is to transcend all *natural limits*—such, for example, as national peculiarities, defects in culture, distinctions in Race, habits,

28 See E. Mätzner, "Die spekulative Philosophie in den Vereinigten Staaten," *Philosophische Monatshefte* (ed. by J. Bergmann, Berlin), Vol. I (1868), 132–39. The first three pages contain a general commentary on how philosophy has taken root in the United States; then Mätzner reviews the contents of Vol. I of the *Journal of Speculative Philosophy*. Lest we forget what our predecessors accomplished, it is well to recall this appreciative sentence (p. 132): "*Hier haben vor allem die in Europa Bedrängten und Beengten, theils dem Glücke, theils der Freiheit, oder Beiden zugleich nachjagend, wenn sie der Noth des Daseins oder kirchlicher und politischer Vergewaltigung zu entrinnen suchten, zunächst mit harter Arbeit den Boden urbar gemacht, und im Dienste der unmittelbaren Bedürfnisse des Lebens eine Kraft und Regsamkeit entfaltet, welche die alte Welt mit Bewunderung zu erfüllen geeignet war.*"

and modes of living—to be *universal*, so that one can dissolve away the external hull and seize the substance itself. . . . Our province as *Americans* is to rise to purer forms than have hitherto been attained, and thus speak a "solvent word" of more potency than those already uttered. If this be the goal we aim at, it is evident that we can find no other means so well adapted to rid us of our own idiosyncracies as the study of the greatest thinkers of all ages and all times.

We have not marshaled before us all the schools and all the men who contributed to the earliest developments of philosophic thought and study in the American Middle West. To do so would be the task of a book, not a brief paper. We have, rather, taken interesting and too little-known samples, and from these we have come to know what the philosophic heritage of the Middle West is. The early Kentuckians of whom we talked were explorers of the tradition of British empiricism; our other examples studied the classical philosophies of Greece and the thought of Europe in the seventeenth, eighteenth, and nineteenth centuries. Other, later middle western schools and students whom we have not mentioned have sought philosophic stimulation in the great medieval Christian thinkers. The philosophic heritage of the Middle West does not bear the label "Made in America." It was made wherever in the world men sought to discipline their thought to the understanding of the ultimate nature of the universe, to penetrate the mysteries of the external world and of man himself. The philosophic heritage of the Middle West is the history of philosophy. Not in their particularistic hours as middle westerners, or even as Americans, but in their universalistic moments as participants in the intellectual adventure of mankind have our philosophers shown themselves faithful to this heritage.

IX

A SOIL FOR THE SEEDS
OF LITERATURE

John T. Flanagan

IN 1841, WILLIAM D. GALLAGHER published at Cincinnati an anthology of western poetry entitled *Selection from the Poetical Literature of the West*. Verse by thirty-eight different poets was included, most of whom have subsequently become obscure, although the names of a few, such as James Hall, Albert Pike, and Gallagher himself, have not been forgotten. In his preface, Gallagher contended that none of his contributors were professional men of letters. Rather, they were journalists, lawyers, merchants, and clergymen who wrote poetry as an avocation. To them, poetry was an emotional release, an exciting artistic contrast to routine existence. The significant thing is not that their work is mediocre in quality, but that they tried to write creatively and chose verse as their medium.

In 1841, of course, the Middle West was fairly well settled. Five of the states that we commonly label middle western (Ohio, Indiana, Illinois, Michigan, and Missouri) were already part of the Union. Indian wars were well in the background, and the military frontier was comfortably to the west of the Mississippi River. Moreover, new routes of immigration had been established—the Ohio Canal and the National Road carried heavy traffic—and a constantly accelerating stream of settlers poured into the new states and territories, engulfing the oases of the old French occupation and introducing a variety of new racial strains. Travelers, once familiar with such towns as Marietta, Detroit, Vincennes, and St. Louis, soon discovered the importance of Cleveland, Indianapolis, and Chicago. Timothy Flint remarked in his discussion of the character of the western people, "The people of this valley are as thorough a combination and mixture of the people of all nations, characters, languages, conditions and opinions, as can well be imagined."[1]

By 1841, too, a great deal of writing in and about the Middle West had appeared. One needs only to consult the extensive bibliographies of Ralph Leslie Rusk and Dorothy Dondore to be convinced of the literacy of the early travelers and settlers.[2] But not much of this work was essentially belletristic. The early books were likely to be codes of laws, tracts, pamphlets, sermons, gazetteers, histories, travel records, reports, and tabulations, all of which had small survival value when their documentation became obsolete. But works with some artistic merit also appeared. Land promoters were often both urbane and persuasive in their propaganda. Soldiers and scientists were literate as well. In the Wabash Valley, Henry Rowe Schoolcraft turned his attention to the culture and folklore of the Ojibwas, and William J. Snelling told fascinating tales of life among the Sioux in what was to be Minnesota. River life, the raw backwoods settlements, and the frontier itself

---

[1] Timothy Flint, *The History and Geography of the Mississippi Valley* (Cincinnati, 1832), 135.

[2] Ralph Leslie Rusk, *The Literature of the Middle Western Frontier* (New York, 1926); Dorothy Anne Dondore, *The Prairie and the Making of Middle America* (Cedar Rapids, 1925).

stimulated writing which had an emotional, as well as a documentary, appeal. It is no wonder that when William T. Coggeshall compiled another anthology of western verse nineteen years after Gallagher's volume, the book was bulky and substantial. One hundred and fifty-two contributors were represented in *The Poets and Poetry of the West*, and they came from nine different western states.[3]

Actually, of course, the story of middle western literature goes back far beyond the middle of the nineteenth century. If one may define the term "literature" loosely and broadly, the first middle western authors were probably the French missionaries who traveled across and around the Great Lakes throughout the seventeenth century and produced the amazing narratives collectively called the Jesuit Relations. Men like Isaac Jogues, Claude Dablon, Claude Allouez, and especially, Jacques Marquette not only suffered incredible privations and even torture in their efforts to bring the Cross to the aborigines, but also left important and revealing journals. From the literary point of view, probably the most interesting of these early scribes was Louis Hennepin, the Recollect priest who accompanied La Salle in 1680, journeyed down the Illinois River to its confluence with the Mississippi, and then ascended that river as far as the cataract which he christened St. Anthony Falls in honor of his patron saint. Hennepin has been justly assailed for his inaccuracy and for his callous appropriation of the data and the deeds of others, yet his *Description de la Louisiane* and his *Nouvelle Découverte* remain fascinating travel narratives. And he himself served to stimulate other writers.

The eighteenth century saw the appearance of many sim-

[3] William T. Coggeshall, *The Poets and Poetry of the West* (Columbus, 1860).

ilar volumes. Travel reports, chronicles, and journals came
from the presses in greater frequency as more and more people
became interested in the interior of the North American continent. Confronted with such a spate of material, one must
choose representative works. A particularly important book,
Histoire et description générale de la Nouvelle France, appeared in 1774 and was written by Pierre Charlevoix. A well-
educated and keenly observant French Jesuit, Charlevoix recorded a great deal of material about Indian life and culture
and produced a work which proved to be a source for many
later writers. He drew mostly on his experiences in the Canadian wilderness, but his knowledge of the continental area was
reinforced by a journey which took him as far south as the
Gulf of Mexico. In contrast to Charlevoix's reliable and still
useful work, there is the widely read *Travels through the Interior Parts of North-America*, published in 1778 and reputedly
the work of Jonathan Carver. Carver, a cobbler turned soldier
and explorer, reached the Upper Mississippi Valley by way of
the Fox-Wisconsin route and saw much of the country just
south of Lake Superior. His *Travels*, virtually a best seller,
pleased readers with its freshness and details, although even a
contemporary audience must have been troubled occasionally
by Carver's credulity. His accounts of personal experience are
lively and vivid, whereas his ventures into history and sociology are obviously derivative from other and better-informed
works. A third volume which, while it did not appear until
1809, was the work of another eighteenth-century traveler
and explorer is the *Travels and Adventures in Canada and the
Indian Territories* of Alexander Henry. The author, a fur
trader and adventurer, survived Pontiac's assault on Mackinac
and went on into the Lake Superior wilderness and even farther

west. His accounts of forest life are reliable and fascinating, and his book was challenging enough to stir the imagination of Henry Thoreau. Somewhere, as Milo M. Quaife observes, Henry had learned a mastery of English, and his sole book "is literature in the best sense of the term."[4]

Men like Hennepin, Charlevoix, Carver, and Henry were obviously not professional writers; they were missionaries, soldiers, explorers, and traders, impelled to write books by a variety of motives. In some cases their superiors or sponsors required reports. Europeans and even seaboard Americans wished to know more about the territory beyond the thin line of settlement. Information about climate, geography, mountain barriers, forest beasts, trade routes, and, above all, the Indians was essential, and no one could provide this better than the early travelers. They thus wrote to inform, to explain, and to insure that their personal experiences would not go unrecorded. They dealt with facts, not with emotions, and if they stirred the imaginations of their readers, it was largely because distance gave a romantic aura to their subjects. Nevertheless, besides owning the clarity of good exposition, these writers often expressed themselves with charm and distinction. Only a very narrow interpretation of the term would deny their work the label of literature.

In the years following the passage of the Ordinance of 1787, immigrants began to flow into the old Northwest Territory and lay the foundation for the maximum of five states which the Ordinance permitted. Stability and permanence of settlement produced differences in the writings emanating from the area. No longer were the books the work of visitors

[4] Milo M. Quaife, Historical Introduction, *Alexander Henry's Travels and Adventures* (Chicago, 1921), xxii.

and travelers who came to see, then quickly left to report else-where. Increasingly, the literary work came from the pens of residents who, to use Cooper's pet term, had a stake in their society. Eventually, of course, western authors would also be native westerners, but one should remember that such representative figures as Mark Twain and Edward Eggleston were not born until 1835 and 1837, respectively. The surprising fact is that an increasingly indigenous literature flourished so quickly. Newspapers appeared in Cincinnati, Vincennes, and St. Louis before 1810,[5] and literary periodicals were not far behind. John P. Foote edited the Cincinnati *Literary Gazette* in 1824 and 1825 with the motto: "Not to display learning, but to excite a taste for it." Timothy Flint inaugurated his *Western Monthly Review* in 1827 and shouldered the editorial burden almost alone for three years while he struggled with a dignified and respectable imitation of the eastern periodicals. In 1830, James Hall established the *Illinois Monthly Magazine* in the little town of Vandalia, sustained it there for two years, and edited it as the *Western Monthly Magazine* for an additional four years at Cincinnati when he moved there. It was Hall, too, who had the courage to issue for the holiday season of 1828–1829 the first literary annual published west of Ohio, the *Western Souvenir,* notable not only for Hall's own contributions to it, but also as the place of publication of one of the first stories about Mike Fink.[6]

But it was some time before a substantial amount of belle-

[5] For example, at Cincinnati, *The Centinel of the North-Western Territory* (1793) and *The Western Spy* and *Hamilton Gazette* (1799); at Vincennes, the *Indiana Gazette* (1804), later called the *Western Sun;* at St. Louis, the *Missouri Gazette* (1808).

[6] Morgan Neville, "The Last of the Boatmen," in *The Western Souvenir* (Cincinnati, 1828), 107–22.

tristic writing came from western pens. Much of the western literature in the early nineteenth century was strictly utilitarian. A particularly familiar early type was the guidebook, or gazeteer, a volume designed to inform settlers of economic and geographical conditions and purporting to give reliable and current statistics. The more pedestrian gazetteers were simple tabulations of villages, counties, and geographical features, but occasionally they would include intelligent surveys of western population and society. One of the most popular was John Kilbourn's *Ohio Gazetteer,* which had at least ten editions between 1816 and 1833. Dr. Lewis Beck's *Gazetteer of the States of Illinois and Missouri* (1823) was a superior work. Equally useful and important were Alphonso Wetmore's *Gazetteer of the State of Missouri* (1837), to which were appended several remarkably vivid sketches of frontier life, and John T. Blois's *Gazetteer of the State of Michigan* (1838). Increase Lapham performed a similar service for Wisconsin in 1844, and Nathan H. Parker published handbooks for Iowa, Minnesota, and Missouri after 1850. One of the best of all these guides was the work of John Mason Peck, the Baptist minister and educator who did so much to raise the cultural level of early Illinois. His first gazetteer was published at Jacksonville in 1834. A second and revised edition appeared in 1837, and in the same year Peck published *A New Guide for Emigrants to the West.* Peck, a well-read classical scholar, was much better informed than most of his fellow editors. He conceived of his gazetteers as being both factual and interpretive, and he did not hesitate to abandon the objectivity which made the gazetteers almost uniform in tone. The following comment suggests Peck's difficulty in reconciling the strictness of his profession with his genuine local patriotism:

Tobacco, though a filthy and noxious weed, which no human being ought ever to use, can be produced in quantity and of the first quality in Illinois.[7]

It was easy to turn from gazetteers to more ambitious historical writing. Probably the first adequate account of any one middle western state was Caleb Atwater's *A History of the State of Ohio, Natural and Civil*, published in 1838. Atwater, both a minister and a lawyer, was something of an antiquarian, and he incorporated a great deal of geological and archaeological data into his narrative. James H. Lannan published his *History of Michigan* in 1839, barely two years after Michigan became a state. John B. Dillon produced several volumes about Indiana, with the usual disproportionate emphasis on military and political events. Two of the early histories of Illinois were the work of former governors of the state, Thomas Ford and John Reynolds, but both volumes suffer from their limited scope and somewhat subjective approach.[8] One of the best of the early middle western state histories, probably because the author was a professional historian, is Edward Duffield Neill's *History of Minnesota*, which appeared in 1858. One of the most appealing and lucid historical works not limited to a definite political unit is James Hall's *Romance of Western History* (1857). The title and, especially, the subtitle of this work, *Sketches of History, Life, and Manners*, well define the book's scope and tone. But certainly the most impressive early middle western historical work, and one which still retains some value as both record and interpretation, is James W. Monette's *History of the Discovery and Settlement of the Valley of the Mississippi*, pub-

[7] J. M. Peck, *A Gazetteer of Illinois* (Philadelphia, 1837), 21–22.
[8] Thomas Ford, *A History of Illinois* (Chicago, 1854); John Reynolds, *The Pioneer History of Illinois* (Belleville, 1852).

lished in two volumes in 1846. Monette, an erudite physician, was reared and trained in the Middle West, although he lived much of his life in Mississippi. Despite his limited access to documents and monographs, Monette's work was accurate and perceptive.

Many of the early Ohio Valley writers, motivated, no doubt, by a desire to preserve the record before the data disappeared, ventured to write accounts of their own lives and in so doing made substantial contributions to the early literature of the region. Timothy Flint's *Recollections of the Last Ten Years*, published in 1826, is still one of the best accounts of life in the river towns and of the society of the time. Despite his prejudices, Flint was an intelligent and keen observer. His accounts of preaching, traveling, and farming are vivid, and he excoriated honestly what he called the two prevalent vices of the western people—gambling and intemperance. James Hall's *Letters From the West* (1828) is an entertaining book but is more fragmentary and subjective. *The New Purchase*, which Baynard Rush Hall published in 1843 under the pseudonym of Robert Carlton, is a rich picture of life in central Indiana shortly after statehood, when the author had aspirations of becoming a college president. Hall was opinionated and scornful of those who lacked his superior education, but his vignettes of the backwoods are both sardonic and hilarious.

Not all the reminiscences of the Methodist circuit riders, and they seem almost legion, deserve the name of literature, but a few are conspicuously successful. As J. Christian Bay observed, the life stories of the itinerant preachers make a special category which well merits study.[9] The autobiographies of Jacob Young, on which Eggleston probably drew, Alfred

---

[9] J. Christian Bay, *A Handful of Western Books* (Chicago, 1835), 40.

Brunson, and James B. Finley are particularly interesting.[10] Probably the best known of such works is the life story of Peter Cartwright, the fiery exhorter and evangelist who once opposed Abraham Lincoln in a political election and who was known for many years as a brilliant preacher in the Sangamon country of Illinois. Cartwright, relatively uncultivated but vigorous and formidable as an evangelist, gives especially vivid pictures of camp meetings in which his goal seemed to be to produce a kind of mass autointoxication as soon as possible. He describes, with satisfaction, scene after scene in which his congregation is twitching, jerking, and even foaming at the mouth, phenomena which to him were convincing proof of seizure by the religious spirit. A more temperate and urbane account of Methodist evangelism is the *Ten Years of Preacher-Life* (1859) of the virtually blind minister William Henry Milburn. Milburn was a competent writer, despite his infirmity, and managed to educate himself in history, literature, and public affairs, notwithstanding an abbreviated formal education. He describes with honesty and emotion the practical training which often was all that he and his colleagues could afford.

> The terms of tuition in Brush College and Swamp University are high, the course of study hard, the examinations frequent and severe, but the schooling is capital.[11]

Travel records, gazetteers, histories and memoirs represent, then, some of the more utilitarian kinds of literature produced by middle western writers in the first half of the nineteenth

---

[10] Jacob Young, *Autobiography of a Pioneer* (Cincinnati, 1857); Alfred Brunson, *A Western Pioneer* (Cincinnati and New York, 1872, 1879); James B. Finley, *Autobiography of Rev. James B. Finley* (Cincinnati, 1854).

[11] William Henry Milburn, *Ten Years of Preacher-Life* (Nashville, 1859), 82.

century. Space does not permit a similar survey of sermons, orations, and scientific treatises, which were also produced in large numbers and which often revealed definite literary competence; on the whole, however, they were inferior to the types discussed. Before we turn to the more belletristic writing, it might be well to note Dr. Daniel Drake's views on the future literature of the West.

Dr. Drake, physician, lecturer, and man of letters, was one of the most distinguished citizens of Cincinnati. Recognized generally as a leading medical man of the Ohio Valley, he was also known for his interest in letters and culture. In 1834, he was invited to address the Union Literary Society of Miami University. In the extraordinary discourse which he delivered at that time, he outlined what directions he thought the future literature of the West would take.[12] In the first place, he asserted, it would be wrong to expect any strong classical influence; the typical western style was rough, rather than elegant, and would probably remain so in the foreseeable future. He sensed a pragmatic quality when he said: "Our literature will be tinctured with the thoughts and terms of business."[13] With Irving and Henry James, he lamented the absence in the United States of certain romantic relics which might inspire emotion and sympathy; America had no ivy-covered ruins. He regretted the absence of any strong feeling for music, a quality which to him imparted a generally refining influence to literature. But these were chiefly negative qualities, and his message was not defeatist. Dr. Drake predicted for future western literature a strong religious tincture. Moreover, he believed that

[12] Daniel Drake, *Discourse on the History, Character, and Prospects of the West* (Cincinnati, 1834).
[13] *Ibid.,* 30.

it would be a literature of and for the people, and therefore he proclaimed it as ultrarepublican.[14] Living as he did in an age of oratory, he probably overvalued the importance of public speaking, yet he emphasized the value of oration and asserted that the literature of a young and free people would necessarily be declamatory. Finally, he felt, the Mississippi Valley, by its very magnitude and importance, would provide inexhaustible themes for future historians, poets, and novelists, themes that at the moment were fresh and untouched. It is curious to add that exactly sixty years after Dr. Drake's address, Hamlin Garland, in his challenging little volume *Crumbling Idols*, made almost the identical point: namely, that the rivers, lakes, and, especially, the cities of the Middle West provided a wealth of subject matter which writers had so far neglected.[15]

It is interesting to apply the criteria which Dr. Drake proposed more than a century ago to the writers of the twentieth century. As we think of Dreiser, Sherwood Anderson, Sinclair Lewis, Masters, and Farrell, we could not disagree with Dr. Drake's prophecy that future literature would lack refinement, elegance, and spirituality. The strongly individualistic and popular flavor which Dr. Drake foretold would seem to be more prevalent, and time has apparently repudiated his emphasis on a declamatory style. At least the singular modern tendency toward "Confederate rhetoric" is limited, as the title implies, to writers south of Mason and Dixon's line. One other striking quality of contemporary writing, its strong feeling of social protest, Dr. Drake never envisaged at all.

To the historical student of literature, perhaps the most important quality shared by the western writers contemporary

[14] *Ibid.*, 31.
[15] Hamlin Garland, *Crumbling Idols* (Chicago and Cambridge, 1894).

with Dr. Drake was their slow but perceptible trend toward realism. In an age which accepted gentility and which preferred imitation to innovation, there were constant efforts to utilize western scenes and western characters. Examine the blank verse of Gallagher's long poem "Miami Woods," obviously inspired by the landscape poetry of William Cullen Bryant, and read the rich descriptions of the Ohio scene, the consciousness of seasonal changes and the strong use of local color. Sample the domestic sketches contained in Alice Carey's *Clovernook*, where, despite the general air of gloom and sorrow, there is a very convincing presentation of rural character. Read James Hall's charming tales of life in the old French settlements of Kaskaskia and Carondelet, where he captures convincingly the indolence, the gaiety, and even the colorful idiom of the residents.[16] Best of all, perhaps, turn to the three books which Mrs. Caroline Kirkland wrote about early days in Michigan. A few miles west of Detroit, she and her husband had speculated in land and had actually founded a crossroad hamlet. Here, for some years, the Kirklands stayed, fighting against both natural and human obstacles. In *A New Home—Who'll Follow?* she told with some acerbity the problems of housekeeping in a backwoods village, while in *Western Clearings* she brought together a number of deft tales about rural swains and speculators, bee hunters, and pedagogues. *Forest Life* was perhaps the least successful, but even here she suggested the flavor of the life she knew first hand. As she remarked in the preface:

Be it remembered that what I profess to delineate is the scarce

[16] Cf. "The French Village," "A Legend of Carondelet," and "Michel de Coucy," in *Legends of the West* (Philadelphia, 1832) and *Tales of the Border* (Philadelphia, 1835).

THE LAND: Still the Basic Resource in America's Heartland. Here It Reveals Wisconsin Strip Cropping.

COTTON IS BIG BUSINESS IN MISSOURI: Picking the Crop, New Model.

NORTH DAKOTA CATTLE: From the Northern Plains,
Beef for the Vast Middle Western Population—and the Nation.

reclaimed wilderness . . . the forest . . . the pioneers . . . the settlers . . . the people who, coming here of their own free will . . . each with his own individual views of profit or advancement . . . have, as a mass, been the mighty instrument in the hands of Providence of preparing the way for civilization, for intelligence, for refinement, for religion.[17]

If other writers turned with fair success to such figures as the Indian and the desperado, figures which the dime novelists of later generations took over as their main stock in trade, these authors chose to portray the life of the people and their physical background.

Complete realism was, of course, difficult to achieve. It might be argued that this goal was not reached until the rise of naturalism at the end of the century. But from the very beginning, the more serious middle western writers were conscious of the need for verisimilitude. First, as one might assume, came a faithful approximation of the landscape. Not only did Pontiac and Tecumseh replace King Philip, and Simon Kenton and Daniel Boone supplant Paul Revere, but the canebrakes, the salt licks, the Indian mounds, the American Bottom, the Ohio, and the Mississippi figured prominently in the geographical background. In Timothy Flint's early novels, *Francis Berrian* and *George Mason,* in the terse sketches which Audubon interpolated between the plates of his *Ornithological Biography,* in such bits of backwoods humor as J. M. Field's *The Drama in Pokerville,* the scene rings true. This could be neither New England nor Virginia.

The next step involved idiom and portraiture. Here progress was spotty and uncertain. Heroes and heroines of the old

---

[17] Caroline Kirkland, *Forest Life* (New York and Boston, 1842), I, 5.

type died hard. The genteel protagonists of Scott and Cooper had a good many descendants, and often they wrenched the plot of a novel. As Henry Nash Smith has pointed out, Cooper never dared to make Leatherstocking the romantic hero of his stories, although he is usually the only Cooper character whom the reader recalls.[18] For a long time the romantic heroes and heroines spoke bookishly and self-consciously, even though their drawingroom language was highly inappropriate to the backwoods. On the other hand, in the effort to make lower-class characters speak authentically, writers were prone to exaggerate their crudities and broken grammar. James Hall's pioneers usually use an uncultivated speech but often employ terms that sound odd, even when reported in Bartlett's *Dictionary of Americanisms*.[19] In general, the more genteel characters, eastern and upper class, speak conventionally and stiffly, while the backwoodsmen, circuit riders, boatmen, peddlers, and hunters, use language which better suits their station. J. L. McConnel, in his *Western Characters*, ventured to draw a series of frontier types and then illustrated them by imaginary portraits which utilized details from various bookish sources, but he was chary of introducing much dialogue. Instead of employing conversation to characterize, he relied on comment and analysis.[20]

Hardest of all for the early western writers to achieve was reality of plot. Stories had to end morally, with the villains properly punished and the hero or heroine properly rewarded. This stereotype lingered, especially in the historical novel,

[18] Henry Nash Smith, *Virgin Land: The American West as Symbol and Myth* (Cambridge, 1950), 65-69.

[19] John Russell Bartlett, *Dictionary of Americanisms* (New York, 1848).

[20] J. L. McConnel, *Western Characters* (New York, 1853).

and appeared in popular works long after serious fiction had drawn closer to the realities of life. Alice Roussillon, for example, the heroine of Maurice Thompson's *Alice of Old Vincennes*, not only flaunts the American flag at the suitable moment, but also learns that she is actually descended from an Old Dominion family and therefore can properly be married to a Virginia cavalier. But the mid-century was a period of sentimentality, a time when, as Hawthorne remarked, literature was in the hands of a damned mob of scribbling women. Despite their proximity to a new scene and new characters, western writers were slow to adjust the patterns of their fiction.

The Civil War brought an end to the literary leadership of Cincinnati. By 1860, the writers who made of the Queen City the cultural center of the Ohio Valley had disappeared from the scene. Dr. Drake, Timothy Flint, and Morgan Neville were dead, James Hall had deserted writing for banking, and William D. Gallagher had turned his attention to politics. During the next few decades, middle western publishing and writing activity would focus briefly in St. Louis and eventually in Chicago. Talented men like Hamlin Garland, Eugene Field, Opie Read, George Ade, and Robert Herrick would eventually gravitate to Chicago and bring it such prominence that H. L. Mencken once referred to it as the literary capital of the United States—a label which, it must be honestly admitted, he quickly withdrew. But in the years between Appomattox and the Spanish-American War, serious western writing became firmly realistic in its approach to life.

The 1870's saw the appearance of various books which were either in the realistic tradition or which pointed strongly in that direction. Five of Eggleston's novels appeared between 1871 and 1878, including the famous *Hoosier School-Master*,

The Circuit Rider, and his best novel, *Roxy.* John Hay published his familiar *Pike County Ballads* in 1871, Maurice Thompson's charming interpretation of Indiana life, *Hoosier Mosaics,* appeared in 1875, and Mark Twain's *Roughing It* and *The Adventures of Tom Sawyer* made the years 1872 and 1876 memorable.

The next fifteen years brought the first stage of realism to a climax. In 1885 appeared *The Adventures of Huckleberry Finn,* which was not only Mark Twain's masterpiece, but also a work of vast influence on such twentieth-century writers as Sherwood Anderson and Ernest Hemingway. A little earlier, E. W. Howe had published the first authentic picture of an American village in his *Story of a Country Town,* a grim, gloomy portrait which anticipated *Main Street* by almost forty years. In 1887 came Joseph Kirkland's *Zury: The Meanest Man in Spring County,* with its astringent picture of an avaricious but hard-working Illinois farmer. And in 1891 appeared Harmlin Garland's *Main-Travelled Roads,* "hard pastorals of the upper Middle West" in Carl Van Doren's striking term but including some of the most significant short stories produced by an American author.[21] By the time the century ran out, Henry B. Fuller had added to the realistic gallery such important Chicago novels as *The Cliff Dwellers,* George Ade had won popularity with his fables in slang, and Finley Peter Dunne had created one of the most memorable characters in the national literature. Mr. Dooley, the inimitable saloon keeper of Archey Road, survives long after the events which excited his fresh and barbed wit have faded away.

In the contributions of Eggleston, Twain, Howe, Kirkland, Garland, and Dunne, the realistic movement reached a

[21] Carl Van Doren, *The American Novel* (New York, 1921), 257.

triumph. Not only did such writers treat landscape, characters, and action with fidelity, but they also introduced themes which had been preciously neglected or untouched. Awkward and distorted as the early novels of Eggleston are, one can still return to them for graphic accounts of backwoods society, of poor whites and Pikes, of political rallies and stump speaking, or rustic weddings and infares. Only too accurately did the author assert in the first sentence of his preface to *The Circuit Rider:* "Whatever is incredible in this story is true." The trials and hardships of the Methodist itinerant, the mania afflicting land speculators, the problems of the rural pedagogue, who often found his miscellaneous pupils superior to himself in size and age—these had seldom been the material for American storytellers before Eggleston's day. It should surprise no one that in the closing decades of his life, Eggleston gave up the writing of fiction for social history.

In like fashion, Mark Twain was an innovator. Although his early sketches were derived from the humorists of the old Southwest and from the newspaper columnists, Twain saw the artistic possibilities in juvenile life, in the games and pranks and folklore of boyhood, and especially in the broad sweep of the Mississippi as he remembered it as a lad on the docks at Hannibal. First from Holliday's Hill and Glascock's Island, later from the deck of a pilot house, he saw the steamboat and knew its kaleidoscopic life, although in later years nostalgia led him to give a rosy color to his memories. Decades after Twain's death, another Missouri-born man of letters paid his own tribute to the Father of Waters but in no way diminished the achievement of Sam Clemens. I quote a few lines from the celebrated middle western poet, T. S. Eliot:

I think that the river
Is a strong brown god . . . sullen, untamed and intractable.
Patient to some degree, at first recognized as a frontier;
Useful, untrustworthy, as a conveyor of commerce;
Then only a problem confronting the builder of bridges.[22]

Nor were the backwoods and the river the only new themes. For the first century and a half of its federal existence, the United States was a predominantly rural country. Indeed, it was not until the Census of 1920 that urban residents (i.e., those living in towns whose population was more than 2,500) reached 51.4 per cent of the total population. Yet our writers had seldom paid much attention to farmers and the farm scene as the raw stuff of fiction.[23] Here, Kirkland and Garland performed a real service. In utilizing the agricultural background—especially in treating the farmer as a worker with his own special chores and problems, not as a musical comedy figure or a romantic idealist musing over the sunset—they widened the scope of fiction and gave it a more solid grounding in reality. To other writers was left the task of interpreting other occupations—lumbering, railroading, mining, business. And to later writers, particularly, fell the burden, or the opportunity, of describing the city, with its economic strife, its heterogeneous races, its constant warfare between materialism and culture, its tensions, and its evils. It was enough for this group of authors to treat faithfully and with durable effect the subjects they chose.

But another comment must be made. Although the middle

---

[22] T. S. Eliot, "The Dry Salvages," in *The Complete Poems and Plays* (New York, 1952), 130.
[23] John T. Flanagan, "The Middle Western Farm Novel," *Minnesota History*, Vol. XXIII (June, 1942), 113–25.

western literature of the nineteenth century was prominently descriptive and expository, it was not uncritical. Read Mark Twain's superb account of the pretensions of an uninformed and provincial culture, symbolized by the Grangerford "house beautiful" described in Chapter XVII of *Huckleberry Finn.* Or read his savage indictment of chicanery and corruption in *The Gilded Age.* Better yet, read Hamlin Garland's sketch, "Under the Lion's Paw," and try to visualize the scene during a Populist convention at Omaha when Garland, instead of addressing the angry delegates, read his story. In other words, the middle western literature of the last quarter of the nineteenth century often had a strongly rebellious note. A full-fledged attack on the *status quo* would follow the publication of such influential volumes as Henry Demarest Lloyd's *Wealth Against Commonwealth* and Thorstein Veblen's *Theory of the Leisure Class.* Later writers would center their criticism on the economic victimization of the farmer, the complacency and frustration of the small town, and the inequities and squalor of urban life. But even before 1900, agrarian unrest, predatory capitalism, and the adoption of a somewhat diluted social Darwinism produced a frankly critical spirit. During the next few decades, this approach was made both familiar and emphatic by the writers commonly associated with literary naturalism.

The middle western literature of our own century, often in full revolt against what the newer voices called a decadent gentility, has been vigorous, experimental, individualistic, and critical. A roll call of those who won literary fame in the last fifty years is not only impressive in itself, but also suggestive of the part played by middle western writers in the national achievement. In 1930, Sinclair Lewis, for example, was the first American writer to be honored with the Nobel Prize in literature. Lewis not only came from a small Minnesota town, but used his native state as a background for a substantial part of his fiction. A later American writer to be crowned by the Swedish Academy, Ernest Hemingway, is less conspicuously middle western, perhaps because his three major novels deal with Italy or Spain and because his own residence in recent years has been Cuba. But Hemingway was born in Oak Park, Illinois, attended high school there, and used northern Michigan as a locale for several of his most impressive stories.

Middle western writers have not been equally successful in all the literary media. Despite such competent playwrights as Augustus Thomas, Booth Tarkington, and Zona Gale, dramatists of stature have not appeared. Serious critical writing has been scarce, and publishing conditions in general have not encouraged the production of either formal or familiar essays. But in other fields, middle western writers have produced significant and lasting works. Probably no biography written by an American—not even Franklin's account of his own life or *The Education of Henry Adams*—has won the general esteem, both popular and scholarly, of Carl Sandburg's study of Abraham Lincoln. A vast work in six volumes, it is a creative biography in the best sense of the term, written by a man who was a successful poet before he turned historian. The autobiographical volumes of Dreiser, notably *A Book About Myself* and *A Hoosier Holiday*, are memorable self-revelations as are, in a different sense, the self-portraits of Sherwood Anderson and Edgar Lee Masters. Floyd Dell's *Homecoming* is a better picture of the age than any of his novels. In his declining career, Hamlin Garland produced several autobiographical volumes which contain, when they do not descend to mere literary gossip, vivid sketches of writers, and William Allen White filled his own life story with sparkling vignettes of political leaders. Nor should one overlook the autobiographies of such disparate figures as the poet and editor Harriet Monroe, the gifted cartoonist John T. McCutcheon, and the famous criminal lawyer Clarence Darrow.

For a time, American poetry in the twentieth century might be said to have centered in Chicago. There, in October, 1912, Harriet Monroe launched her famous magazine, *Poetry*, and opened its columns, at space rates, to whoever had something to say and could say it artistically, regardless of form or style. As an editor, she was both hospitable and eclectic, welcoming William Butler Yeats from Ireland, Sir Rabindranath Tagore from India, and Vachel Lindsay from Springfield. She printed many poems by the three prairie poets, Lindsay, Masters, and Sandburg, and was particularly helpful to Masters, even though the serial publication of his famous *Spoon River Anthology* took place in a St. Louis, rather than a Chicago, periodical. The very differences in the verse of the prairie poets suggest the amazing vitality and richness of the writing which distinguished what Sherwood Anderson termed, derisively, Chicago's robin's egg rennaissance. Lindsay, believing that verse should be essentially rhythmic and musical, emphasized the lyric appeal of his poetry, sometimes at the expense of its meaning. Not only did he chant his verse in public, but he indicated in marginal notes how certain lines should be read, either in a staccato whisper or with the full cadence of the human voice. "The Congo," as Lindsay recited it, may well be the best-known poem of the century. Sandburg, borrowing his technique from Whitman and appropriating from both imagism and the free verse movement, showed triumphantly how the city could supply themes to the poet. To him, a shadow-marked pool in a brickyard at night, or a face on a Halstad Street owl car, or a rivet holding together the girders of a skyscraper could be an image of beauty. The vigor of Chicago struck him—that city which was forever building and tearing down and rebuilding—and without evading its evil and brutality, he could sing its strength. Sandburg celebrated the prairie metropolis in colloquial idiom, praised the steel mills which supported its prosperity, counted the workers who made it polyglot and democratic. Masters, more cynical and bitter, attempted to reaveal the true motives of a typical small town. The epitaphs on the tombstones of Spoon River are a remark-able exhibition of the jealousies, deceptions, hatreds, and lusts possible in the human race, and they are revealed with the candor and bluntness that only death can produce. But it is wrong to think of all of them as sardonic or contemptuous. Idealists and martyrs lived in Spoon River, as did harlots, thieves, and murderers. To all these epitaphs, Masters brought a brittle, terse style and a frank tearing away of illusions. It is no wonder that the impact of the *Spoon River Anthology* on American literature was unequaled by any book of verse since Whitman's *Leaves of Grass*. There were other poets, too, who made a mark. Lew Sarett and Edwin Ford Piper and Paul Engle, for example. Or John G. Neihardt, with his ambitious project of giving epic treatment to the story of the nineteenth-century conquest of the Missouri Valley by soldier and trapper and settler. Neihardt was best of all as a narrative poet, and his stories of Mike Fink and Hugh Glass are dramatic and moving. But the place of the three prairie poets remains unique.

The most important contribution made by the middle western writers of our century, however, lies in the field of fiction. And here, in both theme and technique, the achievement is impressive. Debate over the greatest American novel of the century invariably brings up familiar titles: *Sister Carrie, The Great Gatsby, Arrowsmith, An American Tragedy, Babbitt, Giants in the Earth.* Until the advent of William Faulkner, no writer from any other American region was even mentioned as a rival. And to support these major books, one could always cite the work of Willa Cather, Floyd Dell, Zona Gale, James Farrell, Herbert Quick, Glenway Wescott, Booth Tarkington, Martha Ostenso, and Louis Bromfield.

Similarly, in regard to the short story or the sketch, one can select important writers. Ring Lardner, graduating to literature from the world of sportswriting, drew character deftly and captured cleverly the flappers and the lounge lizards of the 1920's, and, despite recent apologists, will be remembered almost entirely for his pictures of the immature college sophomore, the country-club set, and the social rebels who, in Edna St. Vincent Millay's phrase, wished to burn their candles at both ends. Above all, Sherwood Anderson, in such memorable stories as "I'm a Fool," "I Want to Know Why," and "Death in the Woods," showed how insight and nuance were more important than plot or conventional structure and at the same time remained faithful to milieu and character. In the hands of such writers, the short story became more vivid, more supple, and more meaningful. The tricks of an O. Henry seemed artificial and unworthy of a sincere artist. Fiction had still to be selective, and the writer had still to impose some kind of form on his material, but an organic art could make its own rules.

The serious novels of the period demand a fuller appraisal. One of the literary landmarks of the twentieth century was the appearance of Theodore Dreiser's *Sister Carrie* in 1900. Not only was it an impressive narrative in itself because of its superb picture of character deterioration without mawkish sentimentality, but it was also a pattern for subsequent fiction which was observed almost to the mid-century. James Farrell once remarked, in tribute to Dreiser, "no other writer in America during the present century has exerted as great a moral force on his successors."[24] Dreiser had many faults, mostly stylistic. Grace and verbal precision are commonly lacking in his writing. Moreover, like other naturalists, he was prolix and overly documentary. But Dreiser could conceive character and tell a story, and the cumulative effect of his more ambitious novels is impressive. He also had a vision of life commendably broader than that of the realists and an attitude toward his material which allowed him neither to condone nor to condemn. One of the first reactions to his portrait of Carrie Meeber was that he allowed her material success without punishing her for her indiscretions. And yet only the dullest of readers would accept the final view of Carrie, alone in her comfortable rocking chair, as a symbol of happiness. If evil figured strongly in Dreiser's works, so it is also important in the writings of Nathaniel Hawthorne and William Faulkner, but never is it focal or introduced for its own sake. Dreiser, as a true naturalist, was concerned with human behavior, and only the myopic idealist would deny the element of sin in the life of man. Actually, as Farrell contended, Dreiser was always concerned with morals and was deeply troubled by the inequities and pressures of existence. His sense of determinism led him to part company with the more orthodox writers. To him, the force of environment was so strong that men could not struggle against it, and frequently they became, like his own George Hurstwood and Clyde Griffiths, the helpless victims of society. It was not the

[24] James T. Farrell, in *New York Times Book Review*, July 4, 1943.

centrality of evil that alienated some of Dreiser's early readers; it was the barbaric naturalism, as Stuart Sherman phrased it, that compelled Dreiser to deny responsibility to his characters. The Dreiserian protagonist, living in and suffering from society, was helpless to shape his destiny and at the end, like the novelist himself, could only stop and weep for life.

A very different attitude was that expressed by Sinclair Lewis in such novels as *Main Street, Babbitt,* and *Elmer Gantry.* Where Dreiser was sympathetic, Lewis was satiric. A character member of the group of writers who revolted against the village, Lewis came to fame just at the time that the United States was recovering from the shock of World War I and was well disposed to revalue its own standards. Lewis had seen something of small-town life in his boyhood in Sauk Center, Minnesota. Later he subjected urban life to a clinical diagnosis which was keen, amusing, and, as befitted a satirist, one sided. Lewis had no solution to offer, nor was he scrupulously objective. As William Allen White remarked, he concentrated on the shady side of Main Street. What exasperated Lewis, as it had previously appalled Edgar Lee Masters, was the complacency and smugness of American provincial life. Materialism was dominant, as it usually is in most successful societies, but here it was linked with stolidity, suspicion of new ideas, prejudice against the unfamiliar, and, in particular, contempt for any kind of culture. Lewis thoroughly agreed with the complaint of Vachel Lindsay that the Middle West had crucified the artist. When Carol Kennicott first comes to Gopher Prairie as the wife of the respected and well-liked local physician, she has a little of the zeal of the reformer. She obviously deludes herself when she feels impelled to raise the cultural level of the community, and certainly her methods are gauche and tactless. But the apathy occasionally touching upon hatred which she meets is real enough. Eventually, after a series of frustrations, she flees to Washington, and when she returns as a kind of grudging compromise, the slight change perceptible in the community is less the result of her deeds than a shift in the national temper. Lewis subsequently modified his indictment of the American small town (since to him, Main Street was not a regional phenomenon but a national symbol) but retained his aversion to provincialism, materialism, and complacency until the end of his life.

In *Babbitt,* Lewis created both a character and a term of reproach, for Babbitt has come to represent a kind of obnoxious American businessman who is primarily acquisitive, self-centered, and imitative. On the surface, Babbitt is neither sinister nor objectionable. He is successful in his real-estate business, has engineered no more than his share of shady deals, has a decent wife and a respectable family, and is accepted affably by the other Zenith boosters as a good fellow. Lewis, in the triumph of his portraiture, does not deny Babbitt some virtues. Babbitt is smart enough to realize, occasionally, what he has missed, although he is powerless to change the picture. From time to time, he has aspirations to a culture which he vaguely admires. But his great fault is his lack of originality and independence. He is utterly unable to think for himself, even in his own field of business. His views about everything are second hand, and he quickly accepts the majority approach to everything from politics to the municipal traction system. With broad strokes, Lewis points up Babbitt's character, his admiration for money and authority, his habitual use of clichés, and his passion for glitter and show. Babbitt is a bigger Mainstreeter, just as Sam Dodsworth of a later novel is a traveled Babbitt, but the matrix has not substantially changed, and the qualities that Lewis disliked in Gopher Prairie are just as inherent in the Zeniths of the nation.

Yet Lewis was less of a fatalist that Dreiser. Not only was it possible for men to alter a society for the better, but the novelist introduced figures who won his esteem by their liberality or affirmation of principle. Miles Bjornstam and Guy Pollock in *Main Street*, Seneca Doane in *Babbitt*, Max Gottlieb in *Arrowsmith*, and perhaps Dr. Martin Arrowsmith himself— these are presented sympathetically, and they possibly present the direction that Lewis would have liked society to take. Late in his life, curiously enough, Lewis revealed that he had not been fundamentally antagonistic when he created the character of Babbitt and that his books were less hostile to the United States than their general stridency and savage mimicry would suggest. Most satire is motivated by sincere hatred for the thing satirized, and, usually, no solution is suggested. In his series of books attacking certain aspects of life in the villages and towns of the Middle West, Lewis condemned, but at the same time created. One of the great reporters of modern literature, he used literary photography to capture the milieu and the age.

Another kind of novel done with distinction in the first half of the present century was the historical narrative of settlement, principally involving homesteading in Nebraska and the Dakotas and centering on the adaptation of foreign immigrants to the western prairies. Willa Cather, transplanted from Virginia at an early age to the southern Nebraska range country, found herself surrounded by colonies of foreigners— Czechs, Swedes, Russians, Frenchmen, and Germans. Most of them were city dwellers, unaccustomed to pioneer farming and virtually to farming of any kind, yet struggling heroically against the obstacles of occupation, language, and race in order to make a living. Here, Miss Cather found an important theme and in such memorable novels as *My Ántonia, O Pioneers!* and *The Song of the Lark,* she explored it with distinction. Her heroines are usually romantically successful, and the tone of her books is rather unconvincingly optimistic, yet she wrote with authority and conviction. The feminine side of western settlement has rarely been better shown. Especially memorable is the novelette *A Lost Lady,* which contains not only the superb portrait of Marian Forrester, but also an exposition of one of Miss Cather's deepest convictions: that the true pioneers were a race of giants and that when they reached extinction, the land they had conquered passed into the hands of pygmies. Marian Forrester is truly "lost." Isolated in a large house in southern Nebraska, she pines for the society for which she is best suited. Eventually, her financial position deteriorates, and her social life almost vanishes. When her moral integrity is likewise shattered, she departs from the scene which her husband and his associates had civilized in the distant past.

Other novelists chose similar themes. Martha Ostenso, in *Wild Geese,* dealt with a colony of Finns and Icelanders in the stony country along the Canadian boundary. Herbert Quick, in a trilogy about the settlement of Iowa, introduced almost all the social and political events common to a frontier state and used autobiographical touches in writing several novels about the early fur trade and the Black Hawk War,[25] and Feike Feikema, in a long, ambitious, and somewhat dull chronicle, *This Is the Year,* gave meticulous attention to the plight of a none too intelligent Frisian farmer in northwestern Iowa.[26] But the best of all the fictional attempts to picture the

[25] Cf. *Vandemark's Folly, The Hawkeye,* and *The Invisible Woman.*
[26] Cf. *Bright Journey* and *Wind over Wisconsin.*

FOOD FOR THE SPIRIT: Michigan's Streams Continue to
Afford Some of the Grandest Sport in North America.

MACKINAC BRIDGE: Where the Birch-bark Canoe Once Rode the Waters of the Straits of Mackinac, an Engineering Feat and Pleasure Boats Now Greet the Eye.

coming of the foreigner to the untouched prairie is O. E. Rölvaag's *Giants in the Earth.*

Rölvaag, originally a Norwegian fisherman and for many years a professor of Norwegian and Norse culture at St. Olaf College, actually wrote a trilogy. Although the sequels have their distinction and add much to the final picture, *Giants in the Earth* remains his masterpiece.[27] In the story of Per Hansa and Beret and their children, he not only pictured the successful development of a community on the Dakota prairies, true in almost every historical detail, but also presented two unforgetable characters. Per Hansa is the great actor, lusty and vigorous, cowed by neither the physical nor the intangible, eager to wrestle with the elements, and, at the height of his power, the victim of a prairie blizzard into which he has reluctantly ventured in order to bring a minister to the bedside of a dying friend. His wife, who survives him and becomes the matriarch of the community, is the opposite—timid, irresolute, conscience stricken. She has never quite reconciled herself to leaving her Norwegian heritage behind. She hates the treeless prairie, with its winds and storms, because it provides not even a bush to hide behind. But a malign fate preserves her and kills her husband. *Giants in the Earth* closes with Beret facing the necessity of rearing her child, Peder Victorious, alone. The next two novels tell the story of what happens when Peder matures and slowly repudiates the Norwegian heritage which his mother treasures. Altogether, the novels present a superb picture of western prairie settlement, and they suffer very little from the fact that, originally written in Norwegian, they must be read by the average reader today in translation.

About three decades after the appearance of *Sister Carrie,*

[27] The two other novels are *Peder Victorious* and *Their Fathers' God.*

there arose a group of novelists with a strong interest in the middle western city as a potential theme for fiction and with a desire to continue the naturalistic tradition begun by Dreiser. But naturalism in their hands took a different course. Where Dreiser had been vague, writers like Willard Motley, Nelson Algren, and James Farrell were specific, even redundant. Where Dreiser had treated the sordid aspects of life mostly in passing, these men emphasized the vicious and the seamy. Where Dreiser ignored racial groups as groups and told his stories in terms of individuals, his successors (and to some extent his disciples) exploited urban minorities and limited their attention to Negroes or Poles or Italians or Irishmen. As a representative of these writers and as perhaps the most important middle western writer to appear in the last twenty years, one must select James Farrell.

Farrell's special milieu in the work which brought him fame, the Studs Lonigan trilogy, is that area of South Chicago lying along Prairie and Calumet avenues and bisected by the numbered streets between 55th and 59th. To the east is Lake Michigan and along its curve a boulevard and park strip which provides recreational facilities for the swarming population in the adjacent flats and rooming houses. When Farrell's central characters, Studs Lonigan and Danny O'Neill, were growing up, the area was inhabited mostly by Irish-Americans, lower middle class rather than slum dwellers, with a sprinkling of Jews, Poles, and Italians. On the periphery and gradually encroaching was Chicago's Black Belt, the densely populated and crime-breeding area which provided the background for Richard Wright's memorable indictment of urban life, *Native Son.* Farrell's Irish are not impoverished, nor are they parasitical. Patrick Lonigan, Studs's father, is a boss painter and contractor who owns real estate, can afford radio and motion pictures, lives, like Norris' McTeague, in solid animal comfort, and is only occasionally disturbed by the laxity of the younger generation. But Patrick Lonigan also symbolizes Farrell's basic contentions, for the novelist asserts neither human irresponsibility nor complete environmental determinism. It is true that Studs, originally endowed with a superior physique and an average mind, uses neither. He does not become a priest, to satisfy his mother, or an athlete, to satisfy himself. Instead, he becomes a poolroom loafer, a patron of whorehouses, a political hanger-on, and an alcoholic in imitation of the gangsters and ward bosses, whom he admires. On the other hand, Danny O'Neill, with almost the same ancestry and background, goes the other way. He is interested in sports and plays a fair game of baseball, but he is also studious and industrious. And he manages to avoid the deleterious influences and associations which make Studs, at the age of thirty-two, a moral and physical wreck. Farrell, the naturalistic observer, documents both careers and implies that possibly it is only chance that sends Danny in one direction, Studs in another. But he makes a more specific indictment than Dreiser did, even if he admits that the determinism of society is not inflexible.

To Farrell, the deterioration of Studs Lonigan was the result of three specific failures. First of all, the family was culpable. Here, both the conditions of urban life and the growing lack of interest in the home are operative. The parents can impose neither direction nor control on their children; any kind of authority soon crumbles away, and the generations seek their own companions and entertainment. The modern metropolis has developed a terrific centrifugal force which has all but disrupted the old conception of domestic life.

229

Secondly, the church has failed. Some of the most dramatic scenes in the Studs Lonigan trilogy have to do with religion, and not even Studs himself is altogether unmoved in church. But to him and his kind, the church is sterile, dull, and unimportant, except for an occasional hour on Sunday morning or when marriages or funerals demand ecclesiastical services. The priests whom Studs listens to are nagging and intolerant, or merely mercenary. They offer no guidance and little sympathy. For Studs, the church is cold and impotent, when it should be stimulating and dynamic.

Finally, there is the school. Here again one sees only failure. Not only is classroom work stupid and juvenile, but there is little encouragement for the activities in which Studs is interested. Playgrounds are inadequate, and sports are undirected. Farrell presented here in fictional form a point of view which Sidney Kingsley dramatized vividly in his play *Dead End*. Apparently, to both writers, the real tragedy of the situation was the essential needlessness of the human waste.

The influence of family, church, and school, then, which should have been progressive and stimulating, turned out to be either negative or lacking. The result was degradation, evil, and crime. Farrell has obviously gone beyond Sinclair Lewis' assault on the modern city. Lewis' Zenith is material, stupid, and dull, but Farrell's Chicago (or at least his portion of it) is sinister, depraved, and vicious. In the Studs Lonigan trilogy and some of the related books, the naturalistic revelation of urban life has gone about as far as it can go without becoming simply sensational and melodramatic. Farrell has been accused of being deliberately obscene and pornographic; on occasion he has even had to go to court to defend his books from uninformed attack. But the charge seems absurd. He is an honest craftsman

to whom all human behavior, even the darkest and most inex-
plicable, necessitates attention. The ideological background for
his attack can be challenged. The one-sidedness of the point of
view perhaps needs correction. But the data of his attack on
the evils of the city can be supported by the findings of crimi-
nologists, sociologists, and political scientists.

The depiction of the city (and this usually means Chicago,
since one can hardly name a novel about Cleveland, Detroit,
Minneapolis, or Milwaukee) is the climax of a long development of middle western fiction. Increasingly, as we have seen,
serious writers—from Eggleston and Garland to Dreiser and
Farrell—have striven to present the background, characters,
and events of their novels realistically. As they developed a
technique more suitable to the material and as they dealt more
honestly with their themes, they also began to be more aware
of some of the evils of modern civilization. Very few of them
used the medium of satire, in which Sinclair Lewis excelled, but
many chose to present the more obvious shortcomings of urban
life and, in their effort to prove their case, frequently neglected
vital aspects. Little attention is paid by these writers to cultural
activities or to the advantages the urban resident possesses in his
proximity to museums, libraries, concert halls, and theaters.
Little attention is given the gaiety and color of the Loop. The
virtues of solid industrial productivity are ignored. Whole
areas of metropolitan life are neglected, and the existence of
tens of thousands of decent, simple, hard-working people who
believe in the integrity of the home, the church, and the school
is ignored. The cynic might comment that after all, goodness
makes a rather dull theme; evil is far more interesting. And the
realist might add that if the metropolis of the naturalists were
as essentially ugly and sinister as they depict it, nothing would

stop the full-scale migration of the population to the hinter-
land. A popular song of some years back had as a refrain something like this: "How're you going to keep 'em down on the
farm after they've seen Paree?" Chicago is not Paris, but it has
a magnetism and vitality of its own.

The literature of the Middle West has come a long way
in a short time. In little more than a century it has progressed
from mere reporting and sentimentality to creative work of
durable importance. It has been an honest, a forthright literature, a literature notable for vigor and individuality and originality. Naturally, it is not without faults. To the sensitive
reader, its major defect is surely a definite lack of artistry, of
polish. This limitation is especially apparent to the Anglophiles
among us, who consistently praise the superior finesse of the
British. Perhaps the bluntest rejoinder would be: The English
write better, but the Americans have something to say. But in
all honesty, middle western writing has not been notable for
its literary style. Dreiser was notoriously clumsy and inelegant,
Lewis was strident and sometimes monotonous, Farrell is repe-
titious and overwhelming. One can sympathize with the comment that the best way to read the naturalists is in translation,
where one need not be troubled by solecisms, ineptness, or
aberrations of taste. Of the long and important list of writers
who have made the literature of the Middle West, probably
only Willa Cather was the infallible artist, and many a reader
today would question the lasting impact of her novels. The
majority have been strong and vital and rebellious rather than
graceful.

Some years ago, Harlan Hatcher linked Sherwood Anderson, Theodore Dreiser, and Sinclair Lewis together "as the
three most stimulating and influential authors in the creation

of the modern American novel," and added that "most of the significant work of the twenties and thirties stems in one manner or another from their work."[28] One need not be a regional chauvinist to support this view. And when one adds to such a galaxy some other names—Sandburg, Lindsay, and Masters, Rölvaag and Cather, Suckow and Fitzgerald, Dell and Farrell, perhaps even Hemingway and Dos Passos and Eliot—one can say with assurance that the superiority of American literature of the twentieth century has been due very largely to the contribution of the novelists, poets, and biographers of the Middle West.

[28] Harlan Hatcher, *Creating the Modern American Novel* (New York, 1935), 155.

X

BLAZING A TRAIL
TO HIGHER EDUCATION

Albert Schmidt

THE PROTESTANT liberal arts college holds an honored place
in the epic of America. Originally a frontier institution, it has
achieved excellence as a preserver and transmitter of our European cultural and religious heritage. From the college an
otherwise untutored society learned something of the wisdom
of Greece and Rome and the meaning of the Christian Gospel.
By constantly affirming the significance of this inheritance,
the college has left an imprint on the character of its graduates
that perhaps accounts for the ability and responsibility of the
leaders that it has provided this nation.

The intellectual and spiritual roots of the American college lay deep in sixteenth-century England, where the fruits
of the New Learning and the Reformation ripened for harvest.
During that century, humanist scholars managed to turn the
tide from Scholastic Aristotle to Plato and Cicero in their
endeavors to fashion a new academic curriculum. Cambridge,
the seat of both this learning and reformed religion, sent her
sons throughout Old and New England preaching the gospel
in Ciceronian eloquence. In the wilderness—but in models of
the villages they had left in England—they founded church and

school with the assurance that only by doing so could they preserve the heritage most dear to them.

While the New Englander remained in the East, he founded his Harvards and Yales. When the yearning to follow the ever moving frontier developed, he sought to transplant his New England community to the new site as best he could. Such settlements as those in the Western Reserve, at Marietta, and Oberlin in Ohio; at Beloit in Wisconsin; at Galesburg in Illinois; and at Grinnell in Iowa—to mention but a few—bear witness to the success of his enterprise. And wherever the New Englander brought his village, he was sure to bring his church and college.

The small liberal arts college, though modeled on its English antecedent, was a child of the frontier. Like the community of which it was a part, it was often primitive, rustic, and short of cash—sometimes only laughingly a college. More often than not, it failed ingloriously. But those that failed, as well as the sturdy few which survived, wrote an indelible page in the history of mid-America, where they enriched a frontier society that might otherwise have remained in a state of intellectual and religious sterility. The heritage which the western college preserved becomes more meaningful when we note the trials which this institution faced on the frontier during its formative period—the years preceding the Civil War.

Statistically, the college movement had its most impressive growth during the first sixty years of the nineteenth century, when no fewer than 150 permanent colleges were founded, only a few of which were nonsectarian.[1] These statistics give support to the popular opinion that "a settler could

[1] Donald G. Tewksbury, *The Founding of American Colleges and Universities before the Civil War* (New York, 1932), 16.

hardly encamp on the prairies but a college would spring up beside his waggon."[2]

The need for education was early recognized in the Old Northwest, where the provisions in the Land Ordinance of 1785 clearly provided for public schools. Actual progress was slow, and private sources there, as elsewhere, preceded public in the fostering of education. Itinerant schoolmasters furnished the early preparation for the youngster, while on a higher level, grammar schools, lyceums, seminaries, and other types of preparatory schools made their appearance. Colleges, or at least institutions called "collegiate," were early established. The first west of the Alleghenies was Transylvania Seminary, which was founded in Lexington, Kentucky, in 1785.

The Christian missionary impulse—so vital during the second "Great Awakening"—was largely responsible for the founding of colleges on the frontier. American colleges were just what President Clap of Yale had said that they were in 1754: "Societies of Ministers for training up persons for the work of the ministry." The resumption of the movement westward brought a new challenge to American churchmen and educators. While the uncivilized and lonely frontier of the Middle West was receptive to such religion as the itinerant circuit rider, home missionary, and revivalist could dispense, there was simply not the manpower available to perform such superhuman missionary exploits. Moreover, many of the ministers from the East had great difficulty in adjusting to frontier life. The feeling developed that the frontier ministry should be educated in frontier colleges if the West was to be won for Protestant Christianity. The American Society for the Educa-

[2] Quoted in Louis B. Wright, *Culture on the Moving Frontier* (Bloomington, Indiana, 1955), 178.

tion of Pious Youth for the Gospel Ministry and the American Home Missionary Society (1826) both played prominent roles in the college movement. "Western colleges," declared educator Theron Baldwin, "are a permanently essential part of the great home missionary enterprise at the West—so essential that it is impossible to apply to it the knife of excision without pouring out the life-blood of the whole system."[3] Indeed, how often it was that a solitary home missionary planted the first seeds of a frontier college!

Western missionary activity and the college movement received much of their impetus from competition with Roman Catholicism, which at mid-century gave evidence of interest in this vast region. Nativist and Protestant sentiment evoked loud demands for a western-trained ministry to withstand what they considered a grave threat. One worried educator exclaimed frantically:

> The hosts of Satan are marching upon us in three distinct divisions—the Papal—the Rational—and the Sensual. Who will furnish the munitions of war for the conflict? The majestic west must be educated. If Christianity does not do it through her literary institutions, Infidelity will.[4]

The voluminous speeches and pamphlets of Protestant educators abound in such anti-Catholic diatribes, but religious bigotry was a mark of the ante bellum period and was by no means unique in the field of education.

The egalitarian and democratic stamp of the same period

[3] Society for the Promotion of Collegiate and Theological Education at the West (hereafter cited as SPCTEW), *Seventh Report* (1850), 11–12.
[4] Quoted from R. Smith, *Importance and Claims of the Lawrence University of Wisconsin* (1866), in Tewksbury, *The Founding of American Colleges and Universities before the Civil War*, 74.

pointed to another motive behind the western college movement. Colleges were deemed essential to a republic, for as their
great advocate, Lyman Beecher, put it:

> They break up and diffuse among the people that monopoly
> of knowledge and mental power which despotic governments
> accumulate for purposes of arbitrary rule, and bring to the
> children of the humblest families of the nation a full and fair
> opportunity.[5]

The missionary impulse with its vitality and bigotry, the democracy of the frontier—these were fundamental factors in
shaping western colleges.

Presbyterian Princeton and Congregational Yale took the
initiative in fathering western institutions. They sent their sons,
individually or in bands, to minister the educational and spiritual needs of the frontier. Presbyterian home missionaries in
Indiana were responsible for the founding of Vincennes University and the Bloomington Seminary, (afterwards Indiana
University), as well as Wabash and Hanover colleges. Congregationalists, co-operating with the Presbyterians under the
Plan of Union, directed the founding of Western Reserve,
Ripon, Beloit, Knox, Illinois College, and Grinnell. Both Western Reserve and Beloit, founded as "Western Yales," were designed to serve the New England settlements in their respective
areas. Knox College and Galesburg, Illinois, were founded sim-
ultaneously, with the college designed to serve as a nucleus for
both the community and church. Illinois College was the creation of the "Yale Band," a group of seven young men from

---

[5] Quoted from Lyman Beecher, *A Plea for Colleges* (1836), 15, in
Tewksbury, *The Founding of American Colleges and Universities before the
Civil War*, 6.

Yale who had expressed their "readiness to go to the state of Illinois for the purpose of establishing a seminary of learning such as shall be best adapted to the exigencies of that country— a part of us to engage as instructors in the seminary—the others to occupy—as preachers—important stations in the surrounding country."[6] They did indeed go forth onto the prairies, and they established their college at Jacksonville. Grinnell College was the achievement of the Iowa Band, eleven young men fresh out of Andover Seminary. Answering the pleas of a member from the Yale Band, they determined to dedicate their lives to the ministry in the Iowa country. Their stated purpose was to the point: "Each to found a church and all a college." Iowa College in Davenport, later removed to Grinnell, was the fruit of their effort.

If Presbyterians and Congregationalists were most zealous in their founding of colleges on the frontier, the Methodists and Baptists, traditionally evangelistic, made the greatest headway in gaining religious recruits on the frontier. Their very success made them enter the educational field belatedly, but when they did, it was in full force. By the 1830's, Wesleyan and Asbury colleges were springing up with a note of regularity. In an effort to catch up with the Presbyterians in Indiana, the Methodists founded Indiana Asbury at Greencastle in 1837. In Ohio, a Wesleyan college obtained its charter in 1842, the same year Mount Pleasant Literary Institute, later Iowa Wesleyan, was organized. Cornell College in Mt. Vernon, Iowa, chartered as "Iowa Conference Male & Female Seminary" during the early 1850's, was the fruition of circuit rider George Bowman's dreams.

[6] C. H. Rammelkamp, *Centennial History of Illinois College* (New Haven, 1928), 23-24.

The Methodists' pride in their colleges revealed itself in the case of McKendree College in Lebanon, Illinois, where first instruction began as early as 1828. A traveler recalled that

> in Lebanon everything not connected, either remotely or immediately, with its [the college's] welfare, is deemed of very little, if any importance. "The Seminary! The Seminary" I defy a traveller to tarry two hours in the village without hearing rung all the changes upon that topic for his edification.[7]

Once the Baptist church had formulated its higher educational policy, it entered the field with the same gusto that characterized its vitality among the frontier settlements. "Every state its own Baptist College" became its motto. A Western visitor who traveled through Upper Alton, Illinois, in the mid-thirties wrote with the same enthusiasm:

> What reflecting mind does not hail with joy these temples of science elevating themselves upon every green hill and broad plain of the West, side by side with the sanctuaries of our holy religion! It is intelligence, *baptized intelligence*, which alone can save this beautiful valley, if indeed it is to be saved from the inroad of arbitrary rule and false religion.[8]

On the prairies of Iowa, a number of attempts were made during the ante bellum period to provide institutions of higher learning, but such institutions as were established resembled more often the secondary school than the college. A "univer-

[7] Quoted from Edmund Flagg, *The Far West* (New York, 1838), in Reuben G. Thwaites, *Early Western Travels, 1748–1846* (Cleveland, 1906) XXVI, 252–53.
[8] *Ibid.*

sity" was established at Yellow Springs in Des Moines County in 1844. In Iowa City during the mid-forties, Iowa City College was founded under the auspices of the Methodist Episcopal Church. Also springing up at that time in the same community was an institution termed variously "University of Iowa," "Iowa City University," and "Seminary of Learning." Most of the institutions were ephemeral, but some did endure for long intervals on a very humble level. Lenox College, founded in 1859 as Bowen Collegiate Institute, was originally little more than a high school but by 1870 had evolved to the lower college level. Parsons College in Fairfield, conceived before the Civil War, did not open until 1870 and then only as a preparatory school. Luther at Decorah and Central College at Pella showed the influence of immigrants—in these cases Norwegian Lutherans and Dutch Reformed—on college founding in Iowa before the Civil War.

Coe College in Cedar Rapids provides a good example of an academy's evolving into a college.[9] Indeed, it took Coe nearly thirty years to reach college stature. Its inception is usually traced to the year 1851, when the Reverend Williston Jones of the local Presbyterian church undertook to train a group of young men from the community for the ministry. The need of financial help for the school prompted Jones to travel East, where he found an interested listener in the person of Daniel Coe. Coe, a shrewd business man, insisted on self-help from the community before his donation would become effective. The story of the institute in Cedar Rapids during the intervening thirty years is one of the citizens' struggling to make a going institution in order to collect the Coe donation.

[9] See E. M. Erikson, "The History of Coe College, 1851–1931" (MS in Coe College Library).

During this period, the school was inactive much of the time. For a while it was called Parsons Seminary, with the hope of collecting the legacy that ultimately went to the college in Fairfield. In the mid-seventies, after a period of dormancy, it was resurrected as "The Coe Collegiate Institute." This last attempt in the fall of 1875 proved successful; the Institute, which was actually a preparatory school, flourished until 1881, when it was incorporated as a college.

Despite the heroism and sacrifice which went into the founding of western colleges, their quality generally was not high. American educators and foreign observers alike despaired of their egalitarian character—their tendency to democratize education to the point of mediocrity. The educator Henry Tappan noted that "the idea of fitting our colleges to the temper of the multitude does not promise great results. . . . We have cheapened education so as to place it within the reach of everyone."[10] Foreign visitors—Mrs. Trollope, Dicey, and Tocqueville—all viewed the "universal diffusion of education" with concern. Karl Postel, an Austrian, concluded that western colleges were nothing but names,[11] while Henry Caswall noted that "at the end of the term [the student] receives a degree of A. B. unless notoriously unworthy of that honor."[12] The uncomprisingly anti-American *London Quarterly Review* in 1829 compared the American college with English day schools and added that "the whole construction of [American] society seems opposed to any other system of education, than that of

[10] Quoted from Henry P. Tappan, *University Education* (1850), 65–68, in Tewksbury, *The Founding of American Colleges and Universities before the Civil War*, 8.

[11] R. Carlyle Buley, *The Old Northwest* (Indianapolis, 1950), II, 410.

[12] Henry Caswall, *America and the American Church* (London, 1839), 202.

the most superficial kind."[13] Undoubtedly, there were factors which detracted from the quality of American education in general and western colleges in particular. Poor students, teaching too thinly spread, inadequate facilities, shaky finances, internal cleavages stemming from narrow sectarianism or such national issues as slavery—all shaped the western college during its formative period.

The inadequate academic background of the frontier student frequently necessitated his enrolling in the preparatory department of an institution before receiving collegiate instruction. Within the faculties there were unquestionably mediocrities, but there were also men of broad vision and high ideals who provided unusual leadership. Their weakness as teachers often stemmed less from their inability than from the demands placed upon them. With college staffs small, they performed a multiplicity of tasks. John Finley Crowe, founder of Hanover College, served during a thirty-odd-year period as vice-president, financial agent, member of the board of trustees, and "Professor of Logic, History, Belles Lettres, and Political Economy." A jingle about Bishop Philander Chase tells of his solicitation for funds in England before returning to this country to found Kenyon College almost singlehandedly:

> The King, the Queen, the lords, the earls,
> They gave their crowns, they gave their pearls
>   until Philander had enough
> And hurried homeward with the stuff.
>
> He built the college, built the dam.
> He milked the cow, he smoked the ham,

[13] Buley, *The Old Northwest*, II.

He taught the classes, rang the bell,
And spanked the naughty freshman well.[14]

The material rewards for these versatile educators were hardly commensurate with their mental and physical toil. Five or six hundred dollars per annum was about average. Pay was frequently irregular, and there were instances when instructors forewent part of their salary to keep their college activated. At Oberlin in 1843, one member of the faculty noted that he had not been able to pay for the clothes he had been wearing for a year; another observed that "we have not a dollar in our house, nor have we had for months."[15]

The facilities were generally not conducive to excellence in teaching. Too often the buildings and classrooms were grossly inadequate. The Yale Bandsman Sturtevant described the situation which he encountered at Illinois College in 1830:

> I repaired to the building and found the floors completed, and the building quite enclosed, but no lathing or plastering, no stove, no teacher's desk and only a part of the seats for pupils completed. But we were pledged to commence instruction at that time. . . . Nine students had presented themselves. . . . Our first business was to put up a stove, which occupied us about two hours, carpenters and teacher, and trustee and students cooperating in the work.[16]

Frequently, the whole college was contained in one building. With such compactness, it was no wonder that fires often proved so disastrous.

[14] *Kenyon College Bulletin* (1955).
[15] Robert S. Fletcher, *A History of Oberlin College from Its Foundation through the Civil War* (Oberlin, 1943), II, 489.
[16] Rammelkamp, *Centennial History of Illinois College*, 39.

The problem of books and equipment was especially grave. Libraries and scientific apparatus were lacking, both in quality and quantity. One foreign observer noted that American college libraries in general were inferior even to those of the lesser European institutions. The greatest library deficiency, he added, was in the field of history, where a college library "scarcely furnishes matter for the history of America and is lamentably defective for that of Europe."[17] Many libraries contained but a few thousand volumes, many of which were unsuitable for student use or limited in nature of content. Even where there were libraries, circulation practices often detracted from their value. At Illinois College, for instance, the library was opened infrequently and then for only several hours at a time. Books there circulated in small quantities, and a fee was charged for the privilege of borrowing.[18]

The financial problem was perhaps the most important problem facing the majority of the western colleges. Because many of them started on a shoestring or on risky speculation ventures, their history did not always have a happy ending. For every one which survived, an untold number failed. One specialist on the subject of college mortality has noted that in sixteen states in the East, South, and Middle West, there were founded before the Civil War 516 colleges, of which 104 survived and the remaining 412 died.[19]

Stories describing the sacrifices made in financing these early colleges exist in abundance. Wrote one daughter of a home missionary who aided in the founding of Lawrence Col-

[17] Francis J. Grund, *The Americans in their Moral, Social, and Political Relations* (London, 1837), I, 251.
[18] Rammelkamp, *Centennial History of Illinois College*, 55.
[19] Tewksbury, *The Founding of American Colleges and Universities before the Civil War*, 28.

lege: "My father at that time gave $100 which was a fifth of all his earthly possession, and the rest did likewise."[20] Fire, wind, and epidemics also brought ruin when the shoddy financial structure of the colleges was such that it made them unable to endure such a blow. The Panic of 1837 brought great ruin. In 1838, the steward of Marietta, in order to avert collapse of that college, was "authorized to prepare an enclosure for the purpose of raising mulberries for the culture of silk worms."[21] The officials at Illinois College lamented that "the magnificent sum" raised in the form of subscription notes disintegrated after the Panic of 1837.[22]

"College begging" was commonplace, and it was always directed toward the East. Lyman Beecher made a series of lectures requesting eastern aid for "the religious and political destiny of our nation," which "is to be decided in the West."[23]

When eastern money was not readily dispensed, many western colleges were forced into a ruinous sellout. The problems of hard-pressed Western Reserve, Marietta, Wabash, Illinois College, and Lane Theological Seminary, when considered at a convention of western churches in Cincinnati in 1842, gave rise to the idea of uniting all solicitation of funds under one agency. Before the end of that year, the Society for the Promotion of Collegiate and Theological Education at the West, was established, with the stated object of "afford[ing] assistance to Collegiate and Theological Institutions at the West, in such manner, and so long only as in the judgment of the directors of

[20] S. Plantz, "Lawrence College" (pamphlet published at Menasha, Wisconsin, in 1922), 10.

[21] Arthur C. Beach, *A Pioneer College: The Story of Marietta* (Marietta, 1932), 64.

[22] Rammelkamp, *Centennial History of Illinois College*, 86.

[23] Lyman Beecher, *A Plan for the West* (Cincinnati, 1835), 11.

the Society, the exigencies of the Institutions may demand."[24] As a soliciting agency, the Society sought to meet annual budgetary deficiencies, but in no instance did it provide for the removal of past debts. Sensible direction for the denominational college movement in the West and protection for the East from irresponsible soliciting were its principal aims. Guided by the skillful Theron Baldwin, the Society performed an invaluable function during the quarter-century of its existence.

The millennium climate of the early nineteenth century crystallized into a variety of national issues that left their imprint on the western college. Those same persons who gravitated toward tract and Sabbath-school societies usually agitated loudest for health reform, temperance, woman's rights, pacifism, and abolition of slavery. For these avid Protestant reformers, there seemed no doubt that they would soon witness the ultimate triumph of good. Although the enthusiasm with which these issues were received in the western colleges evidenced the institutions' vitality, such controversial topics often left deep scars. Oberlin, the roost of most of the "isms," was odious to many Northerners, as well as Southerners, for its Garrisonian stand on slavery and its admittance of Negro students. Both faculty and students entered the foray with fervor, never shirking the marks of martyrdom—a rotten egg or even tar and feathers—if it publicized their cause. The slavery controversy left wide cleavages at Western Reserve, where Garrisonians tangled with modern antislavery exponents and split the faculty, administration, and student body alike. The conflict nearly destroyed the college when students boycotted teachers whose views opposed their own. Illinois College, because of

[24] "Western College & Society," *The American Journal of Education,* Vol. XV (1865), 262.

its location, was a meeting ground for the friends and foes alike of the "peculiar institution." Although the Yale-trained faculty did not court disaster as did their colleagues at Oberlin and Western Reserve, they did come under fire from the numerous proslavery partisans in southern Illinois. The association that some of the teachers had with the martyred Elijah Lovejoy only kindled the flames in Jacksonville.

Vitality among the Protestant sects was a fundamental and primarily positive factor in the western-college movement. But in the same way that slavery weakened the college structure, so, too, did differing opinions among the various divisions of Protestant Christianity. The Plan of Union, which had prompted early co-operation on the part of Presbyterian and Congregational missionary enterprises, was disbanded, first by the old-school Presbyterians in 1837 and finally by the Congregationalists in 1852. The increasing number of denominational schisms was followed by intense sectarian competition in establishing colleges. One authority has noted that "colleges came in many cases to be regarded as the agents of a type of denominational imperialism and as a means of sectarian aggrandizement and aggression."[25] Sometimes, institutions were founded for the specific purpose of eliminating a near-by rival. When sectarianism fostered illogical college planning or when it diluted the curriculum with narrow doctrinal courses, it lessened not only the worth of the college, but also its chances of survival.

Student life in the frontier college reflected the democratic but drab atmosphere of the frontier itself. If, indeed, the days were long, the discipline rigid, the living conditions austere, and the recreation meager, it was a situation typical of the frontier as a whole. There were no social restrictions on

[25] Tewksbury, *The Founding of American Colleges and Universities before the Civil War*, 76.

admission to western colleges. What the student needed most was the fortitude to endure the sacrifices which college life entailed. Women were admitted to a number of these colleges, and of course Oberlin shocked even the most liberal-minded by admitting Negroes. Room, board, and tuition costs were by modern standards negligible, but so was the student's budget. Tuition at Marietta College in the early 1840's was in line with that of most western colleges: twenty to twenty-five dollars per annum, while room, board, and incidentals brought the total cost for the year to about ninety dollars.[26] In the early period at Wabash, students obtained their board when they spent two to three hours each day at manual labor. This practice of combining manual with mental exertion enjoyed considerable popularity in the West during the 1830's. It had originated in the East among educators who felt that manual work would improve the student health and reduce college maintenance costs at the same time. George Gales had experimented with the scheme at Oneida Institute in Whitesboro, New York, before embarking for the Illinois prairie. In general, the college farm or shop provided labor for the men, while the young ladies sewed and washed in the boarding house. Student wages varied among colleges, but the average was from six to ten cents per hour. Despite all the optimism which accompanied the initiation of such schemes, they did not endure with success. Incompetent craft teachers, poor quality of work by the students and student irresponsibility, crop failures, and fires in the shops—all these led to the virtual abandonment of the scheme by the end of the 1840's. Small wonder that at one college two workshops were labeled "Do Little" and "Do Less."[27]

[26] Beach, *A Pioneer College*, 48.
[27] Center College in Danville, Kentucky, noted in Beach, *A Pioneer College*, 50.

Student housing, sanitation, and food were frequently inadequate. At Indiana Asbury in 1852, students were "batching" and living on a meager fifty to seventy-five cents a week.[28] These rooms "out" were often dingy and dirty, the beds either hard or of straw and, often as not, infested with vermin. Water came from the nearest well. Sanitation facilities were almost nonexistent: sewers were open and outdoor toilets abounded everywhere. Small wonder that students were often ill and that colleges were caught in frequent edipemics of smallpox, malaria, typhoid, dysentery, tuberculosis, and cholera.

Dormitory food was often pitifully unsavory. The by-laws of Oberlin in 1834 stipulated that "board shall be of plain & holesome [sic] kind; only one dish with its accompaniments shall be eaten at one meal." Such beverages as tea and coffee and fancy meats and pastries were excluded from the commons table. Actually, bread was the basic component of the diet, and it was served variously "with water, salt, milk, gruel, or gravy made from flour and water mixed with 'pot liquor' or ancient butter."[29] It was an accepted dictum at Oberlin that there would be "no pampering men's appetites and making them slaves to their stomachs." But as a student said in 1835: "If I only could have a little coffee and a mouthful of meat now and then, with a pretty respectable room in which to deposit my body, I should consider myself well provided for, as to temporal wants." By 1846, the situation had improved considerably, for meat was then served once a day, with the menus displaying greater variety at the other meals.[30]

[28] William W. Sweet, *Indiana Asbury–DePauw University, 1837–1937* (New York, 1937), 87.
[29] Fletcher, *A History of Oberlin College from Its Foundation through the Civil War*, II, 606–607.
[30] *Ibid.*, 607, 610.

The student day was a busy and long one, beginning about five o'clock with morning prayers. At Illinois College, a student group even petitioned that morning prayers be moved up to four-thirty in order to allow the students more free time afterwards, but a less zealous faculty rejected the plea.[31] Mornings were usually spent in class, the afternoons in manual labor, if such a system was in effect. In the evening, supper was followed by prayers, study, and bed about nine or ten o'clock.

Much of the student's study time was likely to be spent digesting Xenophon, Demosthenes, Cicero or the countervailing Bible. Wherever equipment and trained faculty existed, scientific coarses were introduced. Physiology, phrenology, personal hygiene, and gymnastics penetrated college curriculums at various times throughout the nineteenth century. Oratory and debating held a great fascination for the student who lived during the age of Webster and Hayne. The interest in classical oratory and literature led to the establishment of literary societies which bore such names as Philolethean, Philomathean, Adelphian, or Ciceronian. So important were these groups considered that one college catalogue stated that each was fully equal to a professorship.[32] These societies also improved upon the academic standards of colleges by possessing libraries, some of which nearly equalled those of the colleges themselves.

Rules confronting students were multitudinous and the discipline rigid. The professor was quite as much a policeman as an academician. Religious ordinances, especially chapel attendance, were strictly enforced. Many institutions prompted students by a system of fines. At Western Reserve, for instance,

[31] Rammelkamp, *Centennial History of Illinois College,* 77.
[32] Sweet, *Indiana Asbury–DePauw University, 1837–1937,* 90.

the failure to remove one's hat upon entering a classroom cost the student six and one-half cents; if he fell asleep in a lecture room, he paid twice the amount.[33]

Undoubtedly, the vitality of student life made such rigid discipline necessary. In a day before athletics served as a safety valve for excess energy, pranksters abounded among the students. Student revolts, vigorous student participation in controversial topics, drinking and swearing, despite the devout nature of the students, and above all, fist fights—these were problems confronting the college administrators. Serious offenses merited corporal punishment.

Recreation was indeed meager. Moral disapproval often kept gymnastics from the curriculum. Students did a good deal of hunting or running and jumping—usually on Saturday afternoons, when there was time for it. There was some batting the ball, but baseball did not come into prominence in most colleges until after the Civil War.

In an age of religious emotionalism, the student very often used the revival, or comparable religious activity, as a means to let off excess steam. In colleges where ministers, for the most part, made up the administration, faculty, and boards of trustees and where students in considerable numbers entered the ministry—perhaps a half to two-thirds of the graduates[34]—a display of devotion was encouraged. The western educators delighted in writing of successful revivals held on western campuses during an academic year. Theron Baldwin wrote enthusiastically: "The importance of Revivals in such institutions can scarcely be over-estimated. . . . How great a work then

---

[33] Frederick C. Waite, *Western Reserve University: The Hudson Era* (Cleveland, 1943), 144.
[34] SPCTEW, *Seventh Report* (1850), 11–13.

is achieved when some leading spirit among the students is made the subject of renewing grace!"[35]

In many western colleges, Greek-letter fraternities served as a vehicle for social cohesion. Smaller than the literary societies, they enjoyed a strong following, especially in the colleges of the Old Northwest. The triad composed of Beta Theta Pi, Phi Delta Theta, and Sigma Chi founded at Miami University in Oxford, Ohio, between 1839 and 1855 expanded throughout the West and South as the Union Triad fraternities had in the East. New chapters were founded when the members of one active chapter initiated at least one student from a college proposed for a new chapter, with transportation as it was, this procedure frequently necessitated long and arduous rides to perform the initiation ceremonies. Although secret Greek-letter fraternities were often opposed by the college administrations and were forced underground, they did perform a useful social function for the lonely frontier student. Their gallant display of patriotism—marked by enlistments of whole chapters on occasion—during the Civil War generally won for them a better reception after that conflict.

The Western college in its formative state reflected many of the vital currents of mid-America. Founded during a period of militant Protestantism, it was designed to win the West for that creed. Although deficient in many ways, the early college provided western society with a trained ministry and an acquaintance with our classical past. The Christian impulse which fostered the college's early growth has not been lost on that institution in our own day. Although it has expanded beyond its initial purpose of directing students toward the ministry, the college continues to produce graduates—laymen as well as

[35] SPCTEW, *Fifth Report* (1848), 39.

clergymen—who possess both the moral qualities and the practical ability to meet the crises in an increasingly secular and totalitarian world. For such performance, it deserves high recognition as a priceless part of not only our middle western, but also our American and western heritage.

XI

WHAT USE ART?

Eugene Kingman

ART—THE VISUAL EXPRESSION of the people of the Middle West
—is an integral part of the middle western heritage. It springs
from two distinct backgrounds. We have first of all a deep-
rooted native heritage that reaches back for thousands of years
—a series of Indian cultures that have come in successive waves.
Each was absorbed and modified by environment so that by
the beginning of the nineteenth century and the advent of
Europeans, our native heritage had been firmly rooted and
developed.

To this, then, is added a separate heritage from Europe—
a number of different cultures, each manifest in its own art
and design. Successive decades brought new peoples, a new
spirit, a modified pattern from the East. Native art was absorbed, almost buried, by the end of the century, and the land
was filled with a diverse mixture of imported foreign heritages.
Today, these European cultures have been so absorbed that
we accept them as our native heritage—a composite characteristic of our own land, the Middle West. In recent years, the
original native heritage, that of the Indian, has, fortunately,
reasserted itself in true perspective and joins the others to give
us a rich background in art and design.

Before taking a look at its many aspects, we should recognize the basic factors that condition any work of art; there is the effect of time, the age in which it was produced. Art of any given era, the Victorian era, for instance, has a distinct characteristic, the import of a period, a people, an influence that is inseparable from the artist, no matter how individual it may be.

Then there is the conditioning effect of environment— the surroundings in which art forms are conceived. The land and its climate and resources control, to varying degrees, the living aspects of its people, which effect is permanently stamped in their art. We quickly recognize the contrasting effect of environment in the art of the Northwest Coast Indians, the Pueblo Southwest, or the art of ancient Egypt, all so closely associated with the land.

A third influence is that of the materials themselves, paint, stone, wood, clay, fibre, etc., and the use to which they are put, such as containers, clothes, tools, houses, and pictures. Nowhere were native materials utilized better than on the frontier in the Middle West, where their direct application to living gives us such an effective record of the people who settled here.

So when we consider art forms as the heritage of a region, we can think in terms of time and place, and we can recognize appropriateness and the quality of workmanship and material in the design and function of the object. Art has expressed these factors the world over from the earliest times to the present.

At the Joslyn Art Museum in Omaha, we have set aside a permanent exhibit area for the arts of the Middle West. The exhibit, entitled "Life on the Prairie," presents the subject as it has been recorded by artists and designers in different periods.

It has been arranged as an outline, as an orientation to a subject that is vast and complex. Basic chapters from the various exhibit units lead the visitor from the earliest human settlement on the Plains, some five to ten thousand years ago, to the present day, mid-twentieth century, the main part of the exhibit being directed to the earlier years of the frontier and settlement in the nineteenth century.

The story is well known—the successive migrations, from fur traders to explorers and cross-country gold seekers; new settlements along the way, army posts, and Indian wars; the freighting business, cattle, and then the railroad, which helped to string together the beads of territory as each became a state.

Countless parts of this dramatic story are relived in current fiction and motion pictures, exciting episodes interpreted from the records of history. But we can also turn to these sources—the visual records left by artist-explorers, illustrators, housebuilders, cabinetmakers, and, just as important, the settler himself, who left an imperishable record of his home and community life in the objects of design which he brought with him or made for every-day life.

This record, of course, cannot be illustrated in its entirety. It is sufficient, however, that the materials selected for the exhibit convey a sense of their fitness and character in relation to the Middle West's background. The pictures and objects you see in the exhibit were just as real in their day, and collectively, they tell us a simple, direct story that needs no embellishing.

Let us look briefly at the physical environment of the Middle West. We refer particularly to that vast open country west of the Mississippi River that extends across the Great Plains to the Rockies. It adjoins the eastern woodlands and constitutes a geographic entity in itself. Recognition of this is extremely important because all peoples moving into the area have had to change their mode of living rather drastically. Indians and Europeans alike came from humid, forested areas into treeless, arid regions. Climatic conditions in this open country were severe. Wood and water were scarce. The adjustment to a new way of life on the prairie took time and created special hardships to easterners during the rapid settlement in the mid-nineteenth century.

Design for every-day living was immediately affected, as can be illustrated by a few well-known examples. The horse became a necessity for speedy travel, which promptly brought about a whole new fashion of attire for life on the prairie; the flexible six-shooter replaced the rifle for quick action, especially on horseback; the development of barbed wire became imperative because wood for fencing was unobtainable. Windmills became urgent and soon dotted the prairies, where running water was scarce. The Great Plains had their stern requirements, which, unfortunately, became known to newcomers only after they had arrived. Many items they brought could not be used; others had to be made in haste. Of course, with every caravan load came a few treasured heirlooms that could not be left behind. An elegant, early Victorian dresser, a clock, and perhaps some ornate china often appeared in the log cabin of a homesteader. Countless spinning wheels were preserved. Settlers soon found, however, that they were no longer necessary because the river trade and overland freighters could furnish enough yard goods. Actually, the sewing machine became the treasured piece of household equipment on the frontier.

Such were the land and the conditions it laid down to all who chose to live here. According to latest discoveries, human beings first appeared in the Middle West about ten thousand years ago. Our heritage therefore goes back to these early hunting cultures, to people whose chief livelihood was in the chase, as is indicated by their creative designs—chiefly stone weapons. These people were superseded about fifteen hundred years ago by a new group whose living was more settled, as is evidenced by their large, conical pottery containers. These first potters, as archaeologists term them, were replaced about a thousand years ago by early farmers who fashioned crude hoes and axes and a variety of smaller tools—fishhooks, scrapers, cooking pots, spoons, and delicate ornaments, all made from native materials—bone, shells, wood, stone—and all beautifully expressing a newer way of life. About the time of Columbus, the Plains were extensively populated by town dwellers, whose life was even more stable and ordered—a story we again can read from their well-designed artifacts.

In the sixteenth century came the greatest change of that early day, the arrival of the horse with the first Europeans, Coronado and his party from Mexico. Horses soon spread far and wide and brought the dawn of a new way of life for the Indians. Mounted for the first time, they were free to follow the bison, and soon a new hunting culture extended across the Plains, a culture rich in art forms based on mobility—the tipi and the travois, painted hunting scenes on buffalo skins, embroidery on leather and cloth, first with quills and later with beads traded from whites. This colorful Plains culture reached its climax in the mid-nineteenth century, when it encountered the encroachments of white settlement, and from this point on, the arts of both peoples have been intermixed and have had a deep influence on each other, even to the present day.

Before looking at this new phase, let us consider briefly

the character of our true native art heritage. The American Indian worked out an intelligent adaptation of himself to his physical world, making a balanced use of its geological, topographical, botanical, and zoological arts. Desirous only of existing in Nature and not of conquering her, he had a natural interplay between himself and Nature which resulted in an extremely integrated culture. This occurred whether he was a southwestern Pueblo dry farmer, a Northwest Coast fisherman, an eastern tribes woodsman or a nomadic Plains hunter.

The Indian's mode of self expression—his artistic achievement and his religious practices—were completely tied in with his every-day life and his desire to find himself comfortable and in harmony with his physical surroundings. It was important to him to express himself well in the manufacture and decoration of his dwelling, clothing, food, vessels, weapons, etc., and especially of the articles for ceremonial use; for to him, artistic achievement was closely tied to magic and his relationship with his nature gods.

Thus this highly decorative American Indian art was symbolic, mystic, and religious, for it was connected with prayer. Agriculturists prayed for rain, hunters for an abundance of animals, and the gods were very carefully and ceremoniously thanked for their benevolent gifts. For instance, the deeply significant symbols and semirealistic painted and quilled designs of the early Plains Indians were carefully executed, for their proper manifestation would produce abundant buffalo herds, the mainstay of their food and shelter.

Recognition of this highly stylized and meaningful Indian art has been slow in coming, for to a great extent the explorers and artists who were first to contact the Indian were deeply steeped in the eighteenth- and nineteenth-century realism of European tradition, and not until the twentieth century has Indian art been considered for its creative value apart from its ethnic value.

The first records of native life to be made by Europeans date back to seventeenth- and eighteenth-century engravings, many of which incorporate the inaccuracies of travelers' descriptions rather than following first-hand reports. Some artists, however, penetrated the unknown reaches of America, and an early record from the West is a watercolor of a bison which was subsequently engraved in France in 1746.

Actually, our European heritage in the arts started in the early nineteenth century in the Middle West. My discussion of the subject is planned as a general orientation of the whole field rather than a review of its many artists and designers. Some excellent source material for general reading on the artists of the West has been published in recent years, and there are bright prospects of more to come.

Lewis and Clark had made their memorable trip. The country was open, and the East eager to know more about it. Remember, this was before the days of photography, and the artist-reporter quickly came of age. He was assigned to government expeditions, or he took off on his own. Steeped in the romanticism of the day, the great West stirred his imagination, and for more than a hundred years he went west to collect his source material in the form of invaluable sketches in pencil, watercolor, and oil. Back East they were completed as paintings for exhibitions and printed illustrations for government reports and weekly periodicals. These pictures spread throughout Europe and appeared in such famous publications as Maximilian's *Travels in the Interior of North America*, first printed in Koblenz in 1839. This was the period of the earlier Hudson

River painters in the East, Doughty, Cole, Inness, and the Bar-
bizon painters of France—notably Corot—so it is easy to find
sentiment and a love of nature in the work of our earlier western artists. They thrilled in depicting the bluffs of the Missouri,
the vast buffalo herds, and the Rockies.

The beginning of the story, roughly the first half of the
nineteenth century, was a period of exploration. The artist was
an integral part of every expedition and often found himself
as the chief liaison with the Indians because his sketching
brought about such an informal, friendly relation. Many such
artists were trained in Europe in a period of romantic realism,
and their academic studies stood them well in recording the
pictorial aspects of the great wonders of the West.

In the 1820's, Samuel Seymour, Charles Bird King, and
J. C. Lewis were among the earliest explorer artists. George
Catlin left perhaps the most extensive record of the Indians of
the West. Equally valuable, however, are the superb drawings
and paintings of Karl Bodmer and Alfred Jacob Miller from
their great expeditions in the 1830's. Another noted artist, John
Mix Stanley, was one of the official artist-reporters on the early
government railroad surveys.

By the forties and fifties, much of the work of these artists
had found its way, as lithographs, aquatints, and engravings,
into government reports and popular publications. Their detailed drawings of Indian costumes and customs are a chief
source of study by ethnologists, and they give us a vivid record
of life on the prairie on the eve of white settlement.

These painters came primarily as reporters, but some found
a strength of individuality that gave their work character and
the quality of a work of art. As part of our heritage, it will
live on its own merits. Each artist had his individual approach.

Historical documentation was mixed with the artist's interpretation, but we need not distinguish; the total picture is an
entity in itself. By the middle of the century, other painters
had emerged who added their individual work to the steadily
accumulating visual record. Among these were Carl Wimar,
who followed the fur trade out of St. Louis, George Caleb
Bingham, who so ably documented life on the Mississippi and
its water-front communities, and Seth Eastman, who recorded
Indian life during his army career. Competent illustrative work
has been left by William Ranney and F. O. C. Darley, who
often caught a strong dramatic or romantic flavor.

We come next to that more complex period of settlement
following the Civil War—the rapidly changing conditions
brought on by the onrush of settlers, the army, the Indian resistance, the dwindling bison (the Indian's food supply), the
rise of the cattle industry, and rail and river communication—
and the ultimate linking together of the territory, as each area
became a state, to unify the country. These changes and in-
terrelationships are eloquently recorded by the artist, who reflected at the same time, unconsciously, the major art trends of
the settled world to the East—a continuance of romanticism of
nature in the paintings of Albert Bierstadt, Thomas Moran,
Thomas Hill, William Keith, and others who glorified the
expansion of the West. These painters sometimes worked with
the solid, objective realism of Winslow Homer and Eastman
Johnson in depicting the Indians, trappers, settlers, and freighters against the dramatic background of the West.

The great westward expansion of the late sixties and seventies stimulated the easterner's imagination, and a romantic age
was quick to send more artists into the field to satisfy its thirst
for pictorial news. Publications were profuse with illustrations

brought back by their staff artists. In 1873, *Harper's Weekly* dispatched its illustrators, Paul Frenzeny and Jules Tavernier, on a lengthy rail expedition throughout the West. Four years later, Frank Leslie chartered a special railroad car and conducted perhaps the most elaborate tour of that day for his famous publication. The famous Currier & Ives firm issued a notable series of western subjects covering all phases of its life. One especially characteristic print can be described here. "Across the Continent," a composite scene in 1868 by Fanny Palmer (who never went west), featured the first transcontinental train. In the foreground is a frontier town with a log school, church, and other buildings, a Conestoga train is just starting out, another one is in the distance. A telegraph line is being built, a second track laid. A buffalo hunt is taking place in the far distance, and beyond that stretch the Great Plains. To the right are the mountains, with a lake and woods, and surveying all are two Indian horsemen. These popular concepts of the West made good picture material and found their way into such prints as "Steamboat Race on the Mississippi," "A Check, or Keep Your Distance," "Trapper's Last Shot," etc. William Tait, an English artist, did many of these Currier & Ives westerns. They were not always accurate in detail, but they effectively caught the drama of western life.

Printing techniques at this time made rapid strides with the demands for illustrated, mass-produced publications. The most versatile medium was stone lithography, and the development of the printer's art is apparent in the transition from the earlier hand-colored lithographs and aquatints to the later two-color prints and, finally, to the multicolor, full-blown chromo reproductions which were so popular at the end of the nineteenth century.

The interest in "Westerns" toward the end of the century no doubt spurred on several competent painters to capture the final stages of the Indian wars, the cattle industry, and the last days of the open frontier. The paintings and sculpture of Charles M. Russell and Frederic Remington combine realism and romance to set a new mark for the "Western," a style that has been emulated by painters ever since, notably in the works of the late Frank Tenny Johnson and William R. Leigh. Every western-magazine cover owes a debt to these earlier "greats." Today, a few painters are trying to recapture the romantic era of stagecoaches, buffalo hunts and Indian wars, but in mid-twentieth century, it is difficult to turn back, with any pro-foundness, to those experiences that the old artists actually knew at first hand. Let subject-minded painters of today explore the many facets of present ranch life, of stock raising, dudes, and modern communities. Painters such as Tom Lea and the late Frank Mechau captured the present West—sensitive at the same time to its real heritage.

Returning again to the end of the last century, we find another direction in painting—the romanticists, who were moved by the spirit of the Indian and his lost cause and who idealized him in an ideal setting of deep forests, wide plains, and lofty mountains. They created a poetic serenity of Indian life in their painting of birchbark canoes, love calls, campfire scenes, and peace-pipe ceremonies. We do an injustice to categorize painters too much, but I would include in the foregoing much of the work of George de Forest Brush and Edward Deming, notable painters who wanted to bring to their work spiritual elements over and above factual representation.

The next broad division brings us up to the period following World War I, when artists turned to Europe for study and inspiration. The local scene, the "Western," ceased to hold the artist in a new international world. The famous New York Armory show of 1913 had introduced the moderns from Europe, and the attendant uproar stimulated artists and public alike to new forms of expression. The controversy over modern art was on. Then in the 1920's, the Middle West saw a late chapter of its artistic heritage come into being. Grant Wood, John Steuart Curry, and Thomas Benton, each in his own way, had opposed this European influx of ideas and turned away to their native states of Iowa, Kansas, and Missouri to find, for them, greater significance in the home theme. This caught public fancy, and almost overnight regionalism came into its own. The three artists, independent themselves, were linked together as a trio by the public and widely publicized. Throughout the thirties, regionalism became a major school of American art. The heart of America, the roots of our whole way of life were to be found along every main street, in the harvest, church supper, and floods, and American painters were quick to follow the lead. There was perhaps good reason during the depression years for the artist to turn to the human story in farm and urban communities. In addition to regular easel painting, a vast number of murals appeared in new small post offices under the energetic program of Edward Bruce and Edward B. Bowan of the Treasury Department's Section of Fine Arts. In these competitions the artists were given every freedom, but by and large, the regional, or historical, theme was chosen.

Regionalism finally ran its course, and by World War II, artists were again looking toward Europe. Refugee artists were coming to this country, and the subjective world of individual aspirations and inner feelings took hold. Regionalism became dated in postwar exhibitions as the pendulum swung away until today it is practically impossible to sense an artist's environment in his paintings.

In this survey of the artistic heritage of the Middle West, we must recognize the work of the early photographers, which is significant for both art and history. The documentary rarity of many of the exposures is greatly enhanced by a distinctive artistic quality. One of the most noted photographers, of course, was W. H. Jackson, "the picture maker of the Old West," who worked as early as the sixties and seventies. Recently, some of the finest plate making has been evaluated and published in the work of L. A. Huffman and M. C. Ragsdale, contemporaries of Jackson. Another, but somewhat later, photographer, Erwin E. Smith, was known for illustrative material on cowboy life.

The acceptance of photography as an art form is still in a comparatively early stage. However, many of the old photographers from the above-mentioned photographers would have no peer with respect to print quality, composition, and a myriad of other points on which photographs are judged today by trained jurors. The straightforwardness and flavor, as well as faithful detail, must have been imparted to a great extent from these old "black and whites" to the medium of the good western movie of the last two decades. In these one recognizes the old morality play clothed in new expression. A truly good western movie has high artistic merit, and it is interesting to compare the movie and the old prints on the basis of romantic realism.

Let us now turn to other evidences of our middle western heritage. The essence of frontier life can be found reflected not only in painting, but also in the architecture and crafts of those early days. Objects of every-day use—utensils, tools, clothing, furniture; also vehicles, trains, and steamboats—had a design quality that is deeply rooted in our western consciousness, and they are records of our culture in the true sense of the word.

Their basic character, expressed either in a modified traditional design or something newly invented, shows the interplay of forces employed by the creative spirit. Modifying factors are in the type of material used, its relative abundance, its appropriateness, proper combination with other materials used, and the visual comprehension of the completed object as "right" for its use at the time. These distinctions are important since we all tend to revere or revile the hand-me-downs because we are used to them and are rather indifferent to the contemporary evaluation of a useful object in its own period. The saving of time and labor by use of a new way of manufacture is looked upon too often as merely a means of making more rapidly an object of earlier design rather than as an opportunity to satisfy a new need.

This point is very significant in the settling of the Old West. The 1800's were both a period of lavishness and over-decoration from European baroque overtones in all fields and a period of simplicity governed by straightforward usage.

Thus the early settlers brought or made household objects of pewter, iron, wood, and tin because of their resistance to breakage. Traditional pieces of silver and china were, of course, transported under great difficulty, but it seems to have been a psychological necessity to have them in order to secure ties with eastern origins and family position.

Pewter, generally used from the 1600's to the early 1800's, was imported from England. Later it was made in this country.

Molded tableware was simple and often cast by amateurs using traditional designs.

Iron objects were both cast and wrought. Those intended for every-day use were simple in design (e.g., the iron pot), while the architectural detail of iron trim, when employed in the West, was mostly baroque in feeling.

Tin sconces, lanterns, tea caddies, and trays were often highly decorated with painted designs, and here one begins to see the emergence of individual expression in a few instances.

Wood for rolling pins, trays, butter molds, and kitchen necessities was most often whittled out for hard usage. Here was unpretentious honesty in design, the same as in some of the iron utensils. Furniture naturally achieved more elegance as one approached the more populated centers.

A most interesting aspect of this developing culture was the commemoration, symbolism, and portraiture executed by the glassmakers in both blown and molded glass. Elaborated for us is the westward movement in the famous "Westward Ho," "Log Cabin," and "Grasshopper" patterns, to mention only three of the more noted designs. This romantic viewpoint of the frontier, preserved in the elegance of designed glassware, adds greatly to our knowledge and feeling of what was typical in the nineteenth century.

In weaving, we find the coverlet the artistic expression of many colonial women. Although some patterns were brought from Europe, coverlet patterns were, on the whole, developed in America and traveled in the usual westerly direction. Coverlet designs were also developed locally, with such titles as "Missouri Beauty," "Battle Union," and "Confederate Flag." Because of the vicissitudes of frontier life and the use of manufactured trade goods from the eastern United States, weaving was not a particularly developed craft except in sporadic instances. However, fine needlework found expression in elaborate embroidery, and much sentiment was expressed in the creation of hair wreaths, mounted birds, butterflies, feathers, and shells. An escape into a sort of pseudo gaiety resulted in a great deal of superornamentation and overbrilliance.

The subject of clothing design needs much study and cannot be touched on here because of the even greater psychological factors involved in an accurate study of the differences between men's and women's attire and cross-cultural traits. Only recently have we become aware of the impact of Indian cultures on the white invader, although we all are familiar with the use the American Indian made of white man's trade articles and clothing.

For the final section of this discussion, we shall look briefly at the architecture, especially the development of residential styles, of the Middle West. The earliest houses in the Middle West were built of the most accessible materials and the simplest design—for protection only. Along the rivers, where there were trees, log huts and, later, houses of planed boards were raised. As the settlers moved onto the open plains, sod was, of necessity, used as building material. Sod houses, dugouts built into hills, and adobe shelters were prevalent on the grasslands, and a log cabin was a comparative luxury along the Missouri and Lower Platte rivers. Prairie sod made possible a wall eighteen inches thick, with small windows, roofs thatched or of sod. The walls were usually plastered and a cloth kept the roof dirt from falling into the living room. The floor was earth, pounded hard to keep down the dust.

The cabins were made of native, unhewn or hand-hewn logs held in place by wooden pegs or notches. Open places between the logs were filled with mortar, clay, and sticks. Since the roofs were often of sod or were chinked with sod, the dormant roots in the earth came to life when rain was plentiful, and the houses bloomed with weeds, morning glories, and prairie roses. A cabin usually had only one or two rooms, with a blanket or skins over the doorway and greased paper over the windows. A fireplace made of stone, sod blocks, or wood and clay stood at one end of the room. Although most floors were of dirt, an enterprising homeowner often used rough boards or stone slabs as flooring. Early settlers needed only the bare essentials, usually the few articles brought with them and others made on the spot. More and more objects began to accumulate, and cabins often included some treasured heirloom or elegant piece of furniture that the settlers could not bear to leave behind.

Prior to the middle of the nineteenth century, the more important civic and community structures, such as churches and meeting houses, were frequently constructed of brick, which, at this period, was ordinarily imported up the river from the South. Style was derived either entirely from utilitarian requirements or from the local builder's memory of structures which were found in the East.

The average house in the sixties and seventies still reflected the spirit of the early pioneer who had little interest in architectural style. Homes were simple, almost to the extreme, in design. People of substantial position, however, built larger houses in full Victorian style and used brick which were imported from elsewhere.

Rococco ornamentation was a feature of every room, covering ceilings, floors, and walls. It did not matter whether the embellishment was functional or not. The abundance of bric-a-brac, massive mirrors, baroque picture frames, or the fashionable blackamoors added an ornate but exotic touch to the front and back parlors of the era. The tall, narrow windows of this period were often obscured by wooden shutters, which were kept closed lest the sun fade the velvet-flock wallpaper, the carpet, or the heavily swagged draperies. Glass curtains of costly lace not only diminished the strong outdoor light, but indicated the financial status of the owner. Deep-piled materials were used in draperies and upholstery, although occasional chairs were commonly upholstered in horsehair.

After 1870, the area witnessed a new influx of eastern-bred families, who brought with them wealth, professions, and business. Homes in this period were still compact, still solidly constructed of brick, but were often designed directly by eastern architects, who transplanted literally such design forms as the mansard roof, exterior detailing of somewhat more elaborate millwork, and the first small manifestations of the eventually ever-present front veranda.

During the eighties and nineties, the last quarter of the nineteenth century experienced the arrival of full-blown "Victorian" architecture. The new wealth, which had little in the way of aesthetic background, expressed itself in domestic architecture of great, spreading, frame homes with towers, porte-cocheres, and expansive porches. The most distinctive detail of these houses was always the unrestrained use of elaborate, machine-turned millwork—the more the better.

This was the famous "golden oak" period, when the popularity of the transition from dark to light woods set a new fad in interior decoration. Heavy moldings set off walls covered in fabrics resembling tapestries, brocatels, and leather. Pretentious inlaid furniture vied with mission furniture in all the rooms of the house. Pierced brass articles had a place in draw-ing rooms, and "a Turkish corner," where gentlemen could retire to smoke without sullying the air of the drawing room, was customary in fashionable houses. Pictures, ornately framed, were hung high from the moldings, and bric-a-brac was still an important indication of the owner's travels and interests.

The nationwide depression which occurred during the nineties produced a new architectural style for many families. Restricted funds dictated a return to compact structures and cut down on the use of elaborate detailing. Floor plans were or-ganized on a purely rectangular basis for economy of construc-tion, but these frame houses still retained, in diminished pro-portions, some of the features of the previous Victorian period, much as the porte-cochere and the front porch. The depression, naturally, did not affect all families, and grand homes were still being built. In most cases, these houses drew their inspiration from historical European styles which were adapted for local use.

The 1920's in America were a period of great optimism. In architecture this state of psychological well-being expressed itself in highly imaginative, fairyland styles which were derived primarily from European designs. Wealthy families built taste-ful Moorish palaces, Spanish haciendas, and English manor houses. Many smaller homes took their inspiration during this period from Florida or California and frequently had, there-fore, a slight Spanish flavor. Stucco was a favorite exterior material, and many homes employed tile roofs or had wide overhanging eaves.

Current domestic architecture on the Plains appears to take two forms: the "ranch" house and the regional expression of contemporary design. The ranch house is primarily a child

of the southwestern United States and often nicely comple-
ments the low, rolling plains of the prairie. It is built on one
story, with wide overhanging eaves for protection from the
sun, and it frequently employs large glazed areas which are
sometimes lacking in functional justification. The truly contemporary house of today is less "regional" in spirit. However,
it conforms even more to its immediate natural surroundings
and environmental conditions because it is free from any design
restrictions of traditional style. In the hands of a capable de-
signer, it can achieve a warm simplicity and distinctive "home
atmosphere."

Today, our tempo of life is vastly different than it was
in the last century. Our requirements are varied and highly
technical in a period of accelerated, precision living. To future
historians, this mid-century Middle West will be effectively
presented in all our products of design and artistic creation.
Our region, as an entity, will be less apparent, but researchers
will be aware of our love of the past in countless design carry-
overs with which we live today. We treasure our heirlooms,
our antiques, our collections of those objects which were so
new in their day. Historical museums preserve countless examples of our heritage in these every-day designs as they were
initiated on the frontier and subsequently developed to meet
the changing conditions of settlement.

Even modern design, different as it is, is not a complete
break from tradition, but has gradually grown out from those
elements we call our artistic heritage. It takes little imagination
to reconstruct from this graphic record the various standards
of living achieved on the Plains and, until recently, the close
control laid down by the physical environment. If we add to
this the deep-rooted spirit of nineteenth-century romanticism

274

from the East—that colorful Victorian era in which the Middle West grew up—we can really view our heritage in proper perspective.

XII

◣◣

FOR HISTORIANS,
A LESSON

Walter Johnson

STAND WITH ME at the fork of the Ohio and face to the west. Imagine that the rich prairies stretching to the ninety-eighth meridian—or to the slope of the majestic front range of the Rockies if you insist that the High Plains be included in the Middle West—did not exist. Instead, picture what are today the states of Ohio, Indiana, Michigan, Illinois, Wisconsin, Minnesota, Iowa, Missouri, Kansas, Nebraska, and the Dakotas covered by an inland sea. Now ask yourself the question: How different then would have been development of the United States without the Middle West?

There is some exaggeration in Alexis de Tocqueville's statement that "the valley of the Mississippi is, upon the whole, the most magnificent dwelling place prepared by God for man's abode." He did not exaggerate, however, when he wrote: "That inexhaustible valley of the Mississippi; the whole continent, in short, seemed prepared to be the abode of a great nation."[1]

The Middle West is today the leading industrial center of the nation, with 34 per cent of all manufacturing employ-

[1] H. S. Commager (ed.), *Democracy in America* (New York, 1947), 23, 229, 28.

ment. It is also the leading agricultural region. The farms of the Middle West cover 76 per cent of its area—the highest proportion of farm land in the country. And it is the most populous region of the United States.

A recent study by the Department of Commerce concludes that "the Central region together with the areas eastward to the Atlantic seaboard constitute the most highly industrial area of the World, with a prodigious output of diversified products which are marketed throughout the World."[2]

During the nineteenth century, a unique contribution of the Middle West was that it supplied the foodstuffs necessary for the undergirding of a growing industrialized nation. The abundance from the farms made it possible for cities like Chicago to spring up almost overnight and to expand with breathtaking speed. The growth of Chicago from 4,470 people in 1840 to 298,977 by 1870, to 1,698,575 by 1900, and to 3,620,962 by 1950 is only one manifestation of the fabulous growth of the Middle West. Chicago became the core city of the midland empire with dominance at times or to the present in the grain trade, the lumber market, livestock and meat packing, and iron and steel production.[3]

At the beginning of the nineteenth century, we were an underdeveloped nation. By 1900, we were a new world power, hesitant or uncertain about continuing to develop the industrial, agricultural, and mineral resources which placed us in the front rank of nations.

[2] Department of Commerce, *Regional Trends in the United States Economy* (Washington, 1951), 45–49. The States included in the central region in this study are Ohio, Indiana, Michigan, Illinois, Wisconsin, Minnesota, Iowa, and Missouri.

[3] See Bessie L. Pierce, *History of Chicago* (New York, 1937 and 1940) and *Studies on Chicago Economic History* (Planographed by John S. Swift Company, n.d.).

From 1815 to 1914, there was century of world peace— a century that allowed capital and human resources to be devoted to an amazing economic development rather than to war. The Middle West was a great investment area, not alone of the Atlantic Seaboard, but also of Great Britain and western Europe. Here, for the first time, was an almost unlimited land mass with no pressure of population on its resources and with its riches easily available, first by water transportation and then by railroads.

The United States—a land-mass nation—emerged in the late nineteenth century as a world power and by the mid-twentieth century another land-mass nation—the Soviet Union—had emerged as a rival in material power. One can rest assured that had the Middle West been a sea of water rather than a sea of grass, forests, and subsoil mineral deposits, the United States would have been a much weaker nation in world affairs.

In the internal development of the country, the region was a unifying factor for the larger nation. Without manpower and agricultural and industrial production, could the Northeast alone have won the Civil War and thus held the nation together? Without the lodestone quality of the Middle West, what is now the United States might have developed into a series of small nations. Speaking in 1850 at the installation of the new president of Indian Asbury University, Governor Joseph A. Wright of Indiana said of this feature of the Middle West:

I trust you will inculcate in the minds of the young men who shall come hither for instruction, a burning love for the union of these states. It is too common an occurrence to see our young men in the North and South on examination days and at school exhibitions, engaged in rehearsing the beauties of this, or the evils of that section of the country, at the expense of the other. I have no patience to sit down and hear men talk about this or that section of the Union, or of the peculiar framework of society in this or that State, in opposition to those of other States. This continually speaking of Northern interest, Southern interest, Northern population, and Southern population, is an evil that demands a remedy. This Union is not composed of a few cities in the North or South; the people of this Union consist of something else than iron mills and wooden clocks in the North or of rice and cotton bales in the South. We of the West have something to say as to who and what compose this union. . . . The time has now arrived when the influence of the West, in her conservative spirit, should be felt in the settlement of all our national questions.[4]

We well know that it took more than capital to develop this inland empire. Peoples from the older Atlantic Seaboard, from the Upland South, and from Europe flocked into the area to build cities, towns, and farms. Marcus Lee Hansen has pointed out that "the Mississippi Valley was for fifty years the frontier of Europe as well as of the eastern states" and that "it reacted upon England, Germany and Scandinavia with a force comparable to that which it exerted upon Atlantic America."[5]

The mingling of peoples of diverse origins occurred early in the Middle West. In 1840, a Jesuit priest rode a steamboat from St. Louis up the Missouri River and wrote of this experience:

[4] Joseph A. Wright, *An Address Delivered at the Installation of Rev. L. W. Berry, D. D., as President of the Indiana Asbury University, July 16, 1850* (Indianapolis, 1850). Pamphlet in the Rare Book Room, Indiana University.
[5] Marcus Lee Hansen, "The Problem of the Third Generation Immigrant," in *Augustana Historical Society Publications* (Rock Island, Illinois, 1938), 19.

The craft on which I had embarked was (like all of them in this land, where emigration and commerce have grown to such an extent) encumbered with freight and passengers from every state of the Union; I may even say from the various nations of the earth, white, black, yellow and red, with shadings of all these colors. The boat was like a little floating Babel, on account of the different languages and jargons that were heard upon it. These passengers drop off here and there on the river, to open farms, construct mills, build factories of every kind; they increase day by day the number of the inhabitants of the little towns and villages that spring up as if by magic, on both sides of the river.[6]

In 1952, Governor Adlai Stevenson, in his speech of welcome to the Democratic convention in Chicago, stressed the diverse origins of middle westerners when he said:

As a Democrat perhaps you will permit me to remind you that until four years ago the people of Illinois had chosen but three Democratic governors in a hundred years. One was John Peter Altgeld, a German immigrant, whom the great Illinois poet, Vachel Lindsay, called the Eagle Forgotten; one was Edward F. Dunne, whose parents came here from Ireland; and the last was Henry Horner, but one generation removed from Germany. Altgeld was a Protestant, Dunne was a Catholic, and Horner was a Jew.

That, my friends, is the American story, written by the Democratic Party, here on the prairies of Illinois, in the heartland of the nation.[7]

[6] From a letter dated February 4, 1841, in Hiram Martin Chittenden and Alfred Talbot Richardson, *Life, Letters and Travels of Father Pierre-Jean De Smet, S. J.* (New York, 1905).

[7] Adlai E. Stevenson, *Major Campaign Speeches of Adlai E. Stevenson, 1952.* (New York, 1953), 3.

The fascinating, although at times disturbing and heart-breaking story of the adjustment of different ethnic and racial groups to American life is a dominant theme in American history. Not only the Middle West, but the northern Atlantic Seaboard, the Southwest, and the West Coast all contributed to this process of adjustment of peoples from diverse regions to produce this society we know today.

Perhaps Frederick Jackson Turner exaggerated a bit when he wrote that settlers in the Mississippi Valley of 1830 "shut off by the mountains from the coast, were the first Americans to break decisively with the Europeans, and to a large extent with the tide-water people."[8]

Certainly Frank O. Lowden, later to be governor of Illinois, in a speech delivered in Des Moines in 1900, exaggerated when he said: "I assert that the Mississippi Valley is the home of democracy, because it is the cradle of the American race. There was already the Puritan of New England, the Cavalier of Virginia, the Dutch of New Amsterdam, the Scotch Presbyterian of the mountains, but the American had not yet appeared. . . . We are nothing that ever was before. We are Americans, and it was in the Mississippi Valley that the American people was born. . . . Was it not a distinguished descendant of the Puritan who said of our Lincoln: 'New birth of our new soil, the first American'?"[9]

Governor Lowden was only one of a host who believed that the Middle West was more American than any other section when it began to mature. It is not necessary today to be a regional chauvinist and boast that the Middle West is the

---

[8] *The United States, 1830–1850* (New York, 1935), 19.
[9] I am indebted to Professor W. T. Hutchinson, who has a forthcoming biography of Lowden, for this quotation.

most American part of America in order to set forth the contribution of this region to the nation. What one can emphasize without being provincial is that in the course of settling this land mass, certain characteristics described as American by both foreign and American writers were sharpened. People pulled up their roots from the older America or from Europe and poured into the Middle West, with dreams of improving their lot in life quickly.

For nearly three centuries, Americans, with their habits, ideas, and institutions, knew the experience of movement into the primitive wilderness and then the uneven advance to a more complex social order. The greatest influence of this reversion from a settled, stable existence to frontier living came in the years after 1815, when the Middle West was settled. "American social development has been continually beginning over again on the frontier," Turner has pointed out. "This perennial rebirth, this fluidity of American life, this expansion westward with its new opportunities, its continuous touch with the simplicity of primitive society, furnish the forces dominating American character."

The Middle West, with its abundant resources, furnished a base for material improvement. There was, moreover, a lack of rigid, stratified social lines. Regardless of where he came from and what his social position had been, the pioneer was limited generally by only his own capabilities. As far as government was concerned, the organization of every county and township left a staggering number of posts to be filled.[10] Unlike the settled East, there was no hierarchy of experienced

[10] I am indebted to Stanley Elkins and Eric McKitrick for this stress on political participation as a factor in the Middle West. See their article, "Democracy in the Old Northwest," *Political Science Quarterly* (September, 1954), 321–53.

people to call upon. Perhaps the main reason the Irish immigrant in the growing, urban Middle West took to politics so readily was that for him, it was the quickest way up the ladder to prestige and success.

Politics in the Middle West, whether on the rural or the urban frontier, was dominated by men with unusually scanty prior political experience. With energy and vigor, these pioneers campaigned for office. Among the qualities the campaigner needed was physical prowess. In a society that was advancing by a struggle with nature, brawn and physical skill were the most respected of endowments. Whether it was the ability to shoot straight with a squirrel rifle or the capacity to do well in a wrestling match to quiet a heckler, physical ability payed political dividends. Candidates also took great pains to dress humbly and to appear no better endowed with material wealth than their fellows.

Baynard Rush Hall, a refined easterner, found the political life he saw in Indiana quite distasteful, but his writing reflects the flavor of a new society participating in politics with the same dynamic quality that was devoted to exploiting the physical resources of the region. "Our social state was...always in a ferment; for ever was some election doing, being done, or going to be done; and each was as bitterly contested as that of president or governor," he wrote. "In all directions candidates were perpetually scouring the country with hats, saddlebags, and pockets crammed with certificates, defending and accusing, defaming and clearing up, making licentious speeches, treating on corn whiskey, violating the Sabbath, and cursing the existing administration or the administration's wife and wife's father! And everybody expected at some time to be a candidate for something; or that his uncle would be; or his cousin, or his cousin's wife's cousin's friend would be; so that everybody and everybody's relations, and everybody's relations' friends, were for ever electioneering."[11]

With all his strong individualism, the pioneer knew how to co-operate, to help raise his neighbor's barn or to bring into being a new government. And he was a confirmed believer in progress. He saw change everywhere, and as he transformed the wilderness into farms, towns, and cities, he had immense faith that anything could be done. He indulged in dreams that could and would come true. One of the finest descriptions of the middle western pioneer's faith in progress is this passage from Ole Rölvaag's *Giants in the Earth:* "They threw themselves blindly into the Impossible, and accomplished the Unbelievable. If anyone succumbed in the struggle—and that happened often—another would come and take his place. Youth was in the race; the unknown, the untried, the unheard-of, was in the air; people caught it, were intoxicated by it, threw themselves away, and laughed at the cost. Of course it was possible—everything was possible out here. There was no such thing as the Impossible anymore. The human race has not known such faith and such self-confidence since history began."

Another American characteristic that was sharpened in the Middle West was the strong dislike of special privilege. The American believed in the right of every man to have an equal chance. After this, men could draw apart as far as their abilities allowed. But the game had to be played fairly. When some gained favors at the expense of equal opportunity, the middle westerner was quick to demand action by government. Professor John D. Hicks, in *The Populist Revolt,* has well de-

[11] *The New Purchase: Or, Early Years in the Far West* (New York, 1885), 172.

scribed this reaction on the part of middle western farmers when they found they were not receiving what they considered a fair share of the American bonanza.

There was an openness and fluidity about life in the Middle West. The area was free, flexible, and pragmatic. The host of utopian experiments, the founding of a vast number of liberal-arts colleges and universities, the proliferation of religious sects, the breaking with old traditions, such as Oberlin did when it was the first college to admit women, or the flourishing of the religious revival are only some aspects of the free and open qualities of this region.

From transforming the middle western land mass, the American emphasis on material accomplishments was heightened. The pioneer's achievements were victories over nature. He worked hard and glorified toil. The measure of his success was the size of his barns, the acres he broke to the plow, the towns, cities, and factories he built.

Although big and great tended to become synonymous in the middle western mind, it is misleading to stress only material development. From the Middle West came outstanding writers. Realism in American literature stems from the writings of cranky old Ed Howe, Ole Rölvaag, Hamlin Garland, Joseph Kirkland, and from such observers of the urban frontier as Upton Sinclair, Theodore Dreiser, Sherwood Anderson, Sinclair Lewis, and James T. Farrell. These writers could stand off from the life they had known and, unencumbered by the traditions of polite literature, present many telling criticisms of the changing rural and urban world. With their vitality, rebelliousness, and scorn for the gradeful, these writers and many others sum up much of the spirit of the Middle West.

Many outstanding painters found their inspiration from

their middle western heritage, particularly in recent decades. Thomas Hart Benton, John Steuart Curry, and Grant Wood are perhaps the most familiar. The outstanding achievement in American architecture in the period from the Civil War to World War I was the development of the skyscraper. In Chicago in the decade of the 1880's, a remarkable group of men, with Louis Sullivan in the vanguard, pioneered this new departure in architecture that was soon to spread to many cities of the nation and the world. And Sullivan's disciple, Frank Lloyd Wright, made a telling impact on architecture around the world.

From the outset, there were two Middle Wests—the agricultural and the urban. Although the rural Middle West was more dominant in the last century, the continued growth of Middle western cities has, in the twentieth century, made most people in the region urban dwellers. The bitterness and frustration of farm people as they lost status and power to urban dwellers is no better illustrated in all-American development than in the person of William Jennings Bryan. Bryan was confident that he was called upon to defend the good, Christian yeoman of the agrarian Middle West against the overshadowing dominance of the urban-industrial order.

More than this, however, Bryan, the Populists, the Grangers, and other strident voices from the agricultural Middle West laid the groundwork for what Frederick Lewis Allen has so aptly called *The Big Chance*. Twentieth-century America has faced two immense tasks of adjustment. We have had to readjust thinking developed during the comparatively isolated position of the nation in the nineteenth century to the fact of being a great world power in the present century. At the same time, we have had to re-adapt ideas formed by nearly three hundred years of frontier and rural society to meet the problems created by the rise of the modern industry. We have had to review such hallowed beliefs as isolationism, *laissez faire*, and rugged individualism in terms of the dictates of the machine age.

By the turn of the twentieth century, the power of the new captains of industry and finance stimulated a determined effort to regulate great wealth in the interest of the many. Equal opportunity no longer could be left to chance. The Populists and the Bryan Democrats insisted that the government would now have to curb the greedy in order to insure an equal chance for all. And building on the legacy of the 1890's, the Middle West from 1901 to 1917, contributed a solid base for the Progressive movement. Robert M. La Follette in Wisconsin, Tom Johnson in Cleveland and Golden Rule Sam Jones and Brand Whitlock in Toledo were among the outstanding figures leading the way in extending governmental power to meet the challenges produced by the incredible expansion of the Gilded Age.

During the Progressive era, the base for the adjustment of capitalism to democracy was moving from rural and small-town America to urban America. The reform movement was now broadened beyond dissident farmers to include professional people and small businessmen in the urban centers. By the time of the New Deal, the urban centers were basic to the continuing adjustment of capitalism to democracy. And by this time, too, the dominant influence of metropolitan centers of 500,000 people or more was apparent in presidential elections. Franklin D. Roosevelt was so successful in carrying these metropolitan centers and through them the electoral vote of the states where they were located that in no election was the vote of the South essential to a Democratic party victory.

The ten states containing these metropolitan centers are not located in any one section of the nation. Five of them—Illinois, Michigan, Missouri, Ohio, and Wisconsin—are, however, middle western.[12] By their voting behavior, these urban states strengthened the middle western political heritage, an aspect of which is that people have the right to appeal to government whenever they feel that freedom of the individual, equality of opportunity, and justice have been ignored.

In adjusting to the world-power position of the nation, the middle western record is not as forward looking as it is in the area of domestic political adjustment. The Middle West has had more than its share of isolationists. But the querulous voice of Colonel McCormick as a symbol of the entire area is misleading. It was, after all, another middle westerner, William Allen White, who headed the influential Committee to Defend America by Aiding the Allies.

A recent study of congressional voting from 1933 to 1950 reveals that in the voting in the House of Representatives, North Dakota was the most isolationist in the nation, with Idaho, Kansas, Nebraska, Wisconsin, and Minnesota following in that order. In the voting pattern in the Senate, North Dakota was the most isolationist, followed by Nebraska, Kansas, Ohio, Idaho, and Nevada. Further research on isolationist voting may reveal that there are other factors more significant than geography in determining isolationist behavior. Political party affiliation is one such factor. Another is the behavior pattern of certain specific ethnic groups, regardless of their location. A third is that rural areas are more isolationist than urban cen-

12 See S. J. Eldersveld, "The Influence of Metropolitan Party Pluralities in Presidential Elections Since 1920," *American Political Science Review* (December, 1949).

ters.[13] A recent Gallup Poll would seem to indicate that the continued growth of the urban Middle West has drastically altered the picture of the Middle West as the center of isolationism. It found that while 16 per cent of the respondents in the Middle West thought of themselves as isolationist, 17 per cent in the East, 17 per cent in the South, and 19 per cent in the Far West placed themselves in this category.[14]

With the twentieth-century development of mass transportation, mass communication, and the growth of cosmopolitan centers, the basic problems facing the public have become national and international rather than regional. And the basic attitudes, customs, and habits of middle westerners reflect a national, rather than a regional, norm. Frederick Jackson Turner's description of a region, in *The Significance of Sections in American History*, as "any one part of the national domain which is geographically and socially sufficiently unified to have a true consciousness of its own ideals and customs and to possess a sense of distinction from other parts of the country" is no longer applicable to the Middle West.

Middle westerners, like other Americans, are part of the American pattern of change and adjustment. The Middle West has been, for a century and a half, a mirror of the total American experience of continuous growth, change, and adjustment; of the blending of geographic, ethnic, and racial diversities. Like other Americans, middle westerners have been and are radical in developing new agricultural, manufacturing, and business techniques. Rejecting all other isms, they subscribe to galloping capitalism modified by necessary governmental

[13] Ralph H. Smuckler, "The Region of Isolationism," *American Political Science Review* (June, 1953); Sammuel Lubell, *The Future of American Politics* (New York, 1952).

[14] Washington *Post*, August 18, 1954.

controls. If, however, the Middle West had been a sea of water rather than a rich land mass, there would have been far less rapid change, a slower national growth, less sharpening of American characteristics, and far less opportunity and hope for the common man to improve his lot in America, and the nation would not have emerged as the leading force among the free nations in the tumultuous, turbulent, twentieth century.

INDEX

Ade, George: 214
Agriculture: in Iowa, 34–35, 50–51; changes in, 62–63; government regulation of, 63; economics of 64–65, 83–86; frontier, 87–88; *see also* farming *and* farmers
Allen, Frederick Lewis: 286
Akron, Ohio: 71
Algren, Nelson: 228
Allouez, Claude: 200
Amana, Iowa: 97
Amana Society: 97ff., 103, 105; and communitarian principles, 100; founding of, 106
American Farm Bureau Federation: 65
American Home Missionary Society: 237
American Society for the Education of Pious Youth: 237
Anderson, Sherwood: 218, 219, 221
Arbeiterbund: 111–12
Architecture: 17, 267–68, 270–74, 286
Art: background of, 255–59; in-fluences on, 256; as historical record, 257; native heritage of, 260–61; effect of European tradition on, 261; Hudson River school of, 261–62; romanticism in, 261–62, 263–64, 265; realism in frontier, 263; following Civil War, 263–64; popular western concepts in, 264, 265; techniques in, 264; following World War I, 265–66; photography as, 267; crafts as, 268ff.; architecture as, 270ff.
Artists: as reporters, 261, 262–63, 264
Asbury colleges: 239
Atwater, Caleb: 205
Augustana College (Ill.): 12
Augustana College (Minn.): 12
Augustana College (S. Dak.): 12
Austrian refugees: 135

Baldwin, Theron: 237, 247
Baltic natives in Middle West: 133

The HERITAGE of the MIDDLE WEST

was set into type on the Linotype machine in eleven-point Janson with three points of space between the lines. Janson is one of the most widely used types for fine book work in this country. The fact that it is considered to be Dutch in character, at first glance makes it seem an odd choice for a book about the Middle West. But, like most things Dutch, Janson is practical. It also has a distinctive character of its own that gives good color and legibility to the printed page.

This book is printed on an antique wove paper.

University of Oklahoma Press : Norman